AF505604

Durham Modern Languages Series

Essays in later medieval French literature

MANCHESTER
1824

Manchester University Press

Lizzie Rowe, *Jane Taylor*. Collingwood College, Durham.
Image © Lizzie Rowe, 2007

Essays in later medieval French literature

The legacy of Jane H. M. Taylor

Edited by
Rebecca Dixon

Manchester University Press
Manchester and New York

distributed in the United States exclusively by Palgrave Macmillan

Published by Manchester University Press
Oxford Road, Manchester M13 9NR, UK
and Room 400, 175 Fifth Avenue, New York, NY 10010, USA
www.manchesteruniversitypress.co.uk

Distributed in the United States exclusively by
Palgrave Macmillan, 175 Fifth Avenue, New York,
NY 10010, USA

Distributed in Canada exclusively by
UBC Press, University of British Columbia, 2029 West Mall,
Vancouver, BC, Canada V6T 1Z2

British Library Cataloguing-in-Publication Data
A catalogue record for this book is available from the British Library

Library of Congress Cataloging-in-Publication Data applied for

ISBN 978 0 7190 8192 7 hardback

First published 2010

Printed in Great Britain by TJ International Ltd, Padstow

Contents

List of Illustrations

COVER ILLUSTRATION.
Giovanni Boccaccio, *Les nobles et cleres dames* (Paris: Antoine Vérard, 1493), Manchester, John Rylands Library, 15883, fol. a1ᵛ. Reproduced by courtesy of the the Director and University Librarian, the John Rylands University Library of Manchester.

FRONTISPIECE

Lizzie Rowe, *Jane Taylor*. Collingwood College, Durham. Image © Lizzie Rowe, 2007.

Illustration of the Flash-based prototype image viewer showing two folios from Stonyhurst MS 1 side-by-side. Images © Stonyhurst College, Lancashire, and Scriptura Ltd (digitiser of all the manuscript images).

Using *Virtual Vellum* to compare the frontispiece from 4 different manuscripts that are located at 3 different physical locations. Images © Bibliothèque royale Albert 1ᵉʳ, Brussels (left- and right-most images), Stonyhurst College, Lancashire (second from the left), Bibliothèque municipale de Besançon (second from the right) and Scriptura Ltd.

Two different views of the same folio from Besançon, MS 865. The left window shows the folio in full with the right window magnifying into it. Images © Bibliothèque municipale de Besançon and Scriptura Ltd.

Contributors

Peter Ainsworth is Professor and Head of the Department of French at the University of Sheffield. He has published editions of Froissart's *Chroniques* with Le Livre de Poche and Droz, and numerous articles and essays on medieval historiography. Director of the AHRC-funded *Online Froissart* and EPSRC-funded *Pegasus* projects, he was guest curator for *The Chronicles of Froissart: From Conflict to Cooperation*, a six-month public exhibition at the Royal Armouries Museum (2007–08). With Michael Meredith and Colin Dunn he developed the *Virtual Vellum* manuscript viewing tool funded jointly by the AHRC, EPSRC and JISC under the UK e-Science initiative (2006).

Adrian Armstrong is Professor of Early French Culture at the University of Manchester, and was the inaugural Director of Manchester's Centre for Research in the Visual Cultures of the French-Speaking World (CRIVCOF). A specialist in *grand rhétoriqueur* poetry, he is the author of *Technique and Technology: Script, Print, and Poetics in France 1470–1550* (Oxford: Oxford University Press, 2000), and has published editions of poems by Jean Lemaire de Belges and Jean Bouchet. In addition, he was director of the AHRC-funded project 'Poetic Knowledge in Late Medieval France' between 2005 and 2009.

Rosalind Brown-Grant is Senior Lecturer in French at the University of Leeds. She is the author of *Christine de Pizan and the Moral Defence of Women: Reading Beyond Gender* (Cambridge: Cambridge University Press, 1999) as well as numerous articles on Christine de Pizan in various scholarly journals and edited volumes. Her latest research monograph, *French Romance of the Later Middle Ages: Gender, Morality, and Desire* was published by Oxford University Press in 2008.

Emma Cayley is Senior Lecturer in French at the University of Exeter. She is the author of numerous articles on the poetry of Alain Chartier, and has recently published a monograph on him, *Debate and Dialogue: Alain Chartier in his Cultural Context* (Oxford: Oxford University Press, 2006). She is co-editor, with Ashby Kinch, of *Chartier in Europe* (Cambridge: D. S. Brewer, 2008). Her current research project is an edition and translation of eight later medieval debate poems, with accompanying monograph, *Sleepless Knights and Wanton Women*.

Rebecca Dixon is a Leverhulme Early Career Fellow in the Department of French, University of Leeds. She is the author of several articles on later medieval literature, identity politics, and the relationship between text and image, and co-editor (with Finn E. Sinclair) of *Poetry, Knowledge and Community in Late Medieval France* (Cambridge: D. S. Brewer, 2008).

Catherine Emerson is a lecturer in French at the National University of Ireland, Galway. Her PhD thesis has been published as *Olivier de la Marche and the Rhetoric of Fifteenth-Century Historiography* (Woodbridge: Boydell and Brewer, 2004). She is currently working on representations of Manneken-Pis as a Belgian regional icon and on the work of the sixteenth-century editor and translator, Denis Sauvage.

Douglas Kelly is Emeritus Professor of French and Medieval Studies at the University of Wisconsin-Madison. A specialist in Arthurian literature, his recent publications include *Internal Difference and Meanings in the 'Roman de la rose'* (Madison: The University of Wisconsin Press, 1995), *The Conspiracy of Allusion: Description, Rewriting, and Authorship from Macrobius to Medieval Romance* (Leiden: Brill, 1999), *Christine de Pizan's Changing Opinion: A Quest for Certainty in the Midst of Chaos* (Cambridge: D. S. Brewer, 2007), as well as a supplement to *Chrétien de Troyes: An Analytic Bibliography* (Woodbridge: Tamesis, 2002).

Michael Freeman was Ashley Watkins Professor of French Language and Literature at the University of Bristol until his retirement in 2008. From 1997 until 2007 he was General Editor of French Studies. He is the author of numerous articles on late medieval and sixteenth-century French culture, and has edited works by Coquillart, Jodelle and Larivey, as well as three volumes of essays on Villon, including *Villon at Oxford. The Drama of the Text* (Amsterdam: Rodopi, 1999), with Jane H. M. Taylor. He also published *François Villon in his Works. The Villain's Tale* (Amsterdam: Rodopi, 2000). As this volume was going to press in 2009, we learned of Mike's sudden and untimely death; his legacy as a rigorous and generous scholar, and one of the profession's true gentlemen, will last. He will be sadly missed.

Nancy Freeman Regalado is Professor of French at New York University. She has published *Poetic Patterns in Rutebeuf* (1970), *'Le Roman de Fauvel' in the Edition of Mesire Chaillou de Pesstain* (1990, with Edward Roesner and François Avril) and *Performing Medieval Narrative* (2005, with Evelyn Birge Vitz and Marilyn Lawrence), as well as articles on medieval festive culture, Villon, and Jean de Meun.

Sara Sturm-Maddox is Professor Emerita of French and Italian at the University of Massachusetts (Amherst). She is the author of *Petrarch's Laurels* (Philadelphia: Pennsylvania State UP, 1992), *Ronsard, Petrarch, and the 'Amours'* (Gainesville: University Press of Florida, 1999) and, with Donald Maddox, co-editor of numerous volumes including *Froissart Across the Genres* (Gainesville: University Press of Florida, 1998).

Helen Swift is Fellow and Tutor, and University Lecturer, in Medieval French at St Hilda's College, Oxford. She is the author of several articles on the *querelle des femmes* and on late medieval poetics, and has recently published a monograph entitled *Gender, Writing and Performance: Men Defending Women in Late Medieval France (1440–1538)* (Oxford: Oxford University Press, 2008).

Preface

This volume, in which former colleagues and students of Professor Jane H. M. Taylor honour the contribution she has made to later medieval French studies, marks an important date in the history of Durham Modern Languages Series (DMLS). Over the last twenty-nine years, DMLS has published in excess of fifty books in a wide range of fields that are closely aligned with the research strengths of the School of Modern Languages and Cultures (MLAC), including literary studies, cultural and intellectual history, critical and cultural theory, film and visual culture, theatre and performance studies, gender and sexuality, language and rhetoric, and translation and interpreting. These fields are themselves inflected across a range of languages that reflects the structure of our School: Arabic, French, German, Italian, Russian and Spanish. Knowledge and understanding of other cultures, gained through scholarly analysis of their textual and visual artefacts across time and place, has never been more important, and many DMLS volumes seek to address a wider readership interested in foreign languages and cultures. Starting with this volume, DMLS will continue to provide an outlet for world-class research in the field of Modern Languages – in the form of monographs, critical editions and collections of essays – as a series published by Manchester University Press. It is particularly fitting that this volume, in honour of Jane Taylor, marks this new step in the history of the series, since, as will be evident from Rebecca Dixon's introduction to this volume, Jane's academic life – barring a distinguished interlude at the University of Oxford – has been divided between the universities of Manchester and Durham, and has had a profound effect on both. And yet the influence of Jane's scholarship and collegiality extends well beyond the confines of the north of England, as the range of contributors to this volume attests. In this connection, it is with particular sadness that I record the death of Michael Freeman, formerly Ashley Watkins Professor of French Language and Literature at the University of Bristol, who passed away while this volume was being prepared.

David Cowling (former Jane Taylor DPhil student),
Head of MLAC, Durham University

Introduction
Coming late, coming after?
Later medieval French literature and its legacies

Rebecca Dixon

Que porai-je de nouvel dire?[1]

The later medieval period has not always enjoyed the best of press. Even its name, that 'later' skulking there like a reproach, is reductive-seeming. Later than what, precisely? Have we missed something – something more exciting? For scholars in the early twentieth century, most notably the historian Johan Huizinga, the sense was emphatically that we had: shuffling shamefacedly in on the perky heels of the High Middle Ages, not having been prescient enough to bide its time a little longer and wait for the shimmering new dawn of the Renaissance, the later medieval period was looked at askance, like an unwelcome guest at a particularly lavish banquet. Huizinga's influential *The Waning of the Middle Ages* (1924), whose infelicitous title gains little in translation either from the original Dutch (*Herfsttij der Middeleeuwen* ['Autumn of the Middle Ages']) or into French (as *Le Déclin du Moyen Âge*),[2] was instrumental in shaping a critical stance that prevailed for over half a century, one which lamented the apparent tardiness inherent in the cultural production of the fourteenth and fifteenth centuries, bemoaned their lack of societal progress, and harked back to the glory days of the

---

[1] Jean Froissart, *Le Joli buisson de jonece*, ed. Anthime Fourrier (Geneva: Droz, 1975), v. 433.

[2] The date refers to the English translation. The respective versions of Huizinga's text are *Herfsttij der Middeleeuwen: studie over levens- en gedachtenvormen der veertiende en vijftiende eeuw in Frankrijk en de Nederlanden* (Haarlem: H. D. Tjeenk Willink, 1919), *The Waning of the Middle Ages: A Study of the Forms of Life, Thought and Art in France and the Netherlands in the XIVth and XVth Centuries* (London: E. A. Arnold, 1924), and *Le Déclin du Moyen Âge* (Paris: Payot, 1932).

twelfth and thirteenth centuries when everything was fresh and new (even war and pestilence, apparently, could be appealing in the right circumstances…).

It would be tempting, and reassuring, to view this emphasis on the epigonal status of the fourteenth and fifteenth centuries as a retro-projection on the part of scholars like Huizinga, themselves looking for something new to say after the philological advances of previous decades. But the sentiment had already been vociferously aired by contemporary authors: as the epigraph from Froissart suggests, the literary output of the later medieval period in France is marked by a profound sense of what Jacqueline Cerquiglini-Toulet has called 'la tristesse du "déjà dit"'.[3] Authors like Froissart, or Machaut, Deschamps, and Christine de Pizan, writing in the wake of Chrétien de Troyes or – especially – the innovative, influential and 'inescapable'[4] *Roman de la Rose*, display a deep unease towards the literary past.[5] As Cerquiglini-Toulet underlines, for these writers the past was a source of threat, a crushing weight hanging over their creative endeavours and something to be approached anxiously because, precisely, back then everything had already been said. Fourteenth- and fifteenth-century authors came too late, came after, illustrious predecessors, and were professedly hampered by the perception that the interesting subject-matter had been dealt with, the generic advances made. The later Middle Ages, it seems, were no time to be a writer.

But as might be suggested by a glance at the respective *œuvres* of the individuals mentioned above, as well as those of the writers who came after them (Alain Chartier, Charles d'Orléans, urban dramatists, the *grands rhétoriqueurs*…), later medieval authors appear rarely to have been assailed by writer's block. While the literary past might on the one hand have threatened these authors, on the other it also inspired them to write. Though much of the material Cerquiglini-Toulet adduces in *La Couleur de la mélancolie* bolsters the sense of anxiety and lack experienced by contemporaries, what also emerges – at times despite

---

[3] See Jacqueline Cerquiglini-Toulet, *La Couleur de la mélancolie: la fréqentation des livres au XIVe siècle 1300–1415* (Paris: Hatier, 1993), pp. 57–88.

[4] The term is borrowed from Jane H. M. Taylor, 'Inescapable *Rose*: Jean de Sénéchal's *Livre des cent ballades* and the art of cheerful paradox', *Medium Ævum*, 67 (1998), 60–84.

[5] While later medieval French authors were haunted by the spectre of the *Rose*, and apparently hampered by its all-pervasive innovation, the inception of that literary period is, of course, normally defined in the French context by the date of Jean de Meun's completion of his portion of the text in *c.* 1280.

itself, and despite the protestations of the authors in question – is this positivity, the feeling that sleeves must be rolled up and a job of work pressed on with, the challenges made by earlier periods risen to. The 'réflexion vive … sur l'après'[6] engaged in by these authors implies a futurity, too. The literary legacy with which authors like Machaut, Froissart, or Charles were faced brings with it an authority, but by engaging with this authority – whether by glossing classical models or prior authors, by citing from earlier texts, or by reinventing previously worked genres[7] – later medieval authors became engaged in a process of creativity, and of renewal. Far from being iron rations, the 'mïetes cheans de haulte table' that Christine alludes to in the *Epistre Othea* offer rich pickings for the author willing to indulge.[8]

A similar process of creative (re-)engagement has characterised more recent scholarship on the later Middle Ages. The reductive legacy of Huizinga has gradually, but determinedly, given way to critical approaches that – like the work of the contemporary authors themselves – take a positive approach to these later texts which had come after more interesting, more dazzling, material, and which were apparently so hollow and derivative, so unworthy of serious study. Ensuring the later, and happier, futures of these fourteenth- and fifteenth-century texts on which all that was either valuable or necessary (for earlier scholars, the two were not always synonymous) had been said has, in recent decades, taken various complementary forms. Like the medieval authors, modern scholars have focused on issues connected with later strategies of reworking earlier texts, particularly the Burgundian recastings of earlier material known as *mises en prose*.[9] More broadly,

---

[6] Cerquiglini-Toulet, *Couleur de la mélancolie*, p. 11.

[7] For more on these elements as evinced in the work of later medieval authors see below, as well as the essays in Rebecca Dixon and Finn E. Sinclair (eds), with Adrian Armstrong, Sylvia Huot, and Sarah Kay, *Poetry, Knowledge and Community in Late Medieval France* (Cambridge: D. S. Brewer, 2008), especially the pieces by Deborah McGrady, Nancy Freeman Regalado, Jennifer Saltzstein, and David J. Wrisley.

[8] Christine de Pizan, *L'Epistre Othea*, ed. Gabriella Parussa (Geneva: Droz, 1999), p. 196 (Prologue, v. 41).

[9] For more on these approaches, see: Norris J. Lacy, 'Motivation and method in the Burgundian *Erec*', in Keith Busby and Norris J. Lacy (eds), *Conjunctures: Medieval Studies in Honor of Douglas Kelly* (Amsterdam: Rodopi, 1994), pp. 271–80; Jane H. M. Taylor, 'The significance of the insignificant: reading reception in the Burgundian *Erec* and *Cligès*', *Fifteenth-Century Studies*, 24 (1998), 183–97; Rosalind Brown-Grant, *French Romance of the Later Middle Ages: Gender, Morality, and Desire* (Oxford: Oxford University Press, 2008); and Maria Colombo Timelli, 'Refaire Doutrepont? Projet pour un

these reappraisals take in aspects of contemporary responses to earlier legacies in their considerations of the ways in which 'coming after' earlier avatars encourages poetic competition, and the establishment of literary communities; these communities can grow up around a single charismatic author, as in the example of Charles d'Orléans, or in much larger urban contexts, such as those constructed around urban drama or various poetic competitions.[10] Further, through such avenues of enquiry modern scholarship has engaged with the later medieval revivification of genres, whether romance, debate, or lyric,[11] as well as with broader questions of retransmission and literary exchange, especially in terms of the materiality of the book.[12]

Engagement with such issues of lateness and textual afterlife has been foundational in the work of Jane H. M. Taylor, whose academic legacy this volume celebrates. *Essays in Later Medieval French Literature* brings together original contributions from just some of the scholars who have worked alongside Jane in various capacities – as departmental colleagues, co-researchers, and/or former students – and who have benefitted from her example. The articles demonstrate their authors' link to this illustrious predecessor, and in so doing underline the

---

nouveau répertoire des mises en prose des XVe et XVIe siècles', *Le Moyen Français*, 63 (2008), 109–17, as well as Rebecca Dixon, '"Homs sui je dame, vraiement": sex, chivalry and identity in *Jehan d'Avennes*', *French Studies*, 61 (2007), 141–54, and the essays by Brown-Grant and Sturm-Maddox in the present volume.

[10] On these diverse issues see: Gérard Gros, *Le Poète, la Vierge et le Prince du puy. Etude sur les Puys marials de la France du Nord du XIVe siècle à la Renaissance* (Paris: Klincksieck, 1996); Alan Hindley (ed.), *Drama and Community: People and Plays in Medieval Europe* (Turnhout: Brepols, 1999); Denis Hüe, *La Poésie palinodique à Rouen (1486–1550)* (Paris: Champion, 2002); Emma Cayley, *Debate and Dialogue. Alain Chartier in his Cultural Context* (Oxford: Oxford University Press, 2006); Jane H. M. Taylor, *The Making of Poetry. Late-Medieval French Poetic Anthologies* (Turnhout: Brepols, 2007); Mary-Jo Arn, *The Poet's Notebook. The Personal Manuscript of Charles d'Orléans (Paris BnF MS fr. 25458)* (Turnhout: Brepols, 2008); and Adrian Armstrong, *The Virtuoso Circle: Competition, Collaboration and Complexity in Late Medieval French Poetry* (Tempe: Arizona Center for Medieval and Renaissance Studies, forthcoming), as well as the essays in Dixon and Sinclair (eds), *Poetry, Knowledge and Community*.

[11] See Cayley, *Debate and Dialogue*, and Brown-Grant, *French Romance*, as well as Jane H. M. Taylor, 'Research on the French medieval lyric', *French Studies*, 61 (2007), 69–83. Also relevant here is Helen J. Swift, *Gender, Writing, and Performance. Men Defending Women in Late Medieval France (1440–1538)* (Oxford: Oxford University Press, 2008).

[12] See, for example, Adrian Armstrong and Malcolm Quainton (eds), *Book and Text in France, 1400–1600. Poetry on the Page* (Aldershot: Ashgate, 2007).

vibrancy and breadth of approach which is the hallmark of current later medieval studies.

The book is divided into two parts, the chapters in each being arranged in chronological order of their principal subject-matter's publication. The first section, 'Coming late' responds to an explicit sense of lateness or pastness within the texts in question, and the presence in them of the (positive) weight of a pre-existing tradition ripe for creative engagement. Helen J. Swift's essay, 'Splitting heirs: wrestling with the *Rose* in the *querelle des femmes*' sets the tone, examining the legacy of the *Roman de la Rose* that so preoccupied contemporary authors in three later medieval texts drawn into intertextual dialogue with it, and its misogyny. As Swift argues, the later authors ostensibly reject the anti-feminine stance of the *Rose*, but even as they do so they must also engage with it in order that their reworkings of it might be the better appreciated. Similar notions of engagement and (partial) rejection of earlier models concern Rosalind Brown-Grant and Sara Sturm-Maddox, both of whom discuss Burgundian *mises en prose*. In her '*Gérard de Nevers*: a *Roman de la Violette moralisé*? *Mise en prose* and the revalorisation of the courtly lady in the 'cycle de la gageure'', Brown-Grant examines the prose author's reworking of the text's heroine, Euriaut. The anonymous author takes on, and rejects, pre-existing tradition as he transforms Euriaut from an ambiguous courtly female in the earlier text into a moral exemplar, in ways that, as Brown-Grant argues, reflect the taste of the Burgundian audience. In similar vein, in 'The (other) worlds of *Mabrien*' Sturm-Maddox discusses issues of pastness and imaginative intertextuality in *Mabrien*'s creative re-engagement with its source, the epic cycle of Renaut de Montauban, privileging issues of lineage in order to appeal to a new public, the court of Burgundy, for whom genealogy was of crucial importance. Intertextual relationships with the weight of tradition are at the heart of Nancy Freeman Regalado's 'Saying your prayers: poetic expression of secularism in Villon's *Testament*'. Regalado examines a hitherto unrecognised source for the prayers woven into Villon's poetic will, the parodic *Pater Noster à l'usurier*, and demonstrates the ways in which Villon in a sense parodies the parody in his turn, substituting secular for spiritual concerns and in so doing shakes the very foundations of belief. The section closes with Emma Cayley's 'Le chapperon tousjours dure': the language of ageing desire in the *Debat de la damoiselle et de la bourgoise* and *Debat du viel et du jeune*', focusing on ageing (an issue which preoccupied Villon) in two fifteenth-century debate poems attributed to Blosseville and often collected in manuscript with the work of the earlier author Alain Chartier. In their negotiating of questions of ageing, desire, gender and language, Cayley argues, these poems engage in dialogue with the authority of Chartier in the material space of the codex.

The book's second part, 'Coming after', contains those chapters which offer a recontextualisation of later medieval material via transhistorical literary engagement, or via the explicit application to them of modern scholarly tools. Douglas Kelly, '*Fictio personæ* and subtle rewriting in later medieval French poetry', opens the section with his recontextualisation in later medieval texts of personifications, abstractions and/or specialisations found in the inescapable *Rose* among other earlier texts, taking modern linguistic and hermeneutic (as well as text-based) approaches to the changes these figures undergo. Modern approaches are central to Peter Ainsworth's 'Editing, e-Science and exhibitions', a fascinating excursus into the legacy or afterlife of an editorial project the author was involved in, the digitisation of a number of Froissart manuscripts and the concomitant development of an open access demonstrator, *Virtual Vellum*. Ainsworth's chapter reminds us not only of the wider (and sometimes unexpected) knowledge-transfer potential of modern scholarly endeavours, but also indicates, through its discussion of how new technological tools are used to facilitate research already grounded in rigorous scholarship, that modernity does not replace the traditional; rather, it complements it. Transhistorical recontextualisation, albeit at a much narrower temporal remove, characterises Michael Freeman's 'Did Ronsard really read Coquillart?', which offers a case-study for the re-examination of the sixteenth-century reception of later medieval authors. Freeman discusses the possible links between Ronsard, darling of the Pléiade poets, and the fifteenth-century Coquillart, and in so doing challenges long-held critical views that the dawn of the Renaissance brought with it a radical and permanent break with prior literary traditions. Similar questions of transhistorical literary engagement are addressed in Adrian Armstrong, 'Printing and metrical naturalisation: Jean Molinet's *Neuf Preux de Gourmandise*'. Armstrong discusses the retransmission of Molinet's poem in an anonymous sixteenth-century pamphlet, in which the poem's oringinal heptasyllabic lines are transformed into octosyllables; this, he argues, offers insights into linguistic and translational attitudes of the period, as well as the editorial practices current in the early decades of French printing. Related issues of reframing in the early years of printing are the focus of the final chapter in this section, Catherine Emerson's 'A question of paternity: Denis Sauvage, Philippe de Commynes and Olivier de La Marche'. Emerson looks at the birth of the 'mémoire' genre, first used by La Marche and Commynes in the 1470s but later denied to Commynes's work until some fifty years later when his editor Sauvage recuperated it for him, and focuses on the afterlives and later futures of the term in the work of the two authors, as well as the role of the editor in its recontextualisation.

Both parts, in terms of the subject-matter of the essays they contain as well as the dialogue they encourage between their respective chapters and with the work of Jane Taylor, underline the importance of communities established between writers and/or scholars, in the terms suggested by Jacqueline Cerquiglini-Toulet. In *La Couleur de la mélancolie*, she discusses the horizontal and vertical axes on which such relationships can operate: horizontality concerns more amicable exchange between contemporaries, while verticality implies genealogies, and the taking of material from illustrious predecessors.[13] Both of these axes characterise the legacy of Jane Taylor: her intellectual and personal generosity nourishes those privileged to have worked closely with her, while, more broadly, her scholarship continues to inspire future generations. Jane's example, and the chapters in this volume written to honour it, show that far from there being, as Froissart feared, nothing new to say, later medieval literature is in fact, as Guillaume de Lorris had it at the beginning of his *Rose*, 'bonne et nueve'.[14]

---

[13] Cerquiglini-Toulet, *Couleur de la mélancolie*, p. 145.

[14] Guillaume de Lorris et Jean de Meun, *Le Roman de la Rose*, ed. Felix Lecoy (Paris: Champion, 1965–70), v. 39.

The legacy of Jane H. M. Taylor

Rebecca Dixon

It is a well-known, if well-worn, topos of academic discourse to suggest, when chairing a conference session or seminar presentation, that one's colleague needs no introduction – and then proceed to give just that. There is no need to deviate from this time-honoured principle here, except in one important respect: perhaps surprisingly, Jane Taylor *does* need an introduction.

The fine portrait of Jane by Lizzie Rowe reproduced at the front of this volume captures admirably her physical appearance; but what of her scholarly and professional incarnation? Those of us working on later medieval French literature think we know her: as a specialist of long standing in the vast *Roman de Perceforest*, part of which she edited in 1979, or on the gleefully complex and wilfully ludic poetry of François Villon, on whom she published a monograph in 2001 (details of all Jane's publications appear at the end of this section). Whether at the universities of Manchester (1966–89), Oxford (1989–2001) or Durham (from 2001 until her retirement in 2008), her students – amongst whose number many of the contributors to this volume are privileged to have been able to count themselves –, would rightly identify her as an enthusiastic, generous, and rigorous teacher. No-one would dispute either of these claims; but there are deeper levels to Jane's scholarly, and wider professional, contributions. .

As the Introduction suggested, this volume and the essays in it bear witness to Jane's role in redefining our understanding of later medieval French culture. Her early career allegiance to the *Perceforest*'s cause is but one breathtaking example of this. Subsequently, she has done much to plead the case for and revivify interest in texts such as fifteenth-century prose versions of earlier classics of Arthurian derring-do which, for not always comprehensible reasons, had languished in the shadow of more illustrious and/or canonical works, as well as to offer fresh (textual as well as modern-theoretical) approaches to better-known figures such as Villon, Machaut, or Christine de Pizan. Books and articles, of course, demonstrate clearly this commitment to the rehabilitation of the literary past; but other publicly oriented enterprises are no less revelatory. Her half-century tally of reviews and notices, some of which she would doubtless modestly claim to be the consequence of her editorship of Romance languages for *Medium Ævum* (2002–08), impressively illustrates her verve for and investment in medieval French literature and its wider promulgation. Further, throughout her career, Jane has been a stalwart conference participant. She has given nearly one hundred papers, at international meetings as well as at more local or institutional events, and has played a considerable part in the organisation of more than half a dozen colloquia on later medieval themes in Manchester (1983), Oxford (1993, twice in 1998), Durham (2003, 2004) and beyond (Bangor, 2002).

Those who know Jane from conferences would attest to her scholarly and personal spirit of collegiality, to her intellectual generosity as giver of and listener to papers, to her guidance and inclusivity as head of scholarly societies (she was Vice-President and President of the International Arthurian Society from 1996 to 2002, and is now its Honorary President; and she also fulfilled a presidential role in the International Courtly Literature Society), and to her whole-hearted participation in more social aspects of academic gatherings. Less apparent to the wider community, though, is the way in which these qualities extend to other aspects of Jane's engagement with colleagues and students. She has held visiting scholarships in Europe and the United States (École Normale Supérieure, Paris, 1987; Harvard University, August 1995 to January 1996, and July 1998 to January 1999); University of California at Berkeley, December 2003 to January 2004) that allowed her collegial talents to transcend national and institutional boundaries. Moreover, as many of the contributors to this volume have cause to reflect, Jane is enormously supportive of younger colleagues, most notably (though not, of course, exclusively) as a research supervisor. She has successfully supervised, at either master's or doctoral level, some thirteen research students – a number which has proved anything but unlucky both for those who have benefitted from her ability to see value in their individual capabilities and research topics, and for Jane herself, not least because (directly or indirectly) the enterprise won her Durham University's Vice-Chancellor's Award for Excellence in Postgraduate Research Supervision in 2005.

Less obvious still to the more casual observer are Jane's considerable successes in what might all too narrowly be called administration: the very term fails to do justice to her guiding involvement in and ability to serve, shape and sustain institutions of many kinds, whether colleges and departments, societies, or journals. Anyone reading this volume will know something of Jane Taylor's scholarship; some will have been taught by her and be aware of her previously adduced merits as a teacher; but fewer individuals will have had the benefit of, or have seen in action, her skills in the pastoral support of students. Her deployment of the Dean's Lock, used on illegally parked bicycles in St Hilda's College, Oxford, during her four-year-and-a-term tenure as Dean, was regarded as firm but (usually) fair; more galling, though, was her ability to look wide-awake during early-morning college fire-drills, at which she was surely the only person of the assembly not wearing a coat hastily pulled on over pyjamas. More recently, and more significantly, Jane's contribution to student support as Principal of Collingwood College in Durham (2001–08) has been exemplary: she instigated a programme of study skills workshops for Collingwood students, and was instrumental in and supportive of the more socially and culturally oriented college film nights, 'Collingwood Wednesdays'. Her commitment to widening access to higher education, evident throughout her career, received its fullest and most impressive expression in Durham with the institution and development of the Collingwood Partnership Programme of mentoring for Key Stage 3 and 4 pupils (aged 11 to 14 and 14 to 19 respectively) in schools across County Durham by Collingwood students, and a further scheme in which looked-after children in the region are monitored and mentored by Durham students. 'Working to remove the barriers to social progress', the motto of the Royal Society for the Encouragement of Arts, Manufactures and Commerce (RSA), of which she was elected a Fellow in 2005, could have been written with Jane's endeavours in mind.

Other of Jane's less widely known professional activities have a more readily perceptible link to the academic work for which she is justly fêted. At Manchester in the 1980s she was responsible for setting up the Vinaver Trust which holds and administers funds for the dissemination (through publication or in a biennial lecture) of Arthurian scholarship, and of which she was appointed a Trustee in 2003. She was awarded an honorary doctorate by the Université de Reims-Champagne-Ardennes in 2001, while her critical acumen has earned her editorial and advisory roles in Britain, Europe and North America. Further, these qualities informed her appointment to serve on Sub-panel 52 – French in the 2008 UK Research Assessment Exercise (RAE).

Jane's work on the mid-fifteenth-century Burgundian *mises en prose* draws closely and to illuminating effect on translation theory; and she has a broader serious academic interest in translation demonstrated through her involvement, with the late Edith McMorran and Toby Garfitt, in TRIO (Translation Research in Oxford) and its thrice-yearly themed symposia and numerous publications. But less common knowledge in academic circles is Jane's professional practical interest, and publication record, in translation. She was a founder member of the Institute of Translation and Interpreting (ITI) in the United Kingdom, and served on its Board from 1987 to 1990. Given her commitment, as outlined above, to teaching, learning and mentoring, it comes as little surprise that she chaired the ITI's Education and Training Committee in this same period, when her expertise was brought to bear in the design and implementation of a part-time diploma in translation and interpreting, or that she was responsible for setting up a framework by which new entrants are introduced to the profession.

Jane's influence throughout a career spanning five decades has been immense, both in academic and in more personal terms. A successful research career demands drive, discipline, and imagination; it requires an ability to think outside the box, and to see value in a subject where others have failed to recognise it; and it needs the selflessness to identify a topic's benefits not simply for one's own advancement, but for the community as a whole. Jane Taylor encapsulates these processes in respect not only of her research output, but also of her whole professional life. Her legacy extends into, and beyond, the field of later medieval French literature, and continues to touch and shape the lives and careers, academic or otherwise, of all those who have come into contact with her.

Publications (to 2008)

Books (authored)

The Poetry of François Villon: Text and Context (Cambridge: Cambridge University Press, 2001).

The Making of Poetry: Poetic Anthologies at the End of the Middle Ages (Turnhout: Brepols, 2007).

Books (edited)

Le Roman de Perceforest. Première Partie (Geneva: Droz, 1979).

Dies Illa: Death in the Middle Ages (Liverpool: Francis Cairns, 1984).

(with Lesley Smith) *Women, the Book and the Godly* (Cambridge: D. S. Brewer, 1995).

(with Lesley Smith) *Women, the Book and the Worldly* (Cambridge: D. S. Brewer, 1995).

(with Lesley Smith) *Women and the Book: Assessing the Visual Evidence* (London: The British Library/Toronto: University of Toronto Press, 1997).

(with Edith McMorran and Guy Leclerq) *Translation: Here and There, Now and Then* (Exeter: Weald & Downland Open Air Museum, 1996).

(with Michael Freeman) *Villon at Oxford: The Drama of the Text* (Amsterdam: Rodopi, 1999).

Double Vision: Essays in Literary Translation (Durham: Durham Modern Languages Series, 2002).

(with Toby Garfitt and Edith Franck McMorran) *The Anatomy of Laughter* (Oxford: Legenda, 2005).

Journal Articles

'Aroès the Enchanter: an episode in the Roman de Perceforest and its sources', *Medium Ævum*, 47 (1978), 30–39.

'The pattern of perfection: Jehan de Saintré and the chivalric code', *Medium Ævum*, 63 (1984), 254–62.

'Villon et la danse macabré: "défamiliarisation" d'un mythe', *Publications de l'École normale supérieure des jeunes filles*, 29 (1988), 179–96.

'Mother-tongue enhancement: a survey', *Professional Translator and Interpreter*, 1 (1989), 3–12.

'*Danse macabré* and *bande dessinnée*: a question of reading', *Forum for Modern Language Studies*, 25 (1989), 356–69.

'Poésie et prédication: la fonction du discours proverbial dans la *Danse macabré*', *Medioevo Romanzo*, 22 (1989), 215–26.

'The dialogues of the Dance of Death and the limits of medieval theatre', *Fifteenth-Century Studies*, 16 (1990), 215–32.

'Que signifiait danse au quinzième siècle? Danser la *Danse macabré*', *Fifteenth-Century Studies*, 18 (1992), 259–78.

'Arthurian cyclicity: the construction of history in the late French romances', *The Arthurian Yearbook*, 2 (1992), 209–23.

'Contrasts in courtly patronage: the Dame du Lac and Madame des Belles Cousines', *Medieovo Romanzo*, 19 (1995), 277–92.

'La Fonction de la croisade dans *Jehan de Saintré*', *Cahiers de recherches médiévales*, 1 (1996), 192–204.

'*Le Roman de la Dame a la Lycorne et du Biau Chevalier au Lion*: text, image, rubric', *French Studies*, 51 (1997), 1–18.

'Translation or adaptation?', *The Linguist*, 36 (1997), 167–68 (published in French as 'Traduction ou adaptation?', *Translittérature*, 14 (1998), 71–74).

'Inescapable rose: Jean de Sénéchal's *Livre des cent ballades* and the art of cheerful paradox', *Medium Ævum*, 67 (1998), 60–84.

'Metonymy, montage and death in François Villon's *Testament*', *New Medieval Literatures*, 2 (1998), 133–58.

'The significance of the insignificant: reading reception in the Burgundian *Erec* and *Cligès*', *Fifteenth-Century Studies*, 24 (1998), 183–97.

'The lure of the hybrid: Tristan de Nanteuil, chanson de geste arthurienne?', *Arthurian Studies*, 18 (2001), 77–87.

'Anatomie du rire', *Translittérature*, 22 (2002), 80–84.

'Research on the French Medieval Lyric: an *état présent*', *French Studies*, 61 (2007), 69–83.

'Antiquarian Arthur: publishing the Round Table in sixteenth-century France', *Cahiers de Recherches médiévales*, 14 (2007), 127–42.

Book Chapters and Articles in Conference Proceedings

'Reason and faith in the *Roman de Perceforest*', in W. Rothwell (ed.), *Studies in Medieval Literature and Languages in Honour of F. Whitehead* (Manchester: Manchester University Press, 1973), pp. 303–22.

'Faith and austerity: the ecclesiology of the *Roman de Perceforest*', in Alison Adams, Armel H. Diverres, Karen Stern and Kenneth Varty (eds), *The

Changing Face of Arthurian Romance (Cambridge: D. S. Brewer, 1986), pp. 47–65.

'The fourteenth century: text, context, intertext', in Norris Lacy, Douglas Kelly and Keith Busby (eds), *The Legacy of Chrétien de Troyes* (Amsterdam: Rodopi, 1987), pp. 267–332.

'*Le Roman de Perceforest*', in Brian Moffat and Joy Fulton (eds), *SHARP Practice: the third report on researches into the medieval hospital at Soutra, Scotland* (Edinburgh: Soutra Hospital Archaeoethnopharmacological Research Project, 1989), pp. 76–78.

'La *Danse macabré*: une relecture', in Pierre Citti (ed), *Fins de siècle. Colloque de Tours 4-6 juin 1985* (Bordeaux: Presses Universitaires de Bordeaux, 1990), pp. 99–110.

'The lyric insertion: towards a functional model', in Keith Busby and Erik Kooper (eds), *Courtly Literature: Culture and Context* (Amsterdam: John Benjamins, 1991), pp. 539–49.

'Translator training: a survey', in Catriona Picken (ed.), *Institute of Translation and Interpreting Conference 4: Proceedings* (London: Aslib, 1991).

'Machaut's *Livre du Voir Dit* and the Poetics of the Title', in Jean-Claude Aubailly [*et al.*] (eds), '*Et c'est la fin pour quoy sommes ensemble*': *hommage à Jean Dufournet*, 3 vol. (Paris: Champion, 1993), III, pp. 1351–62.

'Image as reception: Antoine de la Sale's *Le Petit Jehan de Saintré*', in Donald Maddox and Sara Sturm-Maddox (eds), *Literary Aspects of Courtly Culture: Selected Papers from the Seventh Triennial Congress of the International Courtly Literature Society* (Cambridge: D. S. Brewer, 1994), pp. 265–79.

'Order from accident: cyclic consciousness at the end of the Middle Ages', in Bart Besamusca [*et al.*] (eds), *Cyclification: The Development of Narrative Cycles in the Chansons de Geste and the Arthurian Romances* (Amsterdam: Royal Netherlands Academy of Arts and Sciences, 1994), pp. 59–73.

'The parrot, the knight and the decline of chivalry', in Keith Busby and Norris Lacy (eds), *Conjonctures: Medieval Studies in Honor of Douglas Kelly* (Amsterdam: Rodopi, 1994), pp. 529–44.

'Translation as Reception: *La Danse macabré*', in Karen Pratt (ed.), *Shifts and Transpositions in Medieval Narrative: A Festschrift for Dr Elspeth Kennedy* (Cambridge: D. S. Brewer, 1994), pp. 181–92.

'The sense of a beginning: genealogy and plenitude in late medieval narrative cycles', in Donald Maddox and Sara Sturm-Maddox (eds), *Transtextualities: Of Cycles and Cyclicity in Medieval French Literature* (New York: Medieval and Renaissance Texts and Studies, 1995), pp. 93–123.

'*Grosse Margot* and *Sotte Chanson*: François Villon's art of adaptation', in Douglas Kelly (ed.), *The Medieval Opus: Imitation, Rewriting and*

Transmission in the French Tradition (Amsterdam: Rodopi, 1996), pp. 139–54.

'Mélusine's progeny: patterns and perplexities', in Donald Maddox and Sara Sturm-Maddox (eds), *Mélusine of Lusignan: Founding Fictions in Late Medieval France* (Athens/London: The University of Georgia Press, 1996), pp. 165–84.

'Les "huitains scolastiques" du *Lais* de Villon: vers une lecture intertextuelle', in Serio Cigada [*et al.*] (eds), *Actes du 1er colloque internationale sur la littérature en moyen français (Milan, 5–7 mai 1997): Facoltà di lingue et letterature straniere, Università Cattolica del Sacre Cuore* [*L'Analisi linguistica e letteraria*, 1 (1998)], pp. 241–56.

'*Le Roman de Fauvain*: manuscript, text, image', in Margaret Bent and Andrew Wathey (eds), *Fauvel Studies: Allegory, Chronicle, Music and Image in Paris, Bibliothèque nationale de France, MS français 146* (Oxford: Clarendon Press, 1998), pp. 569–89.

'*La Ballade des Seigneurs du temps jadis*: la poétique de l'incohérence', in Jane H. M. Taylor and Michael Freeman (eds), *Villon at Oxford: The Drama of the Text* (Amsterdam: Rodopi, 1999), pp. 35–50.

'*Le Chevalier des Dames du Dolent Fortuné*: image and text, manuscript and print', in Adrian Armstrong and David Adams (eds), *Word and Image: Studies in the French Illustrated Book from the Middle Ages to the Present Day* [*Bulletin of the John Rylands University Library of Manchester*, 81 (1999)], pp. 153–76.

'*Le Roman van Walewein*: man into fox, fox into man', in Bart Besamusca and Erik Kooper (eds), *Originality and Tradition in the Medieval Dutch Roman van Walewein* (Cambridge: D. S. Brewer, 1999), pp. 131–45.

'Guerre et fin des temps: lecture intertextuelle de la Bataille du Franc-Palais dans le *Roman de Perceforest*', in Alain Labbé, Daniel W. Lacroix and Danielle Quéruel (eds), *Guerres, voyages et quêtes au Moyen Âge: mélanges offerts à Jean-Claude Faucon* (Paris: Champion, 2000), pp. 413–21.

'Lire l'illisible: le *Lay* et le *Bergeronnecte* du *Testament* de Villon', in *La Recherche: bilan et perspectives. Actes du Colloque internationale, Université McGill, Montréal, 5–6–7 octobre 1998*, II [*Le Moyen Français*, 46–47 (2000)], 527–40.

'Translation as Reception: Boccaccio's *De mulieribus claris* and *Des cleres et nobles femmes*', in Keith Busby and Catherine M. Jones (eds), '*Por la soye amisté: Essays in Honor of Norris J. Lacy* (Amsterdam: Rodopi, 2000), pp. 491–507.

'*Les Albums poétiques de Marguerite d'Autriche*: the dynamics of an early Renaissance court', in Martha C. Driver with Cynthia J. Brown (eds),

Women and Book Culture in Late Medieval and Early Renaissance France [*Journal of the Early Book Society*, 4 (2001)], pp. 150–71.

'Mimesis meets artifice: two lyrics by Christine de Pizan', in John Campbell and Nadia Margolis (eds), *Christine de Pizan 2000: Studies in Christine de Pizan in Honour of Angus J. Kennedy* (Amsterdam/Atlanta: Rodopi, 2001), pp. 115–21 (notes pp. 319–22).

'Alexander Amoroso', in Donald Maddox and Sara Sturm-Maddox (eds), *The Medieval French Alexander* (New York: SUNY, 2002), pp. 124–41.

'Christine de Pizan and the poetics of the envoi', in Angus J. Kennedy [*et al.*] (eds), *Contexts and Continuities: Proceedings of the IVth International Colloquium on Christine de Pizan (Glasgow 21-27 July 2000), Published in Honour of Liliane Dulac*, 3 vol. (Glasgow: University of Glasgow Press, 2002), pp. 842–54.

'Alain Chartier and the unstable discourses of love', in Alex Vanneste [*et al.*] (eds), *Mémoire en temps advenir. Hommage à Theo Venckeleer* (Leuven: Peeters, 2003), pp. 167–79.

'Embodying the *Rose*: an intertextual reading of Alain Chartier's La *Belle Dame sans mercy*', in Barbara K. Altman and Carelton W. Carroll (eds), *The Court Reconvenes: Courtly Literature Across the Disciplines. Selected Papers from the Ninth Annual Congress of the International Courtly Literature Society, University of British Columbia, 25-31 July 1998* (Cambridge: D. S. Brewer, 2003), pp. 325–43.

'The Reine Fée in the *Roman de Perceforest*: rethinking, rewriting…', in Bonnie Wheeler (ed.), *Arthurian Studies in Honour of P. J. C. Field* (Cambridge: D. S. Brewer, 2004), pp. 81–91.

'Le Défi de la modernité: François Villon et Basil Bunting', in Jean Dufournet, Michael Freeman and Jean Dérens (eds), *Villon et ses lecteurs: actes du colloque internationale des 13-14 décembre 2000 organisé à la Bibliothèque historique de la Ville de Paris* (Paris: Champion, 2005), pp. 251–66.

'The knight and the parrot: writing the quest at the end of the Middle Ages', in Norris J. Lacy (ed.), *The Fortunes of King Arthur* (Cambridge: D. S. Brewer, 2005), pp. 181–94.

'"A rude heap together hurl'd": disorder and design in Vérard's *Jardin de Plaisance* (1501)', in Keith Busby, Bernard Guidot and Logan E. Whalen (eds), *'De sens rassis': Essays in honor of Rupert T. Pickens* (Amsterdam: Rodopi, 2005), pp. 629–44.

'La Double Fonction de *l'Instructif de seconde rhétorique*: une hypothèse', in Tania van Hemelryck and Cécile van Hoorebeeck (eds), *L'Écrit et le manuscrit à la fin du Moyen Âge* (Turnhout: Brepols, 2006), pp. 343–51.

'Inventer le recueil lyrique à l'époque de l'imprimerie: quelques jalons', in Nathalie Dauvois and Daniel Martin (eds), *Le Recueil poétique à la Renaissance* [*Réforme, Humanisme, Renaissance*, 62 (2006)], pp. 21–30.

'Late Medieval Arthurian Literature' (chapter edited by Jane H. M. Taylor, with contributions from Peter F. Ainsworth, Norris J. Lacy, Donald Edward Kennedy and William W. Kibler), in Glynn S. Burgess and Karen Pratt (eds), *The Arthur of the French. The Arthurian Legend in Medieval French and Occitan Literature* (Cardiff: University of Wales Press, 2006), pp. 488–527.

(with Keith Busby) 'Medieval French Literature', in Norris J. Lacy (ed.), *A History of Arthurian Scholarship* (Cambridge: D. S. Brewer, 2006), pp. 95–121.

'Mise en mélange au quinzième siècle: feuilleter le *Jardin de Plaisance*', in Danielle Régnier Böhler (ed), *Le Goût du lecteur à la fin du Moyen Âge* [*Cahiers du Léopard d'Or*, 11 (2006)], pp. 47–63.

'Courtly gatherings and poetic games: "coterie" anthologies in the late Middle Ages in France', in Adrian Armstrong and Malcolm Quainton (eds), *Book and Text in France, 1400–1600: Poetry on the Page* (Aldershot: Ashgate, 2007), pp. 13–29.

'"Flables couvertes": poetry and performance in the fifteenth century', in Eglal Doss-Quinby, Roberta L. Krueger and E. Jane Burns (eds), *Cultural Performances in Medieval France: Essays in Honor of Nancy Freeman Regalado* (Cambridge: D. S. Brewer, 2007), pp. 45–53.

'Lyric poetry of the later Middle Ages', in Simon Gaunt and Sarah Kay (eds), *The Cambridge Companion to Medieval French Literature* (Cambridge: Cambridge University Press, 2008), pp. 153–66.

'The thirteenth century', in Elizabeth Archibald and Ad Putter (eds), *The Cambridge Companion to the Arthurian Legend* (Cambridge: Cambridge University Press, forthcoming).

Reviews

Le Roman de Mélusine ou Histoire de Lusignan, ed. Eleanor Roach (Paris: Klincksieck, 1982), *Medium Ævum*, 54 (1985), 339–40.

Le roman de Floriant et Florete ou Le chevalier qui la nef maine, ed. Claude M. Lévy (Ottowa: Éditions de l'Université d'Ottowa, 1983), *Medium Ævum*, 55 (1986), 318–19.

Jacqueline Picoche, *Le Vocabulaire psychologique dans les 'Chroniques' de Froissart* (Amiens: Presses Universitaires de Picardie, 1984), *Zeitschrift für romanische Philologie*, 102 (1986), 209–13.

Cleriadus et Meliadice. Roman en prose du XVe siècle, ed. Gaston Zink (Geneva: Droz, 1984), *Medium Ævum*, 56 (1987), 146–47.

Le Roman de Perceforest. Quatrième Partie, ed. Gilles Roussineau (Geneva: Droz, 1987), *Speculum*, 64 (1989), 496–98.

George Chastellain, *Le Temple de Boccace*, ed. Susana Bliggenstorfer (Bern: Franke, 1988), *Medium Ævum*, 59 (1990), 329–30.

Littera et Sensus. Essays on Form and Meaning in Medieval French Literature Presented to John Fox, ed. D. A. Trotter (Exeter: Exeter University Press, 1989), *Medium Ævum*, 60 (1991), 134–36.

Guillaume de Machaut, *The Judgement of the King of Navarre*, ed. and trans. R. Barton Palmer (New York: Garland, 1988), *Medium Ævum*, 61 (1992), 341–42.

Peter F. Ainsworth, *Jean Froissart and the Fabric of History. Truth, Myth, and Fiction in the Chroniques* (Oxford: Clarendon Press, 1990), *Medium Ævum*, 61 (1992), 342–43.

La Geste du Chevalier au Cygne, ed. Edmond A. Emplaincourt (Tuscaloosa: University of Alabama Press, 1989); *La Chanson de Jérusalem*, ed. Nigel R. Thorp (Tuscaloosa: University of Alabama Press, 1992), *Speculum*, 68 (1993), 569–71.

Anne Paupert, *Les Fileuses et le clerc. Une étude des 'Evangiles des quenouilles'* (Geneva: Droz, 1990), *French Studies*, 47 (1993), 438–39.

Christiane Deluz, *Le Livre de Jehan de Mandeville. Une 'géographie' au XIVe siècle* (Louvain-la-Neuve: Publications de l'Institut d'Études Médiévales, 1988), *Medium Ævum*, 62 (1993), 149–50.

Daniel Poirion and Nancy Freeman Regalado (eds), *Contexts: Style and Values in Medieval Art and Literature* [*Yale French Studies*, 80 (1991)], *Fifteenth-Century Studies*, 21 (1994), 390–92.

Kathryn Gravdal, *Ravishing Maidens: Writing Rape in Medieval French Literature and Law* (Philadelphia: University of Pennsylvania Press, 1991), *French Studies*, 48 (1994), 87.

Michel Stanesco and Michel Zink, *Histoire européenne du roman médiéval. Esquisse et perspectives* (Paris: Presses Universitaires de Paris, 1992), *French Studies*, 48 (1994), 36.

Charles d'Orléans, *Ballades et rondeaux*, ed. and trans. Jean-Claude Mühlethaler (Paris: Livre de poche, 1992), *Medium Ævum*, 63 (1994), 151–52.

Paul Imbs, *Le Voir Dit de Guillaume de Machaut* (Paris: Klincksieck, 1991), *Medium Ævum*, 63 (1994), 149–51.

Sylvia Huot, *The Romance of the Rose and its Medieval Readers. Interpretation, Reception, Manuscript Transmission* (Cambridge: Cambridge University Press, 1993), *French Studies*, 59 (1995), 443–44.

Christine de Pizan, *The Book of the Body Politic*, ed. and trans. Kate Langdon Forham (Cambridge: Cambridge University Press, 1994), *Revue des langues romanes*, 99 (1995), 168–69.

Simon Gaunt, *Gender and Genre in Medieval French Literature* (Cambridge: Cambridge University Press, 1995), *Revue des langues romanes*, 100 (1996), 324–30 (review article).

Antoine de la Sale, *Saintré*, ed. Mario Eusebi, 2 vol. (Paris: Champion, 1993 and 1994), *Medium Ævum*, 65 (1996), 330–31.

Guillaume de Machaut, *Le Livre de la fontaine amoureuse*, ed. Jacqueline Cerquiglini-Toulet (Paris: Stock, 1993), *Medium Ævum*, 65 (1996), 145–46.

Jacqueline Cerquiglini-Toulet, *La Couleur de la mélancolie. La fréquentation des livres au XIVe siècle 1300–1415* (Paris: Hatier, 1993), *Medium Ævum*, 65 (1996), 142–43.

François Villon: Complete Poems, ed. Barbara N. Sargeant-Baur (Toronto: University of Toronto Press, 1994), *Modern Language Review*, 91 (1996), 470–71.

Sarah Kay, *The 'Chansons de Geste' in the Age of Romance. Political Fictions* (Oxford: Clarendon Press, 1995), *French Studies*, 51 (1997), 305.

The Danse Macabre of Women. Ms fr 955 of the Bibliothèque Nationale, ed. Ann Tukey Harrision (Kent: Kent State University Press, 1994), *Medium Ævum*, 66 (1997), 152–53.

Joël Blanchard (ed.), *Représentation, pouvoir et royauté à la fin du Moyen Âge. Actes du colloque organisé par l'université de Maine les 25 et 26 mars 1994* (Paris: Picard, 1995), *Medium Ævum*, 66 (1997), 187.

John Fox, *The Poetry of Fifteenth-Century France* (London: Grant and Cutler, 1995), *Medium Ævum*, 66 (1997), 346.

Christine de Pizan, *Le Livre du corps de policie*, ed. Angus J. Kennedy (Paris: Champion, 1998), *Medium Ævum*, 68 (1999), 349.

Claude Thiry (ed.), *'A l'heure encore de mon escrire': aspects de la littérature de Bourgogne sous Philippe le Bon et Charles le Téméraire*, ed. Claude Thiry [Les Lettres romanes, special number, 1997)], *Medium Ævum*, 68 (1999), 180–81.

Le Purgatoire d'Amours, ed. Sandrine Thonon (Louvain-la-Neuve: Presses Universitaires de Louvain, 1998), *Medium Ævum*, 68 (1999), 181

Le Roman de Ponthus et Sidoine, ed. Marie-Claude de Crécy (Geneva: Droz, 1997), *Medium Ævum*, 68 (1999), 144.

Deborah M. Sinnreich-Levi (ed.), *Eustache Deschamps, French Courtier-Poet. His work and his world* (New York: AMS Press, 1998), *Medium Ævum*, 69 (2000), 182–83.

Isabelle Bétemps, *L'Imaginaire dans l'œuvre de Guillaume de Machaut* (Paris: Champion, 1998), *Medium Ævum*, 69 (2000), 157–58.

Mabrien. Roman de chevalerie en prose du XVe siècle, ed. Philippe Verelst (Geneva: Droz, 1998), *Medium Ævum*, 69 (2000), 183–84.

Marilyn Desmond (ed.), *Christine de Pizan and the Categories of Difference* (Minneapolis: University of Minnesota Press, 1998), *Medium Ævum*, 69 (2000), 364–65.

The Love Debate Poems of Christine de Pizan. 'Le Livre du debat des deux amans', 'Le Livre des trois jugemens', 'Le Livre du dit de Poissy', ed. Barbara K. Altmann (Gainesville: Florida University Press, 1998), *French Studies*, 54 (2000), 496.

Roberta L. Krueger (ed.), *The Cambridge Companion to Medieval Romance* (Cambridge: Cambridge University Press, 2000), *French Studies*, 55 (2001), 222.

Guillaume de Machaut, *The Capture of Alexandria*, trans. Janet Shirley (Aldershot: Ashgate, 2001); *La Prise d'Alixandre (The Taking of Alexandria)*, ed. and trans. R. Barton Palmer (New York and London: Routledge, 2002), *Medium Ævum*, 70 (2001), 154–55.

Mary-Jo Arn (ed.), *Charles d'Orléans in England* (Cambridge: Cambridge University Press, 2000), *Medium Ævum*, 71 (2002), 154.

Patricia Victorin, '*Ysaïe le triste: une esthétique de la confluence* (Paris: Champion, 2002), *Speculum*, 79 (2004), 576–78.

Le Conte du Papegau: roman arthurien du XVe siècle, eds Hélène Charpentier and Patricia Victorin (Paris: Champion, 2004), *Medium Ævum*, 74 (2005), 172–73.

Le Devisement du Monde. Édition critique publiée sous la direction de Philippe Ménard. Tome II: Traversée de l'Afghanistan et entrée en Chine, ed. Laurence Harf-Lancner (Geneva: Droz, 2003), *Medium Ævum*, 74 (2005), 173–74.

Recueil générale des Isopets. Tome IV: Les Fables d'Eude de Chériton, ed. Pierre Ruelle (Paris: SATF, 1999), *Medium Ævum*, 74 (2005), 363.

Roger Pensom, *Le Sens de la métrique chez Villon. 'Le Testament'* (Oxford: Peter Lang, 2004), *French Studies*, 74 (2005), 384–85.

Virginie Minet-Mahy, *Esthétique et pouvoir de l'œuvre allégorique à l'époque de Charles IV* (Paris: Champion, 2005), *Les Lettres romanes*, 110 (2006), 126–28.

La Conquête de Constantinople, ed. Peter Noble (Edinburgh: Société Rencesvals British Branch, 2005), *Medium Ævum*, 75 (2006), 362.

Denis Hüe and Hélène Gallé, *Rutbeuf* (Neuilly-sur-Seine: Atlande, 2005), *Medium Ævum*, 75 (2006), 337.

Le Devisement du Monde. Édition critique publiée sous la direction de Philippe Ménard. Tome IV: Voyages à travers la Chine, ed. Joël Blanchard (Geneva: Droz, 2005), *Medium Ævum*, 75 (2006), 175–76.

Le Roman d'Eustache le Moine, ed. Anthony J. Holden (Leuven: Peeters, 2005), *Medium Ævum*, 75 (2006), 176.

Le Roman de Gliglois. Récit arthurien du XIIIe siècle, ed. Jean-Charles Lemaire (Liège: Éditions de l'université de Liège, 2005), *Medium Ævum*, 75 (2006), 362–63.

Claire Kappler and Roger Grozelier (eds), *L'Inspiration: le souffle createur dans les arts, littératures et mystiques du Moyen Âge européen et proche-oriental* (Paris: L'Harmattan, 2006), *Medium Ævum*, 76 (2007), 364–65.

Descente aux enfers, avec Guillaume de Digulleville: Edition et traduction commentées d'un extrait du 'Pelerinage de l'ame', ed. Frederic Duval (Saint-Lo: Archives départementales de la Manche, 2006), *Medium Ævum*, 76 (2007), 169–70.

Dominique Billy, François Clément and Annie Coombes (eds), *L'Éspace lyrique méditerranéen au Moyen Âge: nouvelles approches* (Toulouse: Presses Universitaires du Mirail, 2006), *Medium Ævum*, 76 (2007), 150.

Keith Busby and Christopher Kleinhenz (eds), *Courtly Arts and the Art of Courtliness: selected papers from the eleventh triennial congress of the International Courtly Literature Society, University of Wisconsin-Madison, 29 July–4 August 2004* (Cambridge: D. S. Brewer, 2006), *Medium Ævum*, 76 (2007), 363–64.

Lucien Faggion and Laure Verdon (eds), *Quête de soi, quête de vérité du Moyen Âge à l'époque moderne* (Aix-en-Provence: Publications de l'Université de Provence, 2007), *Medium Ævum*, 76 (2007), 367.

Marco Polo: Le Devisement du monde, edition critique sous la direction de Philippe Ménard, Tome V, eds Jean-Claude Delclos and Claude Roussel (Geneva: Droz, 2006), *Medium Ævum*, 76 (2007), 358.

Thomas Maillet (?): Les Proverbez d'Alain, ed. Tony Hunt (Paris: Champion, 2007), *Medium Ævum*, 76 (2007), 357.

Other Contributions

Norris J. Lacy (ed.), *The New Arthurian Encyclopedia* (New York: Garland, 1991), 3 entries.

Peter France (ed.), *Oxford Companion to Literature in French* (Oxford: Clarendon Press, 1995), 65 entries.

Jocelyn Wogan-Browne (ed.), *Voicing Medieval Women: An Anthology of Texts By, About, and For Women in the Middle Ages*, 2 tapes and accompanying book (Utah and Adelaide: Chaucer Studio, 1996), 2 readings.

Margaret C. Schaus (ed.), *Women and Gender in Medieval Europe. An Encyclopedia* (New York: Routledge, 1996), 2 entries.

Part I: Coming late

1

Splitting heirs: wrestling with the *Rose* in the *querelle des femmes*

Helen J. Swift

In an early sixteenth-century farce, *Le Vendeur de livres* (1515–20), a colporteur presents his literary wares to two female customers, one of whom has a specific request:

> – Av'ous le Roman de la rose?
> – Ouy, ma dame.
> – Montrés le nous.
> – Y est enfermé tout desoublz,
>   Pas ne l'érés sy promptement.[1]

The episode attests to sustained familiarity with 'that best-seller of all medieval best-sellers',[2] and is surely swathed in irony: not only the notion that the *Rose* has been pushed to the bottom of the bookseller's bag as if an obscure choice of text, but also the fact that the request is made by a woman when the most significant contemporary context for the *Rose*'s popularity was the *querelle des femmes*, the literary defence of women in which writers from Christine de Pizan onwards expressed vehement opposition to Jean de Meun's continuation of Guillaume de Lorris's original *Rose* portion.

In a different sense from that immediately intended by the Vendeur,

---

[1] Felix Lecoy, 'Une mention du *Roman de la rose* au XVIᵉ siècle', *Romania*, 87 (1866), 119–20 (p. 119).

[2] Jane H. M. Taylor, 'Embodying the *Rose*: an intertextual reading of Alain Chartier's *La Belle Dame sans mercy*', in Barbara K. Altmann and Carleton W. Carroll (eds), *The Court Reconvenes. Courtly Literature Across the Disciplines* (Cambridge: D. S. Brewer, 2003), pp. 325–33 (p. 325).

Jean de Meun's *Rose* lay at the bottom of things in a large number of *querelle* texts.[3] Writers including Martin Le Franc, Jacques Milet and Pierre Michault delighted in taking issue with the alleged misogyny or sexual immorality of the text, and with the author in person as the totemic *auctor* deemed responsible for the utterances of his personified characters. The eponymous hero from Le Franc's *Le Champion des dames* (*c.* 1442) rails:

> Ha, Jehan de Meun, grandement
> Tu a failly, ce m'est advis,
> Tu as parlé trop baudement.[4]

This sense of hermeneutic zest in challenging the *Rose* stems from the detailed nature of their intertextual engagements: topoi, arguments and individual phrases are picked up, taken apart or transformed with what Jane Taylor has called 'exegetical relish, confidently anticipating a readership textually familiar with the original poem'.[5] The writer's excitement is thus shared by his audience who effectively become co-producers of the texts they read.

This chapter, like its topic, is both indebted to and building on the illustrious work of an antecedent: it seeks to develop in one particular context Jane Taylor's emphasis on the dynamic and dialectical nature of intertextual dialogue with the formidable *Rose*. Taylor has brought out the sophistication of these negotiations in several fifteenth-century works, with regard to the *Rose* and also with respect to Alain Chartier's polemical poem *La Belle Dame sans mercy* (1424), which spawned its own series of vibrant literary responses, the so-called *Cycle de 'La Belle*

---

[3] *Querelle* texts may roughly be divided between two strands of literary inheritance: on the one hand, those which primarily take issue with Jean de Meun's late thirteenth-century *Rose* continuation and/or Matheolus's *Liber lamentationum Matheoluli* (1295), and whose quarrel with the *Rose* acquires intellectual impetus from the famous *querelle du 'Roman de la rose'* at the dawn of the fifteenth century; on the other hand, those which present themselves principally as responses to Boccaccio's *De mulieribus claris* (1361–62). The former usually take the form of narrative (debate) poems, while the latter are more often in (prose) catalogue form, such as Antoine Dufour's *Les Vies des femmes célèbres* (1504). A full range of texts is explored in Helen J. Swift, *Gender, Writing, and Performance: Men Defending Women in Late Medieval France (1440–1538)* (Oxford: Oxford University Press, 2008).

[4] Martin Le Franc, *Le Champion des dames*, 5 vol. (Paris: Champion, 1999), vv. 14389–91. Subsequent references to this work (hereinafter *Champion*) will be incorporated in the text.

[5] Jane H. M. Taylor, *The Poetry of François Villon: Text and Context* (Cambridge: Cambridge University Press, 2001), p. 11.

Dame sans mercy.[6] I seek here to pinpoint some characteristics of this 'poetic of engagement' in the corpus of fifteenth-century *querelle des femmes* texts, where negotiations with the *Rose* become especially conflictual and piquant. My aim is two-fold: firstly, to examine the intertextualities of two selected works, a lesser known, anonymous poem, *Le Chevalier des dames du dolent fortuné* (before 1477), in conjunction with a more familiar reference, Martin Le Franc's *Le Champion des dames*;[7] secondly, to consider the theoretical models of intertextuality that may most fruitfully help to unpick the negotiations represented in these works. Taylor has usefully drawn on the work of Michael Riffaterre, whose definition of intertextuality as 'un phénomène qui oriente la lecture du texte'[8] captures nicely Taylor's sense of the 'inescapable *Rose*' which seems to 'impose' an intertextual mode of reading on subsequent imaginative literature.[9] In other words, we are looking towards a model of intertextuality that integrates a measure of influence:[10] the *Rose* is, of course, just another text, but one that is represented within *querelle* texts contesting its authority as exercising an almost palpable force on its heirs. In the allegorical landscape of Jacques Milet's *Forest de Tristesse* (1459), the paragon of ladies, 'le chief des dames', is depicted knelt in prayer to the Virgin Mary, lamenting the burden exerted upon her soul by 'l'ung des chapitres' which 'propose / contre my':[11]

Me fait tant de mal sur mon ame
Qu'au vray dire je n'en puis plus.[12]

---

[6] See Alain Chartier, Baudet Herenc, Achille Caulier, *Le Cycle de 'La Belle Dame sans mercy'*, eds David F. Hult and Joan E. McRae (Paris: Champion, 2003).

[7] On a more personal note, I have included the *Champion* in homage: as the text that Jane suggested to me as I embarked upon my Master's degree, it ignited my research interest in the *querelle des femmes*.

[8] Michael Riffaterre, 'L'Intertexte inconnu', *Littérature*, 41 (1981), 4–7 (p. 5).

[9] Jane H. M. Taylor, 'Inescapable rose: Jean le Seneschal's *Cent Ballades* and the art of cheerful paradox', *Medium Ævum*, 67 (1998), 60–84 (p. 60).

[10] See also Mary Orr, *Intertextuality: Debates and Contexts* (Cambridge: Polity Press, 2003), p. 172.

[11] The contentious 'chapter' is the misogynistic tirade voiced by Le Jaloux (Guillaume de Lorris and Jean de Meun, *Le Roman de la rose*, ed. Armand Strubel (Paris: Librairie Générale Française, 1992), vv. 8459–9496 (hereinafter *Rose*)) which contains the infamous universal condemnation of women as 'putes' (*Rose*, vv. 9159–60).

[12] Jacques Milet, *La Forest de Tristesse*, in *Le Jardin de plaisance et fleur de rethorique*, eds Eugénie Droz and Arthur Piaget, 2 vol. (Paris: Firmin-Didot, 1910–25), I, fols 204[r]–24[v] (fol. 208[r]).

Oppressed by this anti-feminist inheritance, but wishing to repel it, she proceeds to address the crux of the matter:

> Dame vous scavez mon affaire
> Et les choses que j'ay affaire
> Pour trouver remede en ce cy.
> Je ne puis honneur reffaire
> Sans leur mauldiz livres deffaire
> Et leurs escriptz: il est ainsi.[13]

The 'chief des dames', serving as a diegetic echo of Milet himself as a pro-feminine writer, depicts herself in a sticky semiological situation: she cannot restore ('reffaire') her honour without first engaging with the text of the *Rose*, dismantling ('deffaire') the arguments against her, but by doing so she as it were contaminates herself. Later in the *Forest*, her advocate, Noble Vouloir, is similarly troubled by the stain upon his language caused by repeating the rhetoric of Jean de Meun, whom he addresses directly:

> Et reciter grant mal me fait
> Tes villains motz entre mes ditz.[14]

In Riffaterre's terms, 'l'intertexte laisse dans le texte une trace indélébile, une constante formelle qui joue le rôle d'un impératif de lecture'.[15] The pro-feminine case experiences this trace and imperative as a nefarious infection and a burden against which it must struggle. In this light, we find ourselves heading towards a Bloomian understanding of intertextuality, seeing 'the poetic text as psychic battlefield', in which combatants are locked in anxiety-inducing intertextual warfare.[16] Bloom's emphasis on the interpersonal dimension of relations between texts seems not inappropriate to the situation of the *Rose*'s heirs who, as mentioned above, seem to operate with a double understanding of their antecedent as *auctor* and *auctoritas*, perceiving the shadow of the authorial person Jean de Meun looming behind his work. I shall discuss each text in turn, before bringing them together in conclusion to con-

---

[13] *Ibid.* Her reference to 'leur' embraces both Jean de Meun and Matheolus, author of the misogamous *Liber Lamentationum Matheoluli*, who is often paired with the *Rose* author as a double target of pro-feminine argument: see Swift, *Gender, Writing, and Performance*, p. 132 n. 90.

[14] *Ibid.*, fol. 220ᵛ.

[15] Michael Riffaterre, 'La Trace de l'intertexte', *La Pensée*, 215 (1980), 4–18 (5).

[16] Harold Bloom, *Poetry and Repression: Revisionism from Blake to Stevens* (New Haven/London: Yale University Press, 1976), p. 2.

sider the most appropriate intertextual model for drawing out the imaginative zeal with which each author wrestles with the *Rose*.

In the course of some 24,000 lines, Martin Le Franc's *Le Champion des dames* stages a verse debate, divided into five books, between the ladies' Champion, Franc Vouloir, and various delegates of his adversary the arch-misogynist Malebouche. Through the discourse of his Champion and his pro-feminine narrator-persona, Le Franc challenges, condemns and rewrites the *Rose* on several levels, from the dissection of individual offending phrases, through quarrel with whole speeches by Jean de Meun's provocative characters Raison and La Vieille, to the dismantling of entire episodes. The present discussion will focus on one such episode, the *Rose*'s infamous conclusion where the Amant plucks the rose in a passage laden with sexual innuendo, and in particular the suggestion of rape. Casting himself as a pilgrim worshipfully approaching a shrine, the Amant describes his penetration of the inner sanctuary:

> Le paliz au bourdon brisai;
> Sui moi dedenz l'archiere mis
> [...]
> Outre l'ai [= bourdon] passé sanz demeure,
> Mais l'escharpe dehors demeure
> O les martlez rebillanz.[17]

There are two main points in the *Champion*, in Book III and Book V, at which Le Franc takes issue with the propriety of this conclusion. In Book III, Franc Vouloir offers critical comment on the dishonourable abuse of allegorical fiction demonstrated by this passage. The propriety of such fiction, as described by Boccaccio, is that text and gloss, literal and allegorical senses, should be quite distinct.[18] The Champion contends that the *Rose*'s sexual meaning is neither properly clothed in a garment of fiction, nor expressed openly and honestly. He sums up his case by anticipating his opponent's counterargument:

> Or vous direz: 'Meün couvry
> Le fait de rosier et de roses'.
> Je vous respons que tant ouvry
> Le texte qu'il n'y fault ja gloses. (*Champion*, vv. 12425–28)

---

[17] *Rose*, vv. 21644–45, 21651–53.

[18] Giovanni Boccaccio, *Genealogie deorum gentilium*, in *Tutte le opere di Giovanni Boccaccio*, ed. and trans. Vittore Branca, 10 vol. (Milan: Mondadori, 1964–98), VIII, 14.13, p. 1438.

The Champion also finds himself caught up in the same double-bound relationship to the *Rose* as that experienced by Milet's lady and advocate. In order to make his point Franc Vouloir needs to invite familiarity with the passage under debate:

> Veez le ribault en son livre
> A quel fin Amours a mené (*Champion*, vv. 12249–50),

but, by pursuing his argument, he finds himself dealing in the very terms of 'bourdon' and 'martellés rebillans' (vv. 12283, 12286) that he wishes to repel, concluding: 'J'en dis trop, ce parler est ort' (v. 12289).

The subject is, however, not dropped, being picked up again in Book V by a different personified character this time: Dame Virginité. She does not offer detached commentary, but, as if bearing in mind and implementing the Champion's comments, presents the episode rewritten in a proper manner. The entirety of Book V's debate is devoted to the Virgin Mary, and specifically to a theological justification of the doctrine of Immaculate Conception.[19] It is in this light that the reader should approach the recuperation of the *Rose*'s conclusion that is performed most aptly by the embodiment of sexual purity, one of eleven personified virtues who round off the debate with *chansons* in praise of the Virgin. Virginité rewrites it both as a hermeneutic recovery of the rose-maiden's defloration, and as a theologically oriented defence of one, holy woman's honour:

> Vierge, il entra ta chambre close,
> Close, reclose et close arriere.
> Pas ne pouoit estre desclose,
> Je le sçay, devant ne derriere.
> [...]
> Ainsy nonobstant la barriere
> Entra ton clos sans flour corrumpre.
>
> Au venir rien ne deffermay:
> Lui estant o toy tout fu clos.
> Au retour rien ne refermay
> Car n'y avoit eu riens desclos.
> Par ainsy ton precieux clos
> Eust tousjours entiere closture,

---

[19] To Le Franc's delight as a supporter of doctrinal reform, this tenet had recently been ratified by the Council of Basel in 1439: *Champion*, vv. 23425–32.

Car cil qui l'eust clos et reclos
En yssy bien sans descloture. (*Champion*, vv. 24161–64, 26167–76)

Her song is a rhetorical tour de force of verbs of closure and concealment. Her virtuoso manipulation of interlaced antitheses ('close'/'desclose' with 'devant'/'derriere') and synonyms ('arriere'/ 'derriere'), together with extended use of *traductio* ('reclose'/ 'close'/'desclose'/'clos'/'reclos') and *polyptoton* ('clos'/'closture'; 'desclos'/'descloture'), makes her song a masterful interpretative performance to be applauded. It is, after all, a contribution to an intratextual poetic celebration as well as being, on an intertextual axis, a spectacular piece of one-upmanship in Le Franc's competitive engagement with his illustrious ancestor Jean de Meun. Virginité's metaphor for specifying entry 'sans flour corrumpre' (v. 26168) picks up on Marian floral symbolism that has featured prominently throughout Book V,[20] and can thus be seen to trigger a two-fold intertextual context for her song: the two rose-maidens – the *Rose*'s 'rose' and the Virgin Mary as 'la blanche rose' (v. 22419) – intersect and conjure up the inimical spectre of the *Rose*'s sexual conquest together with the positive spectre of the Immaculate Conception.

Riffaterre's vocabulary of intertextual relations may be helpful for articulating Le Franc's manoeuvres here. The feminine figure of the rose, supported by the mention of corruption, serves as a 'connective', a signpost linking text to intertext, while the double intertext implied – the rapacious love ideology of the *Rose* and the Marian theology of the Bible – here supplies conflicting 'imperatives' for reading. The focus for our reading is flagged up through 'overdetermination' in the profusion of lexemes of closure, insisting upon miraculous penetration without rupture of any barrier. These lexemes counter the violent, forced access gained by Jean de Meun's Amant, who burrowed frantically with his staff ('bourdon') in order to break and enter.[21] Virginité's vehement affirmation that the maiden's protective screen remains intact also recalls, within the *Champion*, Franc Vouloir's prefatory description of

---

[20] Mary is 'la blanche rose' (v. 22419), 'le bouton' (v. 23576), 'la flour des flours' (v. 24069). See also Swift, *Gender, Writing, and Performance*, p. 57 n. 98.

[21] Highlighted terms are drawn from Michael Riffaterre, 'Compulsory reader response: the intertextual drive', in Michael Worton and Judith Still (eds), *Intertextuality: Theories and Practices* (Manchester/New York: Manchester University Press, 1990), pp. 56–78.

the 'celeste vergier'[22] where, safely concealed from the treacherous gaze
of Dangier, the eleven virtues may sing in peace:

> Aussy, mes dames, de rosiers
> Est le baing tendu et couvert,
> Et alentour trillié d'osiers
> Siques il n'y a riens d'ouvert.
> Et ne peut on a descouvert
> Pour les feulles et les rainseaux. (*Champion*, vv. 23785–90)

The rhetorical play of antithesis ('couvert'/'ouvert') and *traductio*
('couvert'/'descouvert') emphasises how the Champion's ladies are truly
safe from intrusion, as opposed to the perilously protected maiden of
Jean de Meun's *Rose*, screened by a curtain which yielded readily to the
Amant's battering.

The recuperative re-casting of the *Rose* conclusion performed
conjointly by Virginité and Franc Vouloir transforms the passage by
highlighting and repairing the weaknesses of its poetic structure, its
flimsy fictional veil that should be reinforced if the text is truly to be
read as an allegory operating on two levels: the literal, pilgrim narrative
and the oblique sense of sexual penetration. Virginité goes further: her
chanson redeems the *Rose*'s misuse of sacred images by bringing them
into the proper context of a coherent narrative where the sanctuary is a
not a poetic metaphor for, but the literal truth of, the body being
sexually consummated: either Saint Anne conceiving the Virgin, or
Mary herself at the Annunciation.

As well as recovering the *Rose*-maiden's defloration, the overdetermined vocabulary of closure may also, in a specifically theological
context, encourage connection with the lexical insistence upon
unforced, miraculous entry found in certain Old Testament texts that
anticipate typologically both the Immaculate Conception and the
Annunciation. The image of Mary as an impregnable castle was common currency in exegetical and homiletic tradition as an amplification
of lines in Luke (10:38) that are understood to evoke the incarnate
Christ's miraculous entry into the intact Virgin's womb: 'Intravit Jesus
in quoddam castellum.'[23] Virginité's depiction of a miraculous
consummation not only draws on this general metaphor, but also, with
Le Franc's characteristic textual precision and complexity, interweaves

---

[22] *Champion*, v. 23658. This 'vergier' is itself a purified rewriting of the *Rose*'s uneasy,
earthly paradise of Genius.

[23] '[Jesus] entered into a certain village.'

other, specific echoes. The Song of Songs and the book of Ezekiel prefigure the virginal womb in terms of miraculous opening and secure enclosure which resonate strikingly with Virginité's song.[24] The literal level of both biblical texts implies a courtly context: Ezekiel casts the Lord as a 'prince', while the Song's erotic scenario was often read in the Middle Ages as a sublimation of courtly love.[25] In Book V of the *Champion*, the Virgin's sanctity is itself expressed in a courtly idiom, which promotes an intersection of contexts of courtliness in Virginité's song between the theological *rosa sempiterna* and the redeemed rose-maiden. By interlacing echoes of the *Rose* and scriptural models, the *Champion* recuperates the *Rose*'s conclusion, redeeming it in both literary and theological senses, performing the textual miracle of transforming a rape into miraculous conception.

It is through a similar exercise of purification and deployment of the interface between sacred and secular courtliness that *Le Chevalier des dames du dolent fortuné* performs its recuperation of the *Rose*, redeeming Jean de Meun's ideology of love and misogyny through its portrayal of certain characters. This anonymous 5000-line poem presents a dreamer-narrator who is recruited to transcribe proceedings as Noble Cuer is enlisted by Dame Nature to defend woman's honour against the *Rose*'s misogyny. Inspired by his lady Noblesse Femenine, Noble Cuer defeats Malebouche and Cuer Villain, the embodiments of misogynous writing, and devotes himself thereafter to serving the Virgin Mary. The few scholars who have drawn attention to the *Chevalier* have recognised different aspects of its innovative, corrective response to Jean de Meun's *Rose*.[26] I explore here how the *Chevalier*'s

[24] Song of Songs 5:2–6; Ezekiel 44:1–3.

[25] For the tradition of Marian readings of the Song of Songs, see Ann W. Astell, *The Song of Songs in the Middle Ages* (Ithaca/London: Cornell University Press, 1990), pp. 15, 42–63. Its medieval French inheritance is sketched by E. Ann Matter, *The Song of Songs in Medieval Western Christianity* (Philadelphia: University of Pennsylvania Press, 1990), pp. 190–92.

[26] Helen Phillips explores its reworking of the Fall, exculpating Eve from being the sole agent of humanity's lapse, and observes its foundation on 'sophisticated literary allusion': 'Rewriting the Fall: Julian of Norwich and the *Chevalier des dames*', in Lesley Smith and Jane H. M. Taylor (eds), *Women, the Book and the Godly* (Cambridge: D. S. Brewer, 1995), pp. 149–56. Taylor describes how the poet recovers Jean de Meun's Nature, fountain and tree 'for an unambiguously Christian message': see '*Le Chevalier des dames du dolent fortuné*: image and text, manuscript and print', in Adrian Armstrong and David Adams (eds), *Word and Image: Studies in the French Illustrated Book from the Middle Ages to the Present Day* [*Bulletin of the John Rylands University Library of Manchester*, 81

amorous couple, Noblesse Femenine and Noble Cuer, are intended to be read against their *Rose* antecedents, the rose-maiden and the Amant,[27] as a positive image of the essential holiness of sexual love as opposed to the scurrilous carnal skirmish of Jean de Meun's characters at the *Rose*'s conclusion. By way of preface to this particular analysis, there are two, more general points to observe. Firstly, the example of the *Chevalier* will demonstrate not only the sophistication present in the *querelle*'s engagement with the *Rose*, but also a measure of humour; while both Le Franc and the *Chevalier* stage assiduous efforts to decontaminate the *Rose*, their earnestness is not without wit. Secondly, this example will also show how tackling the *Rose* by no means occurred as an isolated agenda, exclusive of other literary debates. The *Chevalier* combines its pro-feminine quarrel with the *Rose* with a response to Chartier's *Belle Dame sans mercy* through the language of both central characters.

The dynamic of the relationship between Noble Cuer and Noblesse Femenine is set up to be quite different from that of their *Rose* antecedents: Noblesse Femenine is, at first, Noble Cuer's mentor or guide before the pair are united as perfect lovers. This difference accords the lady some practical authority over her suitor, as distinct either from the symbolic, essentially passive authority she would be granted in a conventional *fin'amor* relationship, or from the objectified passivity of Jean de Meun's rose-maiden. Noblesse Femenine's speaks and acts, and in a more assertive capacity than, for example, Milet's 'chief des dames' knelt in prayer. The *Chevalier*'s Lady expresses incisively and concisely how women are not about to bow down and wait upon men:

> Mais les dames, sachez le bien,
> N'ont pas leurs cuers on les genoulz (*Chevalier*, vv. 323–24)

Her authoritative position is reflected in her first dialogue with Noble Cuer. Spanning thirty-one stanzas, with the speaker alternating between each *huitain* stanza, both the form and some content of this couple's sparring exchange conjure up, alongside the *Rose*, another pertinent antecedent, the *Belle Dame sans mercy* (1424). Chartier's sharp-tongued

---

(1999)], pp. 153–76.

[27] A similar suggestion is hinted at, but not developed, by the editor: *Le Chevalier des dames du dolent fortuné: allégorie en vers de la fin du XV*ᵉ *siècle*, ed. Jean Miquet (Ottawa: Les Presses de l'Université d'Ottawa, 1990), pp. 8–9. Subsequent references to the poem (hereinafter *Chevalier*) will be incorporated into the text.

Lady chose to opt out of the game of love by rejecting the advances of her suitor; yielding her heart would, she believes, amount to surrendering her free will 'pour en faire ung aultre le maistre'.[28] The *Chevalier*'s Lady shares the sparky sharp-wittedness of Chartier's; like the Belle Dame, Noblesse Femenine critiques her suitor's language, responding to his gloomy generalisation –

> Et tousjours ne vont point ensemble
> Semblance et cueur, tout en ung pas –

with the authoritative interjection

> Cest argument cy n'est que escume,
> Legier comme fueille en forest,
> Car l'en congnoist bien, a la plume
> L'oiseau de quel affaire il est. (*Chevalier*, vv. 351-56)

The maxim she criticises features, however, in Chartier's poem, in the Belle Dame's own discourse as part of her general pessimism regarding the impossibility of sincerity in amorous dealings.[29] The *Chevalier*'s re-distribution of arguments points up the different ideology of love represented by its Lady: no longer a courtly game played out to woman's disadvantage, nor the debased sensuality of the *Rose*, it is here a straightforward commitment of mutual respect and honesty that allows a woman to be on an equal footing with her lover. Noblesse Femenine's retort above appears peculiarly pertinent to her own love situation. Upon first meeting Noble Cuer, she immediately displays clearly the colour of her feathers by seizing him in a wordless embrace:

> Et elle, plaine de doulceurs,
> Le prist es braz et le baisoit,
> Sans changer contenance ou meurs,
> Ne rien dont blasmer se faisoit. (*Chevalier*, vv. 205–08)

The narrator's insistence that her impulsive conduct is blameless is partly tongue-in-cheek humour, but is also intended to highlight the unusual philosophy of sexual love that the *Chevalier* seeks to advocate: a spontaneous, open devotion. Noblesse Femenine welcomes her beloved

---

[28] Alain Chartier, *La Belle Dame sans mercy*, in *Le Cycle de 'La Belle Dame sans mercy'*, pp. 15–83 (v. 288).

[29] The Belle Dame reveals her distrust of 'Faintise': 'Villain cueur et bouche courtoise / Ne sont mie bien d'une sorte, / Mais Faintise tost les acoise': ibid, vv. 361–63.

sexually with a readiness and openness that recall the rhetoric of the
Song of Songs:[30]

> Tout mon tresor vous est ouvert
> Prenez en la fleur et le chois. (*Chevalier*, vv. 1033–34)

Accordingly, the narrator depicts their union in almost mystical terms,
and allusively plays off their noble first kiss against the corresponding
embrace in the *Rose* through a suggestive floral comparison:

> N'en plus qu'en flerer une rose
> Sur l'arbre y peut avoir offense,
> N'en plus de mal, bien dire je ose,
> N'y ot en leur convenïence. (*Chevalier*, 1073–74)

The rhyme-word 'rose' suffices as a connective, like the mention of
'fleur' in the previous quotation; although the meaning of 'fleur',
coupled in a binomial pair with 'chois', is figurative, denoting 'the best',
a literal understanding is also suggested by the context of amorous
relations. What Riffaterre calls a hermeneutic 'gap' is created between
the fully open 'fleur' of the text and the titillatingly closed rosebud of the
intertext, in turn provoking the reader's intertextual drive to fill out the
meaning of this distinction, and striking a contrast between un-
dissembling uninhibited love and artful seduction.[31] The narrator's
prelude to the lovers' embrace is cast in familiar terms:

> Lors, d'un vouloir incorrompu
> Et d'une amour inreparable,
> Et sans honneur estre rompu
> [...]
> S'entrebesa d'un cuer unysme. (*Chevalier*, vv. 1065–67, 1070)

They come together 'par honneur sans vïolence' (v. 1077), with the
same overdetermined insistence on the absence of fracture as in
Virginité's song in the *Champion*. In the *Chevalier*, this insistence
signals both a refutation of the *Rose* – here performed rhetorically
through repetition of the negative particle 'in-' and its prepositional
equivalent 'sans' – and an affiliation with the perfect love shown to the
Virgin by God acting through the Holy Spirit. In the *Chevalier*, Nostre
Dame herself appears as a character, with her immaculate penetration

---

[30] Song of Songs 5:4.
[31] Riffaterre, 'Compulsory reader response', p. 57.

by the Holy Spirit described in the same rhetorical terms: he enters 'la pucelle rose' (v. 3774) 'sans rompre virginalles trailles' (v. 2541).

The *Chevalier*'s shifting context of love between secular and sacred domains hinges to a great extent on the role Noble Cuer is accorded in the narrative. In the context of *querelle des femmes* literature he has an unusual amalgamation of roles to play: the more conventional is as advocate defending Noblesse Femenine and thereby womankind; the less expected is as Noblesse Femenine's lover, since the defender of ladies is more usually represented as a disinterested party, unbiased by personal feelings. This combination is rendered even trickier by the fact that his lady is clearly articulate and confident enough to speak for herself. Noble Cuer himself endorses her eloquence and, addressing his misogynist adversaries, explicitly opposes the image of abstracted, objectified *fin'amor* femininity:

> Voullez vous que les dames vivent
> Comme ung ymage en ces eglises,
> Et que le monde tout eschivent
> Et soient hors du people mises? (*Chevalier*, vv. 3436–39)

Why, then, does she need a champion? The answer is two-fold. Firstly, in terms of the plot, the poet contrives to have the final showdown between Noble Cuer and women's detractors as a physical rather than a verbal battle, for the hero to prove himself as a military, rather than a rhetorical champion.[32] Secondly, and also tied up with this shift from rhetorical to physical battle, Noble Cuer effects an important transition within the poem's ideology of love: his literal amorous commitment to Noblesse Femenine is translated onto a figurative level when he defends her (i.e. her sex's) honour against Male Bouche and Cuer Villain; he proves himself not only as a secular knight, but also as a spiritual chevalier who then devotes himself to service of the Virgin Mary and thereby advocates quite a different ideology of love towards women as 'le chevalier de toutes dames' (v. 4936). This new role was anticipated in his youth by Dame Nature, who predicted:

---

[32] Narrative progression from physical to verbal combat is more usual. In the *Champion*, for example, an initial assault upon the castle of Amour by Malebouche and his cohort, and a brief duel between Franc Vouloir and Despit le crueux, are followed by extended scholastic debate; physical warfare is sublimated to verbal conflict: see Swift, *Gender, Writing, and Performance*, pp. 100–71.

Toutes les amerez, pas une,
Et leur honneur essaucerez. (*Chevalier*, vv. 625–26)

Far from being an incitement to promiscuity, which is the meaning
such a phrase would hold in the context of Jean de Meun's *Rose*, this is
an exhortation to universal Christian charity, a context of love towards
which Noble Cuer's union with Noblesse Femenine gestured, but which
ultimately transcends the secular couple, at which point Noblesse
Femenine effectively ceases to exist in the narrative on a literal plane,
being present only figuratively, internalised within Noble Cuer's
devotion to the Virgin.

The *Chevalier*'s negotiation with the *Rose* thus appears even more
complex and multi-textual than the *Champion*'s. Both poems act
innovatively upon details of language in the episodes or characters they
rewrite, and both appear aware of an interpersonal dimension to the
intertextual links they forge: the Champion dismantles the text and
impugns the author: 'Jan de Meün, qui te fis maistre / En l'art
d'amours?' (*Champion*, vv. 14497-98); the *Chevalier* remodels
characters and represents Jean de Meun himself as a personified figure
within the diegesis: Cuer Villain, Noble Cuer's antitype:

Car mainte prose
A mis au Roman de la Rose
Qui est de tres villaine glose
Et faulse en soy, bien dire l'ose,
Et faicte a tort. (*Chevalier*, vv. 1372-76)

In his accusations here, Noble Cuer engages in the sort of detached
commentary we saw Franc Vouloir practising in Book III of the
Champion. Their hermeneutic concerns are very similar: they criticise
Jean de Meun's construction of his work, not only at the level of the
gloss, the interpretations to which it gives rise, but, more
fundamentally, at the root of the text itself and the authorial intention
behind its composition, once again underscoring their dual consciousness of the *Rose* as *auctoritas* and *auctor*.

On the one hand, the *Rose* stands as just another text, whose alleged
perverse intention, flawed construction and licentious scope of meaning
may be recuperated through an heir's transformative textual action. On
the other hand, the *Rose* is played up by its respondents to be an
inescapably looming presence to which one remains troublingly double-
bound, needing to entertain its nefarious content in order to be able to

tackle it. How may we, then, most appropriately conceive of this particular kind of intertextual relationship in which the heir seems, as it were, haunted by his ancestor? How may we describe the heir's attitude towards the work he rewrites? I think we may fruitfully speak of the inheriting writer's 'performative interpretation' of the antecedent, understanding 'performative' in two senses. Firstly, it entails a linguistic act on the part of the author (and also on the part of the reader who is drawn to participate in the interaction of present text and prior text) that is conceived of as a 'doing'; the rhetoric of the *Champion* and *Chevalier* is shown working upon the image of sexual penetration to transform its ethical value and purify its artistic presentation.[33] The rhetorically overdetermined presentation of their engagement with the *Rose*'s conclusion portrays this passage as a sort of intertextual 'pressure point': a moment of particular interpretative anxiety. Secondly, it stands as an act to be applauded, a performance in a quasi-dramatic sense. The text's audience, having responded to the author's connectives and pressure points in order to fill out the hermeneutic gap between text and antecedent, is invited to applaud the dexterity and inventive wit manifested in these actions.

This latter aspect of the heir's performative treatment of his ancestor brings us, in conclusion, to address the most basic of questions regarding *querelle* writers' engagement with the *Rose*: why did they bother? If, as I suggested above, wrestling with the *Rose*'s alleged immorality placed the heir's work in an ethically delicate position, risking contamination by Jean de Meun's ordure, why did writers deliberately land themselves in this semiological hot water? Commenting on Machaut's and Froissart's use of the *Rose*, Rosemary Morris remarks that 'to use the *Rose* as subtext while denying the power of sexuality was [...] a dangerous process.'[34] Her remark is equally applicable to the *Champion* and *Chevalier*: why build a message of theological love on the unstable foundations of flawed – or simply lewd – erotic allegory, imposing the need to 'deffaire' the latter before being

---

[33] I take this concept of linguistic performativity operating on an intertextual axis from Jacques Derrida's notion of 'l'interprétation performative, c'est-à-dire d'une interprétation qui transforme cela même qu'elle interprète'; see *Spectres de Marx: l'état de la dette, le travail du deuil, et la nouvelle Internationale* (Paris: Galilée, 1993), p. 89. For further discussion of *querelle* intertextuality according to this model, see Swift, *Gender, Writing, and Performance*, pp. 18–99.

[34] Rosemary Morris, 'Machaut, Froissart and the fictionalization of the self', *Modern Language Review*, 83 (1988), 545–55 (p. 548).

able to 'reffaire' the former? The answer, I think, lies in the competitive spirit of fifteenth-century poetics, what Jacqueline Cerquiglini-Toulet has called its 'jeu sérieux'.[35] *Querelle* writers make a deliberate artistic choice to engage with the *Rose* and choose to present it, through the speech of their characters (including the narrator as a character here), as a troubling presence, perpetuating thereby Jean de Meun's reputation as a totemic figure, a *succès de scandale*. Setting the *Rose* up in this manner as the greatest and most controversial vernacular authority thus boosts the standing of their own works in their readiness to challenge this idol. *Querelle* writers also turned to their profit the contemporary popularity of Jean de Meun's text; being able to rely upon it as part of their audience's intertextual competence, Le Franc and the *Chevalier* poet could render more dramatic and hermeneutically exciting their portrayal of spiritual love by representing it in counterpoint with the *Rose*'s eroticism, using the *Rose* also as a kind of literary fulcrum around which to lever other textual analogies and debates, from the Song of Songs to the *Cycle de 'La Belle Dame sans mercy'*.

If Jean de Meun's *Rose* was being repeatedly reworked, its imagery re-appropriated and its author openly reprimanded, did there not come a point when its authority was broken down and the text finally wrested from its author's control? Not in the fifteenth century, to judge by the description of Jean de Meun in the literary cemetery of Octovien de Saint-Gelais's *Séjour d'honneur* (1494). Saint-Gelais's narrator recounts:

> Peu demouray en ce sejour commun
> Ou tout plaisir et leesse est enclose.
> Si apperceu lors maistre Jehan de Meun,
> Tenant encor son Rommant de la Rose.[36]

Jean de Meun once again looms large, as if cued into the text by the keyword 'enclose' in rhyme position which echoes the *Rose*'s famous title-incipit:

> Ce est li romanz de la rose,
> Ou l'art d'amours est toute enclose.[37]

---

[35] Jacqueline Cerquiglini-Toulet, *La Couleur de la mélancolie: la fréquentation des livres au XIVe siècle, 1300–1415* (Paris: Hatier, 1993), p. 79. See also Taylor, *The Poetry of François Villon*, ch. 1.

[36] Octovien de Saint-Gelais, *Le Séjour d'honneur*, ed. Frédéric Duval (Geneva: Droz, 2002), III.xii, vv. 109–12.

[37] *Rose*, vv. 37–38. The underlying irony is that these lines actually derive from

It is the possessive adjective that is significant in the *Séjour* quotation: the master is envisaged still holding onto 'his' book, the implication being that acts of poetic challenge and hermeneutic revision have not succeeded in wrenching the *Rose* from its author, from whose indomitable spectre the book is indissociable. It is still time to continue wrestling with the *Roman de la rose*.

Guillaume de Lorris's portion. Guillaume plays a varying, usually very minor, role in *querelle* texts: generally entirely eclipsed by concern for Jean de Meun, sometimes lumped in with his continuator as a pro-feminine target, occasionally distinguished from him as an upright promoter of 'pure courtoisie' (*Champion*, v. 11780), and once accorded a starring role, in the anonymous *Le Giroufflier aulx dames* (before 1521): see Swift, *Gender, Writing, and Performance*, pp. 58–65.

2

Gérard de Nevers: a *Roman de la Violette moralisé*? *Mise en prose* and the revalorisation of the courtly lady in the 'cycle de la gageure'

Rosalind Brown-Grant

For many years, the prose reworkings of earlier verse romances or epics (also known as *mises en prose* or *dérimages*) have undoubtedly been the poor cousin of late medieval French literature. Despite the fact that the romances of this type enjoyed enormous popularity at the Burgundian court in the mid-fifteenth century, they have usually been dismissed by modern scholars as merely inferior and repetitious versions of their twelfth- and thirteenth-century originals. Indeed, until recently, Georges Doutrepont, in his ground-breaking study of the *mises en prose* first published in 1939,[1] was almost alone amongst modern critics in discussing the aesthetic conventions of these works in terms of their authors' own narrative purposes rather than simply comparing them unfavourably to the earlier poems. For Doutrepont, the changes that the prose *remanieurs* (or *dérimeurs*) made to their source material was dictated by a desire for greater realism, hence their creation of more logical causal connections between episodes, their development of more psychologically rounded characters and their location of plots within settings that were geographically and historically recognisable. Building on Doutrepont's work, Jane Taylor has been in the forefront of those scholars who have recently begun to challenge traditional negative

---

[1] Georges Doutrepont, *Les Mises en prose des épopées et des romans chevaleresques du XIVe au XVIe siècle* (Brussels: Palais des Académies, 1939; Geneva: Slatkine Reprints, 1969).

assessments of the *mises en prose*, arguing that the transition from verse to prose went hand in hand with an updating of the content of the narrative through a process of acculturation, that is the adaptation of earlier material in accordance with new cultural and ideological norms.[2] In reading the prose reworkings for the valuable information which they provide on the late medieval reception of twelfth- and thirteenth-century romances, Taylor and others have shown how the *dérimeur* felt the need to explain customs and practices that were no longer familiar so as to cater for literary tastes and political agendas which were very different from those of the text's original audience. Moreover, these scholars have stressed how, in line with the more overtly didactic culture of the day, the prose *remanieur* placed far greater emphasis on drawing an explicit moral lesson from the narrative than his verse predecessors had done.

However, although the critical rehabilitation of the *mises en prose* is now well under way, one important aspect of the process of acculturation identified in these works still remains largely unexplored. This is the question of how the gender roles found in the early verse romances were reinterpreted in the later prose works in the genre, this being a key issue given the centrality of gender ideology to romance as a whole.[3] How, then, were the conventions governing the presentation of male and female roles in twelfth- and thirteenth-century romances re-shaped in the very different cultural environment of the later Middle Ages?[4] To what extent does the emphasis on explicit moralisation which scholars have detected in the *mises en prose* inform the way in which gender is represented in the prose reworkings of the fourteenth and fifteenth centuries?

One sub-type of romance which is of particular interest for the study of gender in the *mises en prose* is that of the 'cycle de la gageure' or

---

[2] See Jane H. M. Taylor, 'The significance of the insignificant: reading reception in the Burgundian *Erec* and *Cligès*', *Fifteenth-Century Studies*, 24 (1998), 183–97; Norris J. Lacy, 'Adaptation as reception: the Burgundian *Cligès*', *Fifteenth-Century Studies*, 24 (1998), 198–207; and Maria Colombo Timelli, 'Sur l'édition des mises en prose de romans (XVe siècle): bilan et perspectives', *Le Moyen Français*, 44–45 (1999), 87–106.

[3] See Roberta L. Krueger, *Women Readers and the Ideology of Gender in Old French Verse Romance* (Cambridge: Cambridge University Press, 1993); and Simon Gaunt, *Gender and Genre in Medieval French Literature* (Cambridge: Cambridge University Press, 1995), pp. 71–121.

[4] See Rosalind Brown-Grant, *French Romance of the Later Middle Ages: Gender, Morality, and Desire* (Oxford: Oxford University Press, 2008).

'wager cycle', since it raises important questions about male honour and female sexuality.[5] In this sub-type, a knight who foolishly gambles his lands and title on his lady's fidelity is tricked by another knight into thinking her unfaithful and so abandons her. The hapless hero and heroine then separately undergo a series of perilous adventures before being reunited and restored to their former estate when the disinherited knight reveals his enemy's treachery in a trial by combat which also proves the lady's innocence. As an example of a late medieval 'wager cycle' tale, the anonymous Burgundian romance *Gérard de Nevers* (*c.* 1451), which is a *dérimage* of Gerbert de Montreuil's *Roman de la Violette* (1227–29),[6] provides an excellent opportunity for examining the kind of gendered acculturation that occurs in the reworking of an earlier verse text into prose. In both versions of the tale, the villainous Lisiart wins the wager by claiming to have slept with Euriaut (or 'Euriant' in the *mise en prose*) when in fact it is only by spying on her with the help of her disloyal governess Gondree that he has discovered that she has a violet-shaped birthmark on her breast, one which her lover Gerart has told her never to reveal to another person because he would take it to mean that she had been unfaithful to him.

Predictably, scholars have paid far less attention to *Gérard de Nevers* than to the earlier *Roman de la Violette*, and what studies there have been of the later text have made no mention of gender issues but have tended instead to develop Doutrepont's general claims about the *mises en prose*.[7] Thus, whilst Maciej Abramowicz has noted the emphasis on didacticism in *Gérard de Nevers* in the author's attempt to produce an edifying work of realism which more closely resembles a chronicle than a romance,[8] Mireille Demaules sees the main differences between the two versions as being motivated by the *dérimeur*'s desire to update the verse original, to flatter its fifteenth-century audience by putting up a 'miroir idéalisant de l'aristocratie contemporaine',[9] and to introduce a

---

[5] See Gaston Paris, 'Le Cycle de la *gageure*', *Romania*, 32 (1903), 481–551.

[6] See *Le Roman de la Violette ou de Gerart de Nevers*, ed. Douglas Labaree Buffum (Paris: Champion, 1927); and *Gérard de Nevers: prose version of the Roman de la Violette*, ed. Lawrence F. H. Lowe (Princeton/Paris: Princeton University Press/Les Presses Universitaires, 1928), hereinafter cited as Lowe, *Gérard de Nevers*. All quotations from these two texts will be given in parentheses in the body of the chapter.

[7] See, for example, Lowe, *Gérard de Nevers*.

[8] Maciej Abramowicz, *Réécrire au moyen âge: mises en prose des romans de Bourgogne* (Lublin: Wydawnictwo Uniwersytetu Marii-Curie-Sklodowskiej, 1996), pp. 98–132.

[9] Mireille Demaules, '*Le Cycle de la gageure* au XVe siècle: l'exemple français et

fashionable Arthurian note through an interpolated episode known as 'The Lady in the Water'.[10]

Equally predictably, if scholars writing on *Gérard de Nevers* have omitted to address gender, those who have discussed the earlier romance have focussed almost exclusively on this issue, often comparing the *Roman de la Violette* with other 'wager cycle' romances such as Jean Renart's *Roman de la Rose ou de Guillaume de Dole*, from which Gerbert de Montreuil borrowed both the motif of the tell-tale birthmark and the vogue for extensive lyric insertions. Roberta L. Krueger thus characterises the text as a typical example of a 'wager cycle' romance in appearing to celebrate and glorify women as heroines whilst in fact reinscribing them within the constraints of male courtly values.[11] Similarly, Kathy M. Krause has noted how the heroine in the *Roman de la Violette* is trapped between competing male courtly stereotypes about women as either the erotic 'Amie' or the troubling 'Femme peu fiable',[12] and has argued that Euriaut is represented as a highly ambivalent figure, one whose function as an erotic body which can be voyeuristically violated is at awkward variance with her portrayal elsewhere in the text as a martyr figure clothed in the garb of virtue.[13]

Not only, then, is there a striking discrepancy between the close attention paid to gender in studies of the *Roman de la Violette* and the absence of such attention in studies of *Gérard de Nevers*, but it is in fact misleading to suggest that the prose version differs from its source solely in its greater degree of realism and didacticism. As close analysis of the two texts will reveal, it is precisely on the issue of gender representation that the differences between the verse original and the

---

l'exemple italien', in Danielle Böhler (ed.), *Le Goût du lecteur à la fin du moyen âge* [*Cahiers du Léopard d'Or*, 11 (2006)], pp. 85–99 (p. 88).

[10] See Charles François, 'L'Épisode interpolé du "Roman de la Violette"', *Revue Belge de Philologie et d'Histoire*, 11 (1932), 689–98. For the source of this episode, see Gerbert de Montreuil, *La Continuation de Perceval*, ed. Marguerite Oswald, 3 vol. (Paris: Honoré Champion, 1975), III, vv. 14999–5268.

[11] See Krueger, *Women Readers and the Ideology of Gender*, pp. 128–55 (in particular, pp. 137–40).

[12] Kathy M. Krause, 'L'Héroïne et l'autorité du discours: le *Roman de la Violette* et le *Roman de la Rose ou de Guillaume de Dole*', *Le Moyen Âge*, 102 (1996), 191–216.

[13] Kathy M. Krause, 'The material erotic: the clothed and unclothed female body in the *Roman de la violette*', in Curtis Perry (ed.), *Material Culture and Cultural Materialisms in the Middle Ages and the Renaissance* (Turnhout: Brepols, 2001), pp. 17–39. See also Kristin L. Burr, 'Re-creating the body: Euriaut's tales in *Le Roman de la Violette*', *Symposium*, 56 (2002), 3–16.

mise en prose are most marked. Indeed, whilst the passages concerning Gerart's chivalrous adventures remain remarkably close to those in the early romance, it is the episodes concerning the heroine which have undergone the most substantial modification. What do these modifications consist of in *Gérard de Nevers* and what is their significance for our understanding of the overall moral message of the text?

Even from the dedicatory prologue that begins each of our romances, it is clear that very different expectations are raised in the mind of the reader about what kind of narrative is to follow. Writing for Marie, countess of Ponthieu, the author of the *Roman de la Violette* explains that the chief aim of his text, which he characterises as a 'conte biel et delitable' (v. 33), is to entertain. He thus draws the reader's attention to the aesthetics of his work by stressing the novelty of its treating a non-Arthurian subject (vv. 34–35) and of including lyric sections that complement the action in the narrative (vv. 38–41). Through wordplay, Gerbert also subtly introduces one of the key themes of his poem, namely, the difference between 'avoir' and 'savoir' (vv. 3–5) which he uses here to refer to his status as a poor poet who may lack material wealth but is rich in literary expertise: 'Puis ke scïenche ai et tant vail' (v. 19). However, in the narrative itself, this pair of terms clearly alludes to the carnal knowledge ('savoir') that Lisiart claims to have had of Euriaut's body but which falls far short of actual possession ('avoir') of the lady herself, as he alludes mockingly to Gerart's pact of secrecy with Euriaut concerning the violet birthmark: 'Que se nus, fors il, le *savoit*, / Que ses bons de li fais *aroit*' (vv. 967–68, emphasis added).[14] Exploring this theme of 'avoir' and 'savoir' in terms of the difficulty of retaining possession of the beloved and of being certain in one's knowledge of her fidelity, the couple's actual adventures consist of a series of attempted seductions of both hero and heroine interspersed with set-piece accounts of Gerart's chivalric prowess. Given that these adventures are heavily eroticised through lengthy physical descriptions of female beauty and by snatches of amorous lyrics, the adjective 'delitable' used in the prologue to the *Roman de la Violette* would thus seem to hint at the 'delit', in the sense of erotic pleasure, which the text affords the reader. Thus, despite the flattering parallel that the author seeks to draw in his epilogue between his heroine and his dedicatee, Marie de Ponthieu, on the basis of their 'fois et [...] loyautés' (v. 6625 and v. 6647) which have brought about their shared return to good

---

[14] Krause, 'L'Héroïne et l'autorité du discours', p. 214.

fortune,[15] the sexualised atmosphere of the rest of the narrative creates a highly ambivalent representation of Euriaut herself as, on the one hand, an exemplar of female patience, and, on the other, a courtly lady whose desires and desirability are in part responsible for her misfortunes.

If the prologue of the *Roman de la Violette* raises the expectation that the text is primarily a piece of delectable entertainment hinging on questions of sexual possession and knowledge, that which prefaces *Gérard de Nevers* could not be more different. Stressing that his chief aim in writing this text for his patron, Charles de Nevers, stepson of Philip the Good, is to be didactic and commemorative, the anonymous author creates a direct link between hero and dedicatee through their shared family name and thus presents the deeds of a putative ancestor such as Gerart as a 'bonne exemple, miroir et fondacion aux nobles et vaillans homez' (p. 2) from which the reader can learn. In common with the prologues to other historico-realist Burgundian romances of the period, the author goes on to obscure his actual source, the *Roman de la Violette*, claiming instead that the original on which his work was based was 'en langage prouvençal et moult dificile a entendre' (*ibid.*).[16] Whilst some critics have argued that this reference to Provençal serves to add a kind of exotic Mediterranean flavour to the text,[17] it was perhaps actually intended to signal the author's independence from his real source in terms of both form and content. Thus, in the narrative that follows, he not only rejects the amorous connotations attached to the Provençal language as a medium for talking about passionate love,[18] eliminating most of the love lyrics featured in the *Roman de la Violette* except for those which are clearly motivated by their place in the diegesis,[19] but also resolves the ambiguous representation of the heroine

---

[15] Just as Euriaut had to undergo her various trials before being reunited with her lover, so Marie had had to wait a number of years before the return of her husband, Simon de Dammartin, who had been exiled and stripped of his title and lands for having taken part in a rebellion against the king. See Kara Doyle, '"Narratizing" Marie of Ponthieu', *Historical Reflections/Réflexions Historiques*, 30 (2004), 29–54.

[16] The authors of the *Histoire des Seigneurs de Gavre* (1456) and *Gillion de Trazegnies* (1433–50) both claim to have translated their works from texts originally written in Italian.

[17] See, for example, *Gérard de Nevers*, introduction, p. xiv.

[18] Demaules, '*Le Cycle de la gageure*', pp. 88–90, makes this point but does not relate the author's suppression of the Provençal elements in *Gérard de Nevers* to the idea of moralising its representation of the heroine.

[19] See Christopher Callahan, 'A l'ombre du jongleur disparu. La grammaire de la performance dans deux romans lyrico-narratifs dérimés', *Revue des Langues Romanes*,

as both moral exemplar and sexual being that pervades the earlier poem. Declaring his intention to compose a text that will 'tourner et pourfiter a l'emplifficacion de la vaillance et recommendacion' of his dedicatee (*ibid.*), he undertakes to moralise the verse original in order to draw a clear lesson from this tale of the ill-judged wager and the suffering which it brings to the main couple.

How, then, is the heroine herself portrayed in these two works? First, there are some subtle but important changes made in the *mise en prose* to the way in which the atmosphere of the royal court where Gerart first reveals his love for Euriaut is presented. In the *Roman de la Violette*, the king's court is depicted as distinctly amorous since, it being the month of April, the hero joins a number of courtly ladies all singing of their various loves (many of them implicitly adulterous) by singing and speaking of his own lady as a desiring subject: 'Que plus m'aimme que nule rien / Cele de cui me sui vantés' (vv. 231–32), and it is this thrusting of her name into the public domain which has the disastrous effect of arousing Lisiart's envy. In *Gérard de Nevers*, by contrast, a rather different atmosphere is created as the time of year is Pentecost, a season which is often linked in romance to the idea of questing in a spirit of penance, and the court has just returned from mass. Here, moreover, not only are the actual lyrics sung by the amorous ladies of the court omitted or at most paraphrased, but even before Gerart begins to boast of his love, the narrator intervenes in order to stress Euriaut's fidelity rather than her amorousness, describing her unequivocally as 'la plus leale en amours envers son amy que oncques fust en vye' (p. 5).

This crucial difference between the two texts in the degree to which Euriaut is sexualised by her association with the erotic atmosphere of the court becomes even more marked the first time that the heroine herself actually appears. In the *Roman de la Violette* she is seen through Lisiart's eyes in such a way as to establish her similarity both with the amorous ladies who sang at court and with the archetypal 'amie' of the lyric tradition itself. Perched at the window of a tower at her lover's castle in the classic pose of a lovelorn lady, Euriaut is stimulated to sing of her passion by the sight and sound of the birds, a song which ironically anticipates the actions wrought on lovers by those envious of their passion: 'Si a entendu les oysiaus / Les cans dous et plaisans et biaus. / Lors li souvint de son ami, / Dont souspire et plaint et gemi' (vv. 315–18). Euriaut's amorous pose serves to link her with the most sexually

101 (1997), 211–33.

rapacious woman in this text, Aiglentine, who is frequently depicted atop a tower, as for example when she first glimpses Gerart (vv. 2678–80) and also later when she gives voice to her desire for him (vv. 3428–51). Moreover, Euriaut herself stresses her own status as a desiring subject when she uses a lengthy stanza from an adulterous *chanson de mal mariée* in order to reject Lisiart's advances: 'Amors mi font renvoisier et canter, / Et me semont que plus jolie soie' (vv. 441–42).

In marked contrast to the *Roman de la Violette*, all of these amorous connotations are removed in *Gérard de Nevers*. Here, Euriaut is not proffered to the predatory gaze of Lisiart singing on top of her tower but is instead described in far more virtuous terms as having just returned from church (p. 8). Even the manner in which Euriaut rejects Lisiart's false protestations of love is notably different from that employed by her counterpart in the *Roman de la Violette* since she eschews the use of song to signal that her desires lie elsewhere in favour of stating firmly that he is wholly mistaken in casting her in the role of a potential sexual partner: 'Sachiés que pas ne suis femme pour ce faire' (p. 10). This de-sexualised representation of the heroine is comple-mented by the narrator's emphasis on how, in welcoming Lisiart to Gerart's castle, she is simply acting in her public role as hostess in her lover's absence, a role in which her innocence, hospitality and sense of propriety are foregrounded: 'La noble damoiselle, quy a nul mal n'aloit pensant, le [= Lisiart] festoya et luy fist sy grant chiere come s'il euist esté son frere ou son cousin prochain' (p. 8).

Yet perhaps the most noticeable modification that the narrator makes to his representation of Euriaut in *Gérard de Nevers* occurs in the important passage where she heads off to the royal court in response to her lover's summons after Lisiart has uncovered the secret of the birthmark that will imply that she has been unfaithful. In the *Roman de la Violette*, there is an uneasy discrepancy between the lengthy account of her clothes and jewellery which are associated with such virtuous women as Florence of Rome (vv. 812–56), and the extended, titillating description of her beautiful body that has been spied on by Lisiart, a description which draws the reader's attention to her most intimate parts, from her 'flans deliie et estroite' (v. 865) to her 'Mameletes […] / Ki nouvielement li poignoient' (vv. 899–900).[20] This somewhat contra-dictory representation of Euriaut, which veers awkwardly between her sartorial appearance of virtue and her intensely desirable body, is

---

[20] Krause, 'The material erotic', p.29.

ultimately tipped in favour of her overwhelming sexual allure since all the men who see her making her way to the court are instantly inflamed with a burning desire for her: 'Tout cil de la vile acouroient / Pour li veïr et remirer; / Mais je vous puis pour voir jurer / Que tels le jour le regarda, / Qui mauvaisement s'i garda, / Que maintenant espris en fu' (vv. 901–06).

The way this episode is handled in *Gérard de Nevers* bears little similarity to that in the verse original. Even before mentioning Euriaut's beauty and clothing, the narrator adds new details to his account of her departure so as to stress a different aspect of her character, that of her role as the lady of Nevers who is endowed with a similar authority to that of the absent lord, Gerart himself. The regret with which the people of Nevers watch her depart reinforces her public status as a lady who inspires her future subjects with both affection and respect: 'Des plus grans de la cité fu convoyee. Car tant estoit amee des petis et des grans que se a la verité euissent seu son destourbier, jamais pour riens ne l'en euissent laissye partir' (p. 18). The descriptions of her clothing and beauty which form such bravura set-pieces in the *Roman de la Violette* are reduced here to only their most salient and virtuous elements, as Euriaut is compared in her beauty and, importantly, her humility, to famous examples of virtuous women from classical antiquity and vernacular literature – Helen, Polyxena, Dido, Florence of Rome and the 'Orgueilleuse d'amour' (p. 19) –, and her physical charms are alluded to only in the most generic of terms: 'tant estoit bien faitte et fourmee que en elle Dieu et nature n'avoyent riens oublyé' (*ibid.*). Significantly, there is no mention of her inflammatory effect on men's desires as she passes in the street. Rather, the narrator describes her effect on the *women* who see her and for whom she acts as a model of elegant self-conduct: 'venoient acourant par la rue bourgois, bourgoises et pucelles quy aux fenestres des maisons et des sales estoient, dames et damoiselles moult esmervellees de la tres excellente beaulté que en la belle Euryant veoyent estre' (*ibid.*). Moreover, in an important addition to the text, the narrator highlights not the stir that she, a desirable object, produces amongst the men of the court, as is the case in the *Roman de la Violette*, but rather, in a telling shift of focalisation to Euriaut herself, the fear that is prompted as she finds herself the target of attention in a public space dominated and controlled by men: 'La belle Euryant, come sage et soubtille, veans que layans en la chambre se trouvoit esseullee de femmes, [...] ne se pot assés esmervellier, pour ce que cuida trouver la royne. Prist en elle une freeur moult grande, pensans en elle meisme que pour aulcune chose estoit mandee' (p. 20).

Even when Euriaut has been abandoned by Gerart in a forest and has sought to repel both the honourable advances of the duke of Metz, who has rescued her, and the dishonourable attentions of his vassal Meliatir, by pretending to be a prostitute called Ligiere, the discrepancy between her self-imposed fictional identity and her actual qualities as a virtuous woman is much more explicit in *Gérard de Nevers* than in the *Roman de la Violette*. Thus, in the earlier poem, it is her sexual allure, as displayed in her expensive clothes and 'cors gent' (v. 1176), that attracts the duke to her, whilst his subjects, who try to dissuade him from marrying this woman of unknown origin, refer to her repeatedly as an 'esgaree fole' (v. 1243). Indeed, her desirability is emphasised at every turn, as when she returns from church in order to escape the prurient eyes of the people who want to gaze at her beauty (vv. 3849–51).

In the *mise en prose*, by contrast, Euriaut's position at the court of Metz as a potential sexual prey, both of the duke and of his vassal, is attenuated by emphasising her close link with Ysmaine, the duke's sister. This figure, who merely serves as a plot device in the *Roman de la Violette* (where Meliatir tries to frame Euriaut for the girl's murder in revenge for the heroine's strenuous rejection of his advances), is foregrounded much more in *Gérard de Nevers* as a means of enhancing its representation of Euriaut as virtuous. Thus, as the narrator of the *mise en prose* reiterates several times, Euriaut is given the honour of being Ysmaine's companion with the respectable role of teaching her young charge the worthy occupation of embroidery: 'A Euryant la bailla en garde adfin de l'apprendre et monstrer a ouvrer d'or et de soye, car sur touttes les aultres femmes Euryant en estoit la maistresse' (p. 82). Moreover, the close bond that is formed between the two girls is not only used to stress Euriaut's chastity ('Chascune nuit couchoit avec elle', p. 118), but is also cited by a nobleman of Metz before her trial for Ysmaine's murder as one of the key reasons why she should not be considered a suspect: 'Grant mervelles est en moy dont pouvoyent mouvoir a ceste damoiselle de ainsy avoir murdry celle dont tant estoit amee' (p. 119).

The final transformation of Euriaut's portrayal in the *mise en prose* comes at the *dénouement* when Gerart undertakes two consecutive trials by combat in order to clear Euriaut of both the charge of murdering Ysmaine and the original accusation of infidelity. As numerous critics have pointed out, Euriaut is depicted in the *Roman de la Violette* as a rather passive figure who fails to speak in her own defence, launching instead, in the manner of a virgin martyr, into a very lengthy *prière du plus grand péril* in which she invokes God to have pity on her.[21] However, this likening of Euriaut to a virgin martyr is itself not without ambiguity since scholars of medieval hagiography have long argued that the voyeuristic and sadistic tortures inflicted on female saints are often presented as punishments for the perilous attractions of female sexuality.[22] Such connotations of voyeurism and sadism are certainly present in the sight of Euriaut '[t]restoute nue en sa chemise' (v. 5167) being violently threatened with being 'arse et desfaite' (v. 5355). Furthermore, that Euriaut has been made to suffer precisely for her attractiveness, which has caused her lover to doubt her fidelity to him, is strongly suggested in the reconciliation scene. Here not only does she throw herself on her knees in front of Gerart and beg for his 'merchi' (v. 5672), but his actual response to her confirms that he sees her as having now made reparation to him through her proven loyalty: 'Biele, fait il, ne plourés mie, / Que m'amour avés gaaignie' (vv. 5679–80).

In the *mise en prose*, as opposed to the verse original, Euriaut is not so much a semi-nude martyr-figure as a victim of a miscarriage of justice, as is underlined in the greatly expanded court scene in which the cases for and against her are presented and she herself has the chance to proclaim her innocence: '"Sire, dist Euryant oncques jour de ma vye le criesme ne commys. Se il est trouvé et seu a la verité que celle traÿson et murdre aye commys, j'abandonne mon corps pour en faire telle justice que par vous et voz barons sera advise"' (p. 121). As befits her depiction as victim rather than martyr, the text of her long prayer is suppressed, being replaced with a simple invocation to God to show justice by granting victory to her champion, 'en luy pryant que son champion volsist aidier et secourir aussy vrayement que a tort estoit encoulpee' (p. 122). Her reconciliation scene with Gerart similarly portrays a very different kind of relationship between the lovers. Thus, although, as in the earlier poem, she begs for his pardon, his reply to her gives no indication that he sees her as having been at fault but rather that each of them has been a victim who must take strength from the adversity that has befallen them: '"Belle, ce dist Gerart, prendés resconfort en vous. L'adversité que avés eu, et le mal que vous et moy

---

[21] For an indication of this critical position, see Krause, 'The material erotic', p. 33.

[22] See, for example, Gaunt, *Gender and Genre*, pp. 212–33.

avons souffert, devons prendre en gré et loer Nostre Seigneur, puis que tous deux nous a amené jusques cy"' (pp. 126–27).

This insistence on Euriaut's status as innocent victim in the *mise en prose*, compared to the implicit culpability attached to her troubling sexuality in the *Roman de la Violette*, makes for a very different lesson or set of lessons to be taken from the text. Whilst in both versions Gerart is explicitly told by the wise bourgeoise Marote in whose house he is lodging at Chalon that he should not have tested his lady's fidelity ('Ne doit on esprouver s'amie', v. 2388; 'Celluy quy sent avoir bonne amye ne le doibt jamais esprouver', p. 51), in the *Roman de la Violette* this is made into the central lesson of the text and is developed into a disquisition on the knight's love service to his lady (vv. 2387–408), thus making the couple's adventures into a tale about the trials of love.

In *Gérard de Nevers*, however, this extended lesson on conduct in love is omitted and instead a much more pointed moral message is attached to their sufferings which are deemed to be adversities sent by God to test them. That it is primarily Gerart whose adventures are presented as penitential in the prose version is evident when, after having learnt of Lisiart's trickery, the hero explicitly acknowledges that he has been at fault for having believed the dubious evidence of the birthmark rather than trusting in Euriaut's fidelity: 'Dieux me doinst ceste grace que encores puisse trouver Euryant, m'amye, par qui j'ay eu maint mal et mainte paine. *Mais pas ne m'en doit desplaire, car vers elle l'ay bien deservy'* (p. 112, emphasis added).

This lesson about his lack of faith in Euriaut is given a further dimension in *Gérard de Nevers* that is completely absent from the *Roman de la Violette* when the hero shows himself to be guilty of having lapsed into the kind of misogynistic arguments against women that the villainous Lisiart himself uttered when he denounced Euriaut for her infidelity, claiming that 'est fol cely quy en femme a grant fiance de avoir mys sa terre en gage' (p. 21).[23] Thus, in the scene where Gerart is about to kill Euriaut for having brought disgrace upon him, not only is his manhandling of her much more violent than in the earlier poem, pulling her hair and chaining her to a tree, but he gives vent to similar anti-feminist sentiments to those of Lisiart, saying her fate should be a lesson to all women not to be unfaithful to their lovers ('tel loyer en arés que a touttes aultres sera exemple', p. 22), likening her to other disloyal

---

[23] Compare with the *Roman de la Violette*, vv. 960–69.

women such as 'Briseïda, amye de Troÿlus' (p. 24) and accusing her of 'desordonnee lecherye' (*ibid.*).

The hero's mistake in adopting this negative view of women is made all the more ironic in *Gérard de Nevers* by the fact that, unlike in the *Roman de la Violette* where the constant emphasis on Euriaut's physical attractiveness puts her on a continuum with the sexually rapacious women such as Aigline, Aiglentine and Flourentine, the heroine in the prose romance is presented as their antithesis in terms of her steadfastness, chastity and respectability. This opposition between Euriaut's behaviour and that of these other female characters is evident not only in the moral opprobrium which is explicitly heaped on these women's immodest actions in *Gérard de Nevers* but also in the suppression of much of the titillating detail about their attempts at seduction to be found in the *Roman de la Violette*. For example, in the *mise en prose*, Aiglentine's lack of discretion in casting amorous looks at Gerart is strongly condemned by her father ('Le duc s'en appercheu assés, sy en tint sa fille moins sage', p. 88), and, in the passage concerning the hero's encounter with Aigline, the later text omits all mention of her skimpily-dressed appearance in just a 'chainse blanc' (v. 2054) which the earlier poem describes as being soaked with his blood as she bends over to administer to the wounds that he has sustained in a fight for her family's honour (v. 2090).[24]

Furthermore, in addition to being much more direct about the penitential nature of Gerart's quest and in showing the misguided nature of his misogynistic judgments of Euriaut, the *mise en prose* underlines far more forcefully than the *Roman de la Violette* that, above all, it is the hero's own immoderate boasting which provoked the calamitous wager in the first place, such *vantardise* being a wholly undesirable quality in a knight. Having learnt this lesson the hard way in the amorous domain, Gerart, in turn, teaches it to others in the chivalric domain as a reminder of the correct knightly virtues, as for example when he reproaches Meliatir, Euriaut's accuser, for boasting about his prowess: 'A nul chevalier n'appartient soy vanter ne dire chose dont a aultruy puist desplaire' (p. 121).

Finally, in contradistinction to the *Roman de la Violette* where the text's overall message is limited to expounding the proper conduct in love, the lessons delivered in *Gérard de Nevers* not only depend for their impact on the de-eroticised representation of the heroine but equally

---

[24] Compare with *Gérard de Nevers*, pp. 46–47.

draw out the broader, political repercussions of the hero's failings in his private life. For example, in the prose version there is greater emphasis placed on the consequences for the hero's own subjects of the loss of their legitimate lord as the people of Nevers are described as suffering from the 'malvaises coustumes, tailles et gabelles' (p. 24) unjustly imposed on them by the misrule of Lisiart and his accomplice Gondree. The restitution of Gerart's rightful lands and title is thus greeted with joy not only by his kin but also by his own subjects who are grateful for the re-establishment of a more benign political order (p. 147). Similarly, the later text stresses how Gerart's abandonment of Euriaut and his tarnishing of her reputation have damaged much more than just the lady herself, having deprived her kin of an important figure in their network of alliances with other noble families. Whilst the *Roman de la Violette* simply celebrates the fact that the hero is reunited at the end with his 'amie' (v. 6622), in *Gérard de Nevers* Euriaut is not only fully reinstated in the ranks of her own lineage and shown every possible honour at court, but also attains her social apotheosis by being married to Gerart in a sumptuous wedding organised by the king himself. Thereafter she is referred to by her full title as 'la contesse Euryant, sa femme' (p. 147) and is recounted as having gone on to fulfill her destiny as a loving wife and producer of two male heirs.

The *mise en prose* of the *Roman de la Violette* is thus far from being either an inferior reworking of the verse original or a simple updating of an old tale so as to achieve a greater degree of realism. Rather, the extensive modifications which *Gérard de Nevers* makes to its depiction of Euriaut effectively revalorise the courtly heroine, casting her as a blameless victim and moral exemplar, in marked contrast to the original in which she is presented as a highly ambiguous figure, one who is at once the object of male desires and the troubling, unstable guarantor of masculine honour. If the later version thereby sacrifices titillation for moralisation in using its radically different portrayal of the heroine to deliver lessons in personal and political conduct, it does so as part of the wider process of acculturation with its accompanying changes in literary tastes and cultural *mores*, changes which are so strikingly revealed in the transformation of a thirteenth-century verse romance into a fifteenth-century *mise en prose*.[25]

[25] I am, as ever, indebted to S. H. Rigby for his invaluable comments on earlier drafts of this chapter.

3

The (other) worlds of *Mabrien*

Sara Sturm-Maddox

The story of *Mabrien* unfolds in a late fifteenth-century prose account that results from a generic transposition.[1] It appears in its manuscript context not independently but as part of a lengthy *mise en prose* of a verse *remaniement* of the epic cycle of Renaut de Montauban.[2] The latter rewriting, dating probably from the late fourteenth century, contains numerous amplifications of elements in the cycle, including, in one of its two manuscripts, a very brief summary of the heroic adventures of Mabrien, who is the son of Renaut's son Yvon.[3] The prose account, categorised by its editor as a *roman de chevalerie*, elaborates Mabrien's story in two major segments depicting his chivalric exploits first as Saracen and then as Christian warrior, punctuated by an extraordinary itinerary that includes, among other venues, the land of Faerye ruled by King Arthur and the Earthly Paradise. *Mabrien* combines these disparate elements into a story that builds to a remarkable conclusion of the *geste* of the *quatre fils Aymon*, the famous Rebellious Vassal cycle.

Mabrien's story conflates those of two of his uncles, the principal heroes of late *chansons* of the epic cycle, *Maugis d'Aigrement* and *Vivien de Montbranc*. According to the former poem, Maugin and Vivien, twin

---

[1] *Mabrien*, ed. Philippe Verelst (Geneva: Droz, 1998), based on Paris, Arsenal 5072–75 (*Am*) and Paris, BnF, fr. 19173–77 (*Lf*). Text cited by rubric number and paragraph number in the body of the chapter.

[2] *Renaut de Montauban. Deuxième fragment rimé du ms. de Paris, B. N., fr. 764 ('R')*, ed. Philippe Verelst (Ghent: University of Ghent, 1988). 'L'histoire de Mabrien occupe le cinquième et dernier volume des mss *Am* et *Lf* les rubriques 8 à 55 (fin), et même si elle n'est pas présentée comme telle, elle ne constitue pas moins un tout homogène qu'il est parfaitement possible d'isoler du reste du cycle' (*Mabrien*, ed. Verelst, p. 8).

[3] See François Suard, 'Le Développement de la 'Geste de Montauban' en France jusqu'à la fin du moyen âge', in Hans-Erich Keller (ed.), *Romance Epic. Essays on a Medieval Literary Genre* (Kalamazoo, MI: Medieval Institute Publications, 1987), pp. 141–61 (pp. 148–50). For the *mise en prose* of the 'chanson primitive', see pp. 150–51.

sons of Beuves d'Aigremont, are separately abducted on the day of their birth. Maugis is raised by the fairy Oriande, then immediately departs to seek his parents when she discloses his true identity.[4] Vivien, meanwhile, is raised as a Saracen and leads pagan armies against Christian forces, his father and brothers among them, until he is recognised in single combat by his twin Maugis, made aware of his parentage, and converted to the Christian faith.[5] 'Au fond', *Mabrien*'s editor comments, 'tout se passe comme si Mabrien combinait le sort de Maugis avec celui de son frère jumeau Vivien.'[6] Mabrien is stolen as an infant from his parents, the king and queen of Jerusalem, and raised as the son of the admiral Barré of Persia and his wife Mabrienne. He distinguishes himself first as the greatest warrior among the Saracens, fighting against his own noble lineage before learning his true identity; thereafter he sets out to find his parents in the West, and becomes the leader of united conquering Christian forces.

When, at an early age, Mabrien demonstrates exceptional chivalric aptitude, the narrator invokes the topos of Nature vs. Nurture in anticipation of his future:

> Et s'esprouvoit par Nature, qui l'amonnestoit de ainsi faire, et de retraire et resembler au lignage duquel il estoit, quelque raison que Nourreture voulsist opposer a l'encontre, car telle estoit sa destinee, laquelle nul ne lui eust peu oster. (14.5)

When he learns his true identity, his embrace of Christianity is instant-aneous. In addition to this emphasis on lineage, however, *Mabrien* also engages the characteristic thematic issue of the cycle, the struggle between Charlemagne and the four sons of Aymon, their supporters,

---

[4] The tutelage of Oriande's brother results in his command of magical arts. On this figure, see Philippe Verelst, 'L'Enchanteur d'épopée: prolégomènes à une étude sur Maugis', *Romanica Gandensia*, 16 (1976), 19–162.

[5] In *Vivien de Montbranc*, the continuation of *Maugis d'Aigremont*, Vivien's new-found Christian relatives help him to defeat a vengeful attack by Saracens. Joseph Palermo comments that by engaging these heroes in a holy war against the Saracens, '*Vivien de Montbranc* est le chaînon qui relie la tradition de la guerre sainte de la chanson de *Roland* à celle de la révolte seigneuriale de la chanson des *Quatre Fils Aymon*.' See 'Vivien de Monbranc: personnage épique ambivalent', in *VIIIᵉ Congreso de la Société Rencesvals* (Pamplona: Institución Principe de Viana, 1981), pp. 375–79 (p. 378).

[6] *Mabrien*, p. 11. On the extensive echoes of *Maugis* in *Mabrien* see Danielle Quéruel, 'L'Art des réécritures: de *Maugis* à *Mabrien*', in Jean Dufournet (ed.), '*Si a parlé par moult ruiste vertu*': *mélanges de littérature médiévale offerts à Jean Subrenat* (Paris: Champion, 2000), pp. 455–65 (p. 462).

and their children. In *Renaut de Montauban* the four brothers, having incurred the emperor's enmity, endure years of intense suffering in the Ardennes and then Charlemagne's cruel siege of Montauban. They are obliged to capitulate and flee. As a condition for reconciliation with Charlemagne, Renaut undertakes a pilgrimage to the East, during which he participates in the defence of the Christian kingdom of Jerusalem; he declines the throne of Jerusalem, which his son Yvon later occupies.[7] Mabrien's uncles, sons of Beuve d'Aigrement, are also key figures in the confrontation with the French sovereign: Maugis, a sorcerer as well as a fierce warrior, subjects Charlemagne to ridicule and incurs his implacable hatred through his command of magic,[8] while *Vivien de Montbranc* attributes the antagonism between their father Beuve's lineage and Charlemagne to the latter's refusal to come to the aid of the newly converted Vivien when he is attacked by Saracens.[9]

The opening of Mabrien's story gives us a greatly attenuated version of the legendary struggle between Charlemagne and Renaut's lineage. It is alluded to only twice, both times by perfidious Saracens immediately following the hero's birth. In Jerusalem, the slave who kidnaps the infant Mabrien gains access to his mother's room by pretending to bear a message from King Yvon in France, telling her that the war that opposes him and Charlemagne will be brought to an end, but that its outcome is unknown; then a Saracen attacker tells the knight whom Yvon has left in charge of the city that the king is dead, 'occis en France de la main Charlemaine mesmes, qui plus le hayoit que homme qui fust eu monde' (11.4). This knight, however, as he assists in the queen's escape during the Saracens' conquest of the city, tells her that he has heard from French pilgrims that Yvon and Charlemagne have reached an accord, and soon thereafter, Yvon having made his peace with the

[7] *Renaut de Montauban*, ed. Jacques Thomas (Geneva: Droz, 1989), vv. 12803–983, vv. 13474–84. Another rebellious vassal, Huon de Bordeaux, also travels far to the East to meet near-impossible terms set by the emperor. See the analysis by William Calin in *The Epic Quest: Studies in Four Old French Chansons de Geste* (Baltimore: Johns Hopkins Press, 1966), pp. 172–235.

[8] See Philippe Verelst, 'Le Personnage de Maugis dans *Renaut de Montauban* (versions rimées traditionnelles)', *Romanica Gandensia*, 18 (1981), 73–152.

[9] This contradicts the origin of their enmity as established in *Renaut de Montauban*: the fatal wounding of Charlemagne's son Lohier by Beuve d'Aigrement, Charlemagne's refusal to pardon Beuve, and his acquiescence in the murder of Beuve demanded by Ganelon. See Wolfgang G. van Emden, 'Le Personnage du roi dans *Vivien de Monbranc* et ailleurs', in Madeleine Tyssens and Claude Thiry (eds), *Charlemagne et l'épopée romane*, 2 vol. (Liège: Université de Liège, 1978), I, pp. 241–50 (pp. 247–50).

emperor, and taken leave of him most amicably, Mabrien's parents are reunited in Acre.

The reconciliation between Charlemagne and Yvon is of truly momentous importance in cyclical terms. Like Mabrien's story, however, it receives only a brief mention at the end of the verse *remainement*.[10] In the opening of *Mabrien*, it is reported without comment or emphasis. It nonetheless sets the stage for later events in the East. Yvon retakes Jerusalem, but peace is by no means assured. Years later, a Saracen army lays siege to the city, led by none other than an apparently invincible Mabrien on behalf of his 'father' the admiral. Yvon and other Christian kings send an appeal for aid to Charlemagne in France. It is Roland who urges the emperor to undertake the mission with only a small army, a bold counsel that the narrator explains in an astonishing rewriting account of epic history: Charlemagne's nephew recalls the success of another small band, including himself, Olivier, Ogier, and the sons of Aymon, whom Renaut de Montauban had recently led *outremer* against Marsile, Baligant, and others, who were defeated 'par grace divine'. Charlemagne's response counters the stereotypical image of the irascible, unjust and unworthy sovereign that emerges from the *geste* of the *barons revoltés*:[11] 'Et s'acorda l'empereur a son dit et jura sa couronne que lui mesmes exposeroit son corps et ses hommes en l'ayde des enffans Regnault', as he had pledged when his peace with them was concluded (20.3–4). In the ensuing battles in the East, however, the Christian forces are defeated and obliged to abandon Jerusalem. They flee to Acre, with an enraged Mabrien in close pursuit, and from there they set sail back to France.

Shortly thereafter, this most redoubtable Saracen warrior learns his true identity and vows to find his parents in the West.[12] His reunion with that lineage, however, is long deferred. His quest is a journey into the unknown, related in a sequence of episodes in which he finds himself far from both his Saracen 'homeland' and the French lineage with which he has as yet no contact.[13] It is not the inclusion of the interlude

---

[10] *Renaut de Montauban, Deuxième fragment*, vv. 28324–79.

[11] For the progressive degradation of the emperor's image in the later printed versions see François Suard, 'Charlemagne dans les proses épiques imprimées', in Tyssens and Thiry (eds), *Charlemagne et l'épopée romane*, I, pp. 271–80.

[12] Under circumstances very similar to those of Maugis, his identity is revealed by the beauteous young Saracen he had believed to be his mother and who then demands his love.

[13] The voyage is narrated in rubrics 27–30 of a total of the 55 rubrics containing his

that makes this work singular for, as François Suard points out, the hero's 'visite en féerie est un point de passage obligé de nombreux textes post-épiques'.[14] In *Mabrien*, however, the indeterminate period of the voyage, which is both geographically and temporally liminal, is the time of an initiation. While his *cuyrie* or breastplate, 'd'ouvrage merveilleux', and his enormous axe, both conquered from a Saracen opponent of his surrogate father the Admiral, continue to set the young man apart,[15] this segment affords repeated confirmation of his new identity as Christian knight.

The circulation of motifs and scenes from both epic and romance – the *migration des données* characteristic of late French epics[16] – is particularly pronounced in this segment of *Mabrien*. A remarkable metatextual comment alerts the reader to a radical expansion of the intertextual horizon:

> Pour racompter des merveilles du monde et ouyr parler des avantures, faiz et entreprinses du noble damoisel Mabrien, qui seront fortes a croire a ceulz qui autrefoiz n'auroient ouy recorder les faiz et cronicques du roy Artus, de Lancelot du Lac, de Perceval, de Tristam, de Hue de Bourdeaux et autres livres, esquelz a plusieurs choses que l'en pourroit bien appeller fantosmeryes et mensonges, dit ainsi l'histoire que… (26.1)

The heading of the following rubric confirms the change of orientation: 'Comme Mabrien fut mené par tampeste de mer en l'aymant et en terre faee.' The adventure begins with the hero's separation during a battle at sea from two faithful Saracen companions and from Gloriande, the daughter of the sultan of Mecca, who has rescued him and chosen to follow him and embrace his new faith. His vessel, driven by raging winds for several days and nights, is at last seized by a magnetic force

---

story in the manuscript volume in which it is found.

[14] François Suard, '"Meurvin" et "Mabrian", deux épigones de la "Chevalerie Ogier de Danemarche" et de "Renaut de Montauban"', in Wolfgang van Emden and Philip E. Bennett (eds), *Guillaume d'Orange et la chanson de geste. Essays Presented to Duncan McMillan* (Reading: Reading University Press, 1984), pp. 151–66 (p. 158).

[15] On these fearsome weapons see 15.3. As Bernard Ribémont observes, 'Mabrien tient à conserver cet équipement qui le rend invincible, marquant par là qu'il restera toujours un chevalier d'une catégorie particulière, un peu en marge.' See 'Héros épique ou héros de cour? Une autre vision de l'héroïsme à la fin du Moyen Âge: le cas de *Mabrien* (XVe s.)', *Cahiers de Recherches Médiévales*, 11 (2004), 63–73 (p. 71).

[16] See Claude Roussel, *'D'armes et d'amours*: l'aventure chevaleresque dans les dernières chansons de geste', in Dominique Boutet (ed.), *Le Romanesque et l'épique* [*Littérales*, 31 (2003)], pp. 163–78.

called the Magnet. While an explanation of the phenomenon is offered several paragraphs later, initially the reader's curiosity must be satisfied or suspended by the affirmation that Mabrien's boat was drawn 'droit au rochier ou Hue de Bordeaux avoit esté mené' (27.1).[17]

Indeed, like Huon de Bordeaux in the *Chanson d'Esclarmonde*,[18] Mabrien finds himself amid the wreckage of countless empty vessels. A host of creatures that he first takes to be men swim toward him; as they approach he finds that they are 'diversement deffigurez', with faces like birds'; known as *Becqus*, they prey upon shipwrecked mariners.[19] Mabrien kills many of them with his axe, and the rest retreat to their land, identified as *Femenye*, no doubt suggesting here a land of utter desolation, as described in *Huon de Bordeaux*.[20] Drawn toward the Magnet by the metal in his helmet and his axe, he loses them both to its force; at last, tormented by hunger, he learns from a knight dying of starvation that escape can be made in a barge containing no metal, and that in a nearby land he will find a path up a mountain to a place abounding in food and drink. With great difficulty he ascends the mountain, and falls into a deep sleep.

Mabrien dreams of walking through a pleasant land where he finds 'un grant arbre' bearing a shield, then a castle that must be taken by

[17] Caroline Cazenave proposes that *Esclarmonde* derives the encounter with the Magnet, often exploited in both Arabic and occidental literature in the Middle Ages, from a late twelfth-century German romance of *Herzog Ernst*; both Pliny and Ptolemy place this mountain in the East. See 'L'Imagination au pouvoir: le décor onirique du périple de Huon dans la *Chanson d'Esclarmonde*', in Jean-Michel Racault (ed.), *Ailleurs imaginés: littérature, histoire, civilisations* (Paris: Didier, 1990), pp. 21–55 (p. 29). See also Francis Dubost, *Aspects fantastiques de la littérature narrative XIIᵉ–XIIIᵉ siècles. L'Autre, l'Ailleurs, l'Autrefois* (Paris: Champion, 1991), pp. 353–54.

[18] *Esclarmonde, Clarisse et Florent, Ide et Olive*, ed. Max Schweigel (Marburg: N.G. Elwert, 1889); for *Esclarmonde* see pp. 93–126.

[19] On these creatures see Dominique Boutet, 'Au-delà et Autre monde: interférences culturelles et modèles de l'imaginaire dans la littérature épique', in Denis Hüe and Christine Ferlampin-Acher (eds), *Le Monde et l'Autre Monde* (Orléans: Paradigme, 2002), pp. 65–78. Monstrous warriors called *Becqus* appear in *La Conquête de Jérusalem*, where their name is attributed to their heads of dogs with a strong *bec* (*Mabrien*, p. 465, note to 27.3).

[20] *Huon de Bordeaux*, eds William W. Kibler and François Suard (Paris: Champion, 2003), vv. 2922–26. For other mentions of such a land in epic poems, see Marguerite Rossi, *Huon de Bordeaux et l'évolution du genre épique au XIIIᵉ siècle* (Paris: Champion, 1975), pp. 101–03. The prose version of *Huon de Bordeaux* printed in 1530 adopts the more obvious etymology: a land named Femenie 'pour ce qu'il n'y a nulz hommes: et n'y a que des femmes'; cited in Suard, '"Meurvin" et "Mabrian"', p. 159.

force. Upon awakening, he sets out again, now 'tendant trouver avan-ture'. This is, of course, the vocation of many a knight in courtly romance, and *aventure* is what Mabrien finds. His dream was prophetic: soon he comes across a tree which 'le riche roy' had had planted, and the *ystoire* tells us that he has entered 'en Terre Faee' (27.10). This is the land of 'le roy Artus, lequel avoit la dominacion du royamme et pays de Faerye, ou tant advenoit de diverses choses che merveilles' (27.12), and these 'diverses choses' are to afford both an affirmation of Mabrien's chivalric supremacy and his initiation into more than one facet of courtly culture. Both begin with his successful appropriation of the shield he finds hanging from the tree. Its inscription, to which he pays little heed, warns that 'NUL NE PEULT CEST ESCU PORTER S'IL N'EST VAILLANT ET PREUX SUR TOUS AUTRES, ET S'IL N'EST EN SOY GARNY DE LEAULTÉ E DE PREUDOMMIE.'[21]

Mabrien's venture into Faerie presupposes, on the part of a fifteenth-century reader, curiosity and a considerable intertextual competence. In *Huon de Bordeaux*, whose voyage to the East has already been evoked, that realm is ruled by Auberon. Ogier le Danois, in thirteenth-century versions of his story, enters Avalon, where he becomes the lover of the *fée* Morgain.[22] Nor is *Mabrien* the first work in the epic tradition to associate Arthur with the fairy realm. In the *Bataille Loquifer* in the cycle of Guillaume d'Orange, a sleeping Rainouart is spirited away by three fairies to an Avalon ruled by Arthur.[23] In the fourteenth-century *Batard de Bouillon*, a continuation of *Baudouin de Sebourc,* Baudoin learns from his new vassals, the princes of Mecca, that beyond the Red Sea lies a mysterious land: 'le nostre anchisserie / Avons oï retraire que che est Faërie / Et que la terre Artus et Morgue la jolie / Marchist au les dela', but that from there no

---

[21] The warning is reminiscent of the sententious inscriptions on objects in Arthurian prose romance; Mabrien will fight to free Gracienne 'tout pour l'amour de l'Escu aux Lectres d'or', repeated like a refrain at the end of several paragraphs (28.12, 29.2, 29.3, 29.4, 29.5).

[22] *La Chevalerie d'Ogier de Danemarche*, ed. Mario Eusebi (Milan: Instituto editoriale Cisalpino, 1963). In some versions of the story of *Meurvin*, which has a 'parenté profonde' with *Mabrien*, that hero is the product of this union. See Suard, '"Meurvin" et "Mabrian"', pp. 151–53.

[23] *La Bataille Loquifer*, ed. Monica Barnett (Oxford: Blackwell, 1975); for the Vulgate version containing the episode see pp. 3–29. Jeanne Wathelet-Willem concludes that the episode in this twelfth-century *chanson* was an interpolation, probably introduced in the second half of the thirteenth century. See 'La Fée Morgain dans la chanson de geste', *Cahiers de Civilisation Médiévale*, 13 (1970), 209–19 (p. 218).

boat ever returns.[24] Baudoin and his men undertake the voyage and are met on arrival by Arthur, who tells them that no one has ventured there for two hundred years. All of these texts have clear affinities with *Mabrien*.

Suggesting a shift into a mode more reminiscent of Arthurian prose romance, Mabrien at once confronts the first of many challenges as he approaches the castle, which no one can enter without overcoming sixteen men who guard the bridge. The hero is undeterred, despite his lack of arms, and that handicap is soon remedied when Arthur, learning of the challenger's presence, dispatches a messenger to leave a mass of gold on the Magnet in exchange for Mabrien's axe and his helmet; the king then finds a vantage point from which to watch the combat, accompanied by Morgue and three other fairies with whom he had visited the infant at his birth. The chivalric confrontations are reminiscent of romance tourneys: Mabrien's opponents are attired in armour of various colours – a Vermeil Chevalier, a Blanc Chevalier, a Noir Chevalier, next 'ung jayant' armed all in green, a Chevalier Myparty with arms of *gris* and white[25] – and the terms of combat are those of a *coutume* established by Arthur himself. After Mabrien's eventual triumph, Arthur and his knights and ladies escort him to a splendid courtly celebration. It is evident that the newcomer has achieved full acceptance into courtly society, gaining not only entrance to the castle but 'la grace du roy Artus, avecques l'amour des dames, qui n'estoit mie pou de chose' (28.6).

Arthur's realm in *Mabrien* is a courtly society *faée*. During Mabrien's initial combats, the castle guardians, however gravely wounded, are immediately healed by a magic ointment administered by a *damoiselle faee*.[26] Now in court, he is so enchanted by the singing and dancing of 'demoiselles faees' and their partners that 'il avoit tout sa fain omblyee

---

[24] *Le Batard de Bouillon*, ed. Robert Francis Cook (Geneva: Droz, 1972), vv. 3308–11, vv. 3565–70. Here, as Wathelet-Willem observes, the area of the Red Sea replaces Avalon as the place to which Morgain took Arthur ('La Fée Morgain dans la chanson de geste', p. 212).

[25] The description of armour is here detailed: the knight is 'monté sur ung hault destrier de poil gris sur blanc, pommelé d'autre gris brun, bel et hault, trotant, et armé noblement, et ses armes couvertes, et son escu semblablement, de deux coulleurs figurees et paintes selon le poil donc le cheval estoit; et en son poing avoit une lance de mesmes coulleur' (28.5).

[26] The *chevaliers de Faerye* who confront Mabrien in a later episode (30.1–30.2) are able, when wounded, to renew themselves with 'poisons et medicine de onguement' which they possess 'faeement'.

par la vertu de la grant leesse en quoy son cueur estoit ravy et tramsporté a icelle heure' (28.7). In *Le Batard de Bouillon*, Baudoin and his men are similarly entertained in Arthur's *vergier* by many *fées* who so delight the visitors that

> ne lor souvenoit adonc de leur pais,
> De femmes ne d'enfans ne de lor boins amis;
> De grace et de plaisanche ont les coers rassouffis,
> Jamais ne s'en vausist nuls d'iaus estre partis' (vv. 3589–92).

Such will soon be the fate of Mabrien.

A further experience of enchanted courtliness awaits the hero. A 'Damoiselle Messagiere' bears him a message from the lady Gracienne, described as the most beautiful ever seen, who has hung the shield on the tree because she needed the aid of the best of knights. The identification of the 'meilleur chevalier du monde', a leitmotif of the Prose *Lancelot* and the Prose *Tristan*, will recur frequently from this point in Mabrien's story; here it initiates a rescue of the lady from a pavilion where she is guarded by three extraordinary beasts and a formidable *luiton*, and she desires to give 'l'amour de son gent corps' to the hero in return. Mabrien at once declares himself 'chevalier et servant de la dame' and affirms that the god of Love now commands his heart (28.9–12). Thus inspired, he overcomes the three animal guardians – a lion, a huge serpent, and a dragon – and then the *luiton*. His instinctive comportment in confronting the latter reminds us of his new identity: he ends the creature's terrifying series of shape-shifting transformations by calling on the name of Jesus, after uttering an abbreviated *prière du grant péril* like those of devout Christian warriors in a number of *chansons de geste*.[27] The *luiton* turns at last into a handsome young man who begs him for mercy: he had been condemned to continue his shape-shifting until the arrival of the 'meilleur chevalier du monde', and now, assuming the name of Gaudisse, he becomes Mabrien's faithful helper.[28]

---

[27] 29.8. See Jean Frappier, *Les Chansons de geste du cycle de Guillaume d'Orange*, 2 vol. (Paris: SEDES, 1967), II, p. 132. Mabrien's grandfather utters a lengthy prayer of this type in *Renaut de Montauban*, vv. 6812–37.

[28] On this figure see Christine Ferlampin-Acher, '*Larron* contre *luiton*: les métamorphoses de Maugis', in Danielle Quéruel (ed.), *Entre épopée et légende: Les Quatre Fils Aymon ou Renaut de Montauban*, 2 vol. (Langres: Dominique Guéniot, 2000), II, pp. 101–18 (pp. 112–18).

After Mabrien frees Gracienne, she tells him that she, along with other fairies, had visited him immediately following his birth, and had given him the gift of her love, 'l'amour de moy, qui jamaiz ne vous fera faulte' (29.12). The scene she describes, depicted earlier in the text, resembles that in a fourteenth-century version of the *chanson* of *Ogier de Danemarche* in which Morgain, the last of six fairies who bestow gifts upon Ogier at his birth, promises that he will be her 'drus' and 'amis' and will live with her in Faerie as her husband.[29] Mabrien spends a year with Gracienne, who bears him a son. In the account of this idyllic interlude, the status of both Gracienne the fairy and Gaudisse the former *luiton* is blended fully into the courtly ethos in references to 'la noble fee' and 'le noble luiton' (29.18, 29.19). When Mabrien becomes aware that his stay in Faerie has been prolonged and determines to resume his search for his parents, Gracienne, though saddened by his departure, will repeatedly intervene to protect him after he abandons Faerie.[30]

At last Mabrien arrives at the Earthly Paradise, whose doorkeepers are Enoch and Elijah. Enoch informs him that he has reached 'le lieu euquel Dieu forma Adam et Eve' (30.5). Other accounts too identify Enoch and Elijah as inhabitants of the Earthly Paradise.[31] For Mabrien, however, this association holds particular significance, for it is from the two of them that he hears the stories of the Fall and the Passion.

> Longuement prescherent Enoc et Helye le chevalier Mabrien, qui tant fu de leurs parolles content que merveilles, et moult les mercya, disant par bon et devot courage : 'Moult avez mon cueur esjouy, beau preudoms, fait il, et voullentiers ay vostre langage escouté. Si m'est moult pleasant a ouyr, car oncquesmaiz ne ouys autant parler de la foy chrestienne comme j'ay ores, si en vauldray mieulx, se Dieu plaist, parce que ma creance y sera plus fort fermee que oncquesmaiz'. (30.7)

Knowledge, however, is not his only acquisition in the Earthly Paradise. He is also allowed to take away three of the fruits from the garden, but is

---

[29] For the introduction of the *merveilleux* into the legend of Ogier de Danemark see Laurence Harf-Lancner, *Les Fées au Moyen Âge* (Paris: Champion, 1984), pp. 280–82. Maugis d'Aigremont and Brun de la Montagne, she notes, are also promised the love of a *fée* at the time of their birth.

[30] For example, after he ignores her warning and sounds a magic horn hanging outside an abbey and thus provokes the attack of numerous 'chevaliers de Faerye affolé', she sends Gaudisse to order them to desist. In a particularly exotic note, Gaudisse travels on a *drommadaire*.

[31] For the association of Enoch and Elijah with the Earthly Paradise see Jean Delumeau, *Une histoire de Paradis. Le jardin des délices* (Paris: Fayard, 1992), p. 37.

admonished to use them wisely: they are the *Fruit de Jouvent*, which can restore an elderly person to the age of thirty years.

Mabrien's experience of the Earthly Paradise affords him not only fundamental elements of the Christian faith into which he had been baptised before his abduction as an infant, but also represents divine confirmation of his unique entitlement. To his question of how he may enter the garden, the reply is portentous: 'Sachiez, sire vassal, fait il, que cestui lieu est appellé Paradiz Terrestre; et par ces motz que sur l'uiz povez voir, par lequel il convient dedens entrer, povez savoir en vous mesmes se vous y entreriez ou nom.' The inscription over the door is a peculiarly exclusive formula, proclaiming that none may enter unless he be 'né en leal mariage, de noble lieu extrait, et le meilleur chevalier du monde' (30.5). Elijah then asks him 'qui il estoit, dont il venoit, que il alloit illecques querant et ou il voulloit aller' (30.6). In Mabrien's earnest reply there is no hint of his Saracen years:

> je suis ung chevalier d'estrange contree que Avanture aconduisi ja a assez longtemps par tampeste de mer a l'Aymant, dont je fuz mis hors ne sçay comment, sinon par grace Dieu, qui me mena en ung pays ou j'ay esté l'espace d'un an, et si n'y cuidoye mie avoir esté quatre jours. (30.6)

After Enoch and Elijah instruct him at length in the Christian faith, he enters the garden, 'donc les deux nobles preudoms furent moult joyeulx, disans que s'estoit le meilleur chevalier du monde, et qu'il avoit bien deservy d'avoir du fruit et des biens qui leans croissoient' (30.7) – an entitlement to which we shall return.

As Mabrien leaves the Earthly Paradise, Enoch and Elijah indicate a path to the Mer Perilleuse where he will find a boat, assuring him that he may safely enter it: 'soyez certain que ja mal ne vous advendra tant comme vous ayez en Dieu bonne et ferme creance' (30.8). Remarkably, at this late point in the 'otherworldly' interlude, the divine protection promised by Enoch and Elijah functions through the supernatural agency of Mabrien's fairy mistress and his faithful former *luiton*: the boat, the *histoire* tells us, has been sent by Gaudisse at the behest of Gracienne, and after Mabrien boards it and prays, it leaves the shore 'par le voulloir de Dieu'.[32]

Mabrien's next encounter, with Cain, is like several others anticipated in the adventures of Huon de Bordeaux. In *Huon*, Judas and Cain

---

[32] Again we find a close similarity to *Esclarmonde*, where angels instruct Huon to board a boat that has been brought for him by Auberon, 'li roys faés'.

are invoked together as models of traitors (vv. 2471–79), and Cain is again recalled in the hero's accusation of his own treacherous brother (vv. 10041–53). In *Esclarmonde* Huon speaks with a defiant Judas, who is suffering punishment by inundation in all the water of God's creation, and then with Cain, who is imprisoned in a rolling barrel. The spirited exchange with Cain (vv. 1774–1870) is echoed in *Mabrien* when the hero finds a *tonnel* in his path and strikes it with the hammer attached to it by a chain. From within the cask issues the voice of someone tormented by the reverberations; conjured by Mabrien 'par la vertu des sains noms de Nostre Seigneur', the prisoner identifies himself as Cain, once a living man, 'l'un des premiers qui fu' (30.9). Learning that his defiant interlocutor was imprisoned there by God, Mabrien places himself on the side of divine justice by refusing to free him from his ordained torment.

Mabrien's next adventure is in the realm of Prester John. In the so-called 'Letter from Prester John' which circulated from the twelfth century, this land is depicted as being replete with many wonders, among them flowing streams of milk and honey, vast quantities of gold and precious stones, and a spring with rejuvenating properties, fed by a river flowing from the Earthly Paradise.[33] Believed to be located in Asia and ruled by a priest-king, it inspired both literal and fictional exploration; the vastly popular *Roman d'Alexandre* of Alexandre de Paris, for example, contains an interpolated *Voyage d'Alexandre au Paradis terrestre* in which Alexander himself witnesses the rejuvenation of a number of his men.[34]

Mabrien offers an unusual version of Prester John's realm. The hero finds there an 'Arbre de Vie' that produces a single apple, the 'Pomme de Vie', which nourishes the entire population through sight and smell alone. And he finds not the all-powerful, totally virtuous priest-king of the 'Letter' and subsequent moralising interpretations,[35] but a ruler who is of very small stature, as are his subjects, who marvel like Lilliputians

---

[33] For this realm and its connection with the Earthly Paradise in the popular imagination, see Delumeau, *Une histoire de Paradis*, pp. 99–114.

[34] Alexandre de Paris, *Le Roman d'Alexandre*, pres. and trans. Laurence Harf-Lancner (Paris: Librairie Générale Française, 1994), pp. 518–87.

[35] The text of the 'Letter' configures an 'Orient virtuel' whose alterity is not in its marvels but in the wealth, power, and justice of its priest-king, a spirit preserved in the first two interpolations; see Gioia Zaganelli, 'L'Orient du prêtre Jean et la tradition encyclopédique du Moyen Âge', in *La Géographie au Moyen Âge: espaces pensés, espaces vécus, espaces rêvés* [*Perspectives Médiévales*, suppl. 24 (1998)], pp. 97–107 (p. 105).

at the size of the interloper whom they find sleeping. Having taken possession of the talismanic apple, Mabrien uses it to negotiate his departure. To obtain restitution of the fruit, Prester John himself guides Mabrien to the land of the French lord who holds his friends and Gloriande captive, where the second major segment of the hero's story begins.

Arriving at last in the West, Mabrien inquires about Charlemagne and learns of the recent monumental battle in Spain in which the emperor has suffered the loss of 'la fleur de chevalerye … jusques au nombre de huit mil chevaliers, ducs, contes et barons' (34.1). Raised as a Saracen, Mabrien is presumably ignorant of the bitter feudal and personal conflicts between his grandfather and his uncles, the *quatre fils Aymon*, and the emperor in earlier poems of the *geste*, but he is well aware of the defeat he himself had inflicted on the Christian armies in conquering Jerusalem and Acre, and of the challenge he had hurled at them as they escaped him at Acre:

> Par tous mes dieux, se maintenant ne vous puis ycy avoir, je vous suivray jusques oultremer; et tant vous di qu'il ne vous demourra terre, contree ne seignourie que de moy ne tendrés, et a la loi que je tiens vous feray obbaïr, ou tous vous feray de malle mort finer voz jours! (22.8)

The Christian Mabrien's immediate reaction to Charlemagne's loss in Spain is one of both sorrow and solidarity. 'Dieu! Comme fu dollent Mabrien du dommage Charlemaine!' exclaims the narrator, as Mabrien vows to seek the emperor straight away (34.2).

A series of fortuitous encounters mark his progress. Nearing Orleans, where he expects to find Charlemagne, he encounters Ogier de Danemark; unknown to each other, they fight until the emperor arrives and calls out Ogier's name. Aware that Ogier is both his cousin and – 'comme il avoit entendu autrefoi' – his father's closest friend, Mabrien recounts his story to his former adversary, and Ogier in turn presents him to Charlemagne; there is a touch of convivial humour in this elderly knight's recollection that Mabrien the Saracen had 'promised' them as they fled from Acre that he would very soon come to see them in their own land. Charlemagne too rejoices at the arrival of King Yvon's son: 'Il le baisa et recueilli moult doulcement, et lui pria qu'il demorast a sa court, car pour lors ne desiroit que avoir l'amour des barons et acquerir des amis et serviteurs nouveaux, pource que trop en avoit perdu en Espaigne' (34.10). When Mabrien declines, in haste to fulfill his vow to find his parents, Charlemagne requests that he return with the latter to a 'court nouvelle' to be held at Easter.

Soon another combat incognito pits Mabrien against his father. It corresponds to an earlier confrontation during the Saracen attack on Jerusalem, when he had twice refrained from killing King Yvon, acting, we are told, 'non mie par couardie ne par paour qu'il eust, mais par Nature, qui son cueur amonnestoit de le depporter de mort' (21.12). Mabrien was on those occasions both mystified and profoundly disturbed by his own conduct, but his two close companions, cognizant of his history, suspected that 'c'estoit Nature laquelle besognoit' (19.13) and that he might soon return to the Christian religion of the family whose existence he ignored.[36] Now the father-son combat ends in joyful recognition, as does Mabrien's meeting with his cousin Anssel, the son of Renaut d'Acre whom he himself had killed in the Saracen conquest of Acre.

The last of this series of glad reunions takes place in Paris, where Mabrien and his kinsmen and followers find Charlemagne in the company of Naymes and Ogier. The new arrivals are led before Charlemagne, 'qui mie ne fut apprentis de les recepvoir: ains leur fist si joyeuse chiere que merveilles'. Against the vast background of enmity between the emperor and his rebellious vassals, this scene depicts a euphoric resolution, as Charlemagne's effusive public praise of Mabrien extends to his entire lineage:

> moult grant compte faisoit Charlemaine du chevalier Mabrien, en loant le roy Yvon et son lignage, donc il estoit ung tel chevalier yssu qui tant estoit plain de proesse que il avoit lui et la chevalerye de France chassez du royaume d'Acre et de Surye, et qui encores venoit en aage de valloir de plus en plus. (35.13)

The most remarkable scene of this positive rewriting results from Mabrien's earlier acquisition of apples in the Earthly Paradise. This is reminiscent of a scene in *Esclarmonde*, in which Huon de Bordeaux, on the 'Ile de Jouvent', discovers apples with the marvellous capacity to restore anyone who eats them 'en leage de xxx ans' (v. 1314) and is informed by an angel that he may pick three of them. Later, with results proclaimed to be miracles, Huon bestows them upon an emir who converts to Christianity, upon the Abbot of Cluny, and lastly upon

---

[36] For the two combats between Mabrien and Yvon in the battle for Jerusalem, see *Mabrien* 19.8 and 19.12; 21.11–21.12.

Charlemagne, following his hard-won reconciliation with the emperor: 'Drois emperes dist Huës li membrés / Si maït Dix je vous ferai bonté' (vv. 2390–91).[37]

In *Mabrien* too the hero gives an apple to Charlemagne. The presentation occurs at a strategic moment, when the Emperor has granted Mabrien two requests: that he and Gloriande be baptised and then married at Charlemagne's court, and that he then be given leave to return to the East to engage with his father and his cousin in the reconquest of the lands which he had been instrumental in wresting from them. This apple, unlike the 'vermeille pume' Roland is reported in the *Chanson de Roland* to have presented to the Emperor, is not a symbolic gift of universal dominion.[38] It is a fruit with very specific characteristics, detailed by Mabrien when he summons Charlemagne to receive it:

> Et lors appella Mabrien Charlemaine devant les princes de son hostel, et en tirant de son sain la pomme qu'il avoit apportee de paradiz terrestre, laquelle avoit perdu sa rondeur, sa beaulté et sa verdeur par l'avoir si longuement portee et gardee en challeur qu'elle estoit toute seiche, si qu'il n'y avoit plus sinon la pel et les pepins du meillieu, lui dist: 'Ceste pomme vous ay de moult loingtain pays apportee, sire, fait il, afin de jeunesse recouvrer se vous en mengiez; et sachez qu'elle fu cueillie en l'Arbre de Jouvent. Mais pource qu'elle est ainsi sur moy sechee la convient tres bien laver, et fendre par le meillieu; si la mectez en ung hanap d'or ou d'argent pour soy revenir, et puis la buvez et mengiez, si perdrez vostre viellesse, ainsi comme on le m'a certiffié pour vray.' (35.15)

This detailed depiction of the 'pomme de Jouvente' and the process of its rehydration, revealing an evident concern for verisimilitude, focuses the attention of the reader on the dramatic physical results of Mabrien's gift, Charlemagne's immediate rejuvenation 'comme en l'aage de .xxx. ans'.

This transformation has momentous – and unexpected – consequences. With this event which, we recall, occurs during the immediate aftermath of the defeat at Rencesvals, Charlemagne's epic future is transformed. In the memorable final scene of the *Chanson de Roland*, at

---

[37] This series of bestowals, as Jean Baroin points out, is an important structural feature in *Esclarmonde*. See 'Le Fruit merveilleux d'*Esclarmonde*', in *De l'étranger à l'étrange ou la conjointure de la merveille* (Aix-en-Provence: CUER MA, 1988), pp. 59–70.

[38] *La Chanson de Roland*, ed. Cesare Segre, 2 vol. (Geneva: Droz, 1989), I, vv. 3587–88: 'Tenez, bel sire, dist Rollant a sun uncle, / De trestuz reis vos present les curunes.' Ganelon is evoking what he represents as Roland's dangerous pride.

the corresponding point of his return from Spain in that poem, the angel Gabriel appears to the emperor, telling him that Christians are calling for his aid and summoning him to resume his war against the Saracens. He will go, of course, but, aged and weary, 'li emperere n'i volsist aler mie: / "Deus! dist le reis, si penuse est ma vie!" / Pluret des oilz, sa barbe blanche tiret.'[39] In sharp contrast, the rejuvenated Charlemagne of *Mabrien* is eager to associate himself with Mabrien's announced expedition against the Saracens, swearing that 'encores vengeroit il la mort de Roland et d'Olivier, et des nobles chevaliers qui demourez estoient a Rainssevaulz par la trayson du conte Guennelon et du roy Marcille' (35.15). Ogier will join them, in a united venture merging their forces under Mabrien's leadership as they blend their battle-cries: 'Acre! Mont Joye! Jherusalem! Et Dampnemarche!'

This mission accomplished, Mabrien leads Charlemagne to the Holy Sepulchre in Jerusalem, where the Emperor prays devoutly 'pour les ames de Roland, d'Olivier et des chevaliers qui mors estoient par grant trayson a Raincevaulx' (37.9). Charlemagne and Ogier then return to their lands, leaving Mabrien to conquer and further Christianise cities in Persia and India. He is aided by his son Renaudin, who is crowned king of Cana, as well as by the son he fathered in Faerie, Gracien, whom Gracienne had raised nobly until he was 'en aage de chevalerye recevoir', thus anchoring the *matière de Bretagne* within the *matière de France* through the genealogical principle central to cycle-formation.[40] Mabrien, now king of India, confers knighthood upon Gracien.

Following these triumphs, Mabrien's story rejoins that of earlier heroes of his noble lineage. Both his grandfather Renaut and his uncle Maugis had retreated from the secular world, and he in turn spends his final twenty years as a hermit before engaging in a final battle against the Infidels.[41] Mabrien reappears to aid Renaudin when Cana comes un-

[39] *La Chanson de Roland*, I, vv. 3998–4001.

[40] Rubric 50. In sinister contrast, in the *Bataille Loquifer* the opposition of the hero's two sons, one fathered in a fairy realm, casts a shadow over his adventures. When Renoart leaves to resume his search for his first son, Morgain attempts to have him destroyed because she fears for her child's inheritance; her child Corbon will be '.I. vif diable; ans ne fist se mal non' (v. 3923). See Sara Sturm-Maddox and Donald Maddox, 'Renoart in Avalon: generic shift in the *Bataille Loquifer*', in Karen Pratt (ed.), *Shifts and Transpositions in Medieval Narrative* (Cambridge: D. S. Brewer, 1994), pp. 17–22.

[41] The monastic retreat of the epic hero is found also in the *Moniage Guillaume*, the *Moniage Rainouart*, and *Giraut de Roussillon*; in the first of these, Guillaume returns to the secular world to defend the French king in Paris.

der Saracen attack. The Christians are victorious, but Mabrien is treacherously killed in the battle. During his funeral procession, however, the miraculous pealing of the bells in all the city's churches reveals 'tout plainement la saincteté du glorieux roi et hermite', transforming the mourning of the populace into joy. The glorious end of his story echoes that of Renaut de Montauban, whose life, as Charlemagne acknowledges in Jerusalem, 'avoit deservy la grace Dieu si grandement que il estoit collocqué en la gloire des sains cieulx, et faisoit Dieu pour lui miracles evidens' (37.10).[42] Mabrien too will be revered as a martyr saint and his remains preserved in a *chasse d'argent*, the locus of many miracles.[43]

What, then, is the place of *Mabrien* in the narrative literature of the fifteenth century? As an epico-romance narrative, it is flagrantly intergeneric, sharing with a number of late verse epics a strong tendency to incorporate elements characteristic of medieval romance;[44] at its conclusion, the story of the hero in this *roman de chevalerie* shades into hagiographic romance. These intergeneric elements, however, are here tributary to a powerful dynamic of cyclification. 'The later Middle Ages', as Jane Taylor observed with her accustomed breadth of vision, is in codicological terms 'the "Age of the Narrative Cycle"',[45] and *Mabrien* effects a transformative intervention both within and beyond the *données* of the *geste* of Renaut de Montauban. The repeated public

[42] This ending is elaborated in the epilogue to *Renaut de Montauban*, vv. 14205–308. See Eve-Marie Halba, 'Hagiographie de saint Renaut de Montauban', in Jean-Luc Deuffic (ed.), *Reliques et sainteté dans l'espace médiéval* [*PECIA*, 8–11 (2005)], pp. 281–99.

[43] Its inscription reads 'CY REPOSE LE PRECIEUX CORPS DU GLORIEUX MARTIR MONSEIGNEUR SAINT MABRIEN, JADIZ ROY D'INDE LA MAJOUR, DOMPTEUR ET FLAYEL DES ENNEMIS DE LA FOY, ET EN LA FIN SAINT ET DEVOT HERMITE' (55.7).

[44] For an overview of these elements see Claude Roussel, 'Le Mélange des genres dans les chansons de geste tardives', in Carlos Alvar and Juan Parades (eds), *Actes du XVIe Congrès International de la Société Rencesvals* (Granada: University of Granada, 2005), pp. 65–85.

[45] Jane H. M. Taylor, 'Order from accident: cyclic consciousness at the end of the Middle Ages', in Bart Besamusca *et al.* (eds), *Cyclification:The Development of Narrative Cycles in the Chansons de Geste and the Arthurian Romances* (Amsterdam: Royal Netherlands Academy of Arts and Sciences, 1994), pp. 59–73. On this 'intertextual dialogue of text with text', see also Taylor, 'The sense of a beginning: genealogy and plenitude in late medieval narrative cycles', in Sara Sturm-Maddox and Donald Maddox (eds), *Transtextualities: Of Cycles and Cyclicity in Medieval French Literature* (Binghamton, NY: Medieval & Renaissance Texts & Studies, 1996), pp. 93–123 (pp. 122–23).

celebration of the lineage is set against the anguishing conflicts that mark the stories of those heroes pitted against their sovereign.

At the same time, the totalising tendency of this prose romance is evident in its commemoration of the deeds

> de Mabrien, de Yvon, le riche roy, de son pere Regnault de Montauben et de ses trois freres, Allart, Guichart et Richart, de Maulgis, le noble duc d'Aigremont, qui tint le lieu pappal, et en montant de ligne en ligne jusques a Doon, le seigneur de Mayence, de qui ilz estoient tous descenduz, et lequel estoit du temps et aage de Charlemaine, comme l'istoire le peult avoir veu et leu en autres livres parlans de Doon de Mayence, de Garin de Monglenne et de Charlemaine, desquelz trois issirent les plus vaillans chevaliers du monde. (35.16)

That this identification of three lineages is identical to that of the three major French *gestes* in Bertrand de Bar-sur-Aube's often-cited class-ification in the thirteenth century[46] invites us to reflect further upon the notions of 'jonction de cycles' and 'mélange de cycles', two of the variants of cyclification proposed by Michael Heintze.[47] *Mabrien* writes an end to the legendary struggle between Charlemagne and his famously rebellious vassals that leads to resounding success in the struggle against the Infidel, in a story that may be characterised, as in two of the several early printed editions that attest to its continuing popularity, as 'singuliere et fort recreative'.[48]

---

[46] They are the *gestes* of the *roi de France*, of *Doon de Mayence*, and of *Garin de Monglane*. See the prologue to *Girard de Vienne*, ed. Wolfgang van Emden (Paris: Picard, 1977), pp. 8–69.

[47] Michael Heintze, 'Les Techniques de la formation de cycles dans les chansons de geste', in Besamusca (ed.), *Cyclification*, pp. 46–55.

[48] On these early editions see *Mabrien*, pp. 41–46.

4

Saying your prayers: poetic expression of secularism in Villon's *Testament*

Nancy Freeman Regalado

This study of Villon is my tribute to Jane Taylor, who has expanded our understanding of that Parisian poet through her books and through collegial dialogue. In her *Poetry of François Villon*,[1] she elaborated reading strategies that opened Villon's work to new insights. Equally attentive to the work of fellow scholars, she invited me to speak twice at Oxford and came herself to lecture at New York University. I also participated in the conference she co-organised in 1996 which yielded a volume of important papers, *Villon at Oxford*.[2] This chapter, originally conceived for the Sewanee Medieval Colloquium on 'Secularism in the Middle Ages' (1985), formed part of my 1994 lecture at Oxford. It expresses my admiration and gratitude for, and my warm friendship with, Jane Taylor.

***

Secularism and secularisation are notions defined by elements of change in ideas about the nature of man and the world. What changes is not so much the facts of existence as human beliefs about existence. Secularisation is, in its essence, a cultural shifting in beliefs and in thought. Secularism is the result of that process: it anchors man's ethical and metaphysical beliefs not principally in concepts of a transcendent religious or spiritual nature, but rather within the things of this world.

---

[1] Jane H. M. Taylor, *The Poetry of François Villon: Text and Context* (Cambridge: Cambridge University Press, 2001).

[2] Michael Freeman and Jane H. M. Taylor (eds), *Villon at Oxford: The Drama of the Text* (Amsterdam: Rodopi, 1999).

We can guess at the thoughts and beliefs that inspired ancient cities, medieval cathedrals, great wars and migrations by the monuments and ruins that remain. But it is in the texts preserved from the past that we can read expression of the thoughts and beliefs themselves and witness changes in thinking. We depend on texts to show us the presence of secularism in the Middle Ages, how and where it emerges, and how it was experienced.

There is a group of nine medieval French poems shaped as parodic prayers that reveal the very thought processes of secularisation, for they catch the confrontation of secular thought and spiritual belief within representations of an individual mind at work. Largely neglected since they were edited by Eero Ilvonen in 1914,[3] these poems constitute an important literary expression of secularisation, for they reveal shifts in belief and in interests that gave rise to tensions between spiritual concerns and a secularised world-view in the later Middle Ages.

In literary terms, spiritual and secular matters expressed in the ver-nacular correspond to different discourses. While romances, *chansons*, and *fabliaux* are dominated by matters of love, chivalry, and everyday life, and can be considered secular texts, prayers and sermons are religious and moral in content. There are, however, a number of medieval works that deliberately combine and contrast religious and secular discourses. Among these may be counted Villon's great *Testament*, a poem which depicts a deeply ironic speaker and his world in the form of a civil document, a will, which contains several prayers.[4]

Prayer takes many shapes within the *Testament*.[5] There are relatively straightforward prayers such as the stanzas addressed to Louis XI (vv. 49–72), the *Ballade pour prier Nostre Dame* (vv. 873–909) and the *Verset* which concludes the epitaph (vv. 1892–1903). There are also ambiguous, unstable pieces such as the *Ballade et oroison* for Jehan Cotart (vv. 1238–63), which is at once a prayer and a drinking song, and the *Ballade des langues envieuses* (vv. 1422–56), a prayer of hellish male-diction. There are also, within the *Testament*, two kinds of 'interrupted prayers'. In the first, the poet breaks off, letting us know that what follows will be a curse, as in his prayers for Thibaut d'Aussigny

---

[3] Eero Ilvonen, *Parodies de thèmes pieux dans la poésie française du Moyen Age: Pater – Credo – Ave Maria – Laetabundus* (Geneva: Slatkine, 1975).

[4] *Le Testament Villon*, eds Jean Rychner and Albert Henry (Geneva: Droz, 1974); hereinafter Rychner-Henry.

[5] Evelyn Birge Vitz, '"Bourde jus mise"? Villon, the liturgy, and prayer', in Freeman and Taylor (eds), *Villon at Oxford*, pp. 170–94.

(*Testament*, vv. 16–48, 742–44). In the second, a prayer is interrupted by the muttered thoughts of the poetic voice *saying* that prayer, intruding within the words of the prayer itself. The *Testament* prayer 'Ou nom de Dieu, Pere eternel' (cited in Appendix A) begins twice (vv. 793, 825) before it can be concluded (v. 832). In this interrupted prayer, worldly concerns invade the spiritual words, expressing the insistent pull of thoughts of this world, of secularism. The digressive musings that well up into Villon's prayer seem natural to the reader, since they continue one of the essential tasks of the *Testament*, the convincing characterisation of a poetic voice represented as that of an impoverished ex-student resentful of clerical authority.[6] Yet these digressions have a literary source, as yet unacknowledged, that enables us to trace this poetry of secularisation back over more than two centuries.

Many thirteenth-century authors writing in French had a liking for works combining profane and religious matters: the *Roman de la Rose* and the *Queste del Saint Graal* are works that blur the boundaries between the secular and the religious. It is, moreover, a period with a great taste for parody, including both the pious *contrafacta* of courtly chansons such as those by Gautier de Coincy[7] and also secular parodies of religious works, such as the celebrated drinking song 'Vinum bonum cum sapore / Bibit abbas cum priore' (Good wine with savour the abbot drinks with the prior) which parodies the liturgical hymn to the Virgin, 'Verbum bonum et suave / Personemus, illud *Ave*' (Let us proclaim that word good and sweet, that 'Hail').[8]

Several parodic texts imitate vernacular prayers in which the *Pater noster* is glossed in French. Such pious paraphrases exemplify the de-

---

[6] See Nancy Freeman Regalado, 'Speaking in script: the construction of voice, presence, and perspective in Villon's *Testament*', in W. F. H. Nicolaisen (ed.), *Oral Tradition in the Middle Ages* (Binghamton, NY: Center for Medieval and Early Renaissance Studies, 1995), pp. 209–23.

[7] On Gautier, see Kathryn Duys, 'Books Shaped by Song: Early Literary Literacy in the *Miracles de Nostre Dame* of Gautier de Coinci' (unpublished PhD dissertation, New York University, 1997), and Ardis Butterfield, *Poetry and Music in Medieval France: from Jean Renart to Guillaume de Machaut* (Cambridge: Cambridge University Press, 2002), pp. 103–15. See also *Recueil de chansons pieuses du XIIIᵉ siècle*, ed. Edward Järnström, 2 vol. [(I) Annales Academiae Scientiarum Fennicae, Ser. B, t. III, 1; (II, with A. Långfors) Annales Academiae Scientiarum Fennicae, Ser. B, t. XX, Pp. 4 (Helsinki: Suomalaisen Tiedeakatemian Kunstantama, 1910, 1927)].

[8] Martha Bayless (ed. and trans.), *Parody in the Middle Ages: The Latin Tradition* (Ann Arbor: University of Michigan Press, 1996), pp. 109–10, 339, 342, which supersedes Paul Lehmann, *Die Parodie im Mittelalter*, 2ⁿᵈ ed. (Stuttgart: A. Hiersemann, 1963).

votional urge, inspired by the Fourth Lateran Council of 1215, to strengthen lay piety,[9] as in *La Patre nostre farsie*:

> *Pater noster* doit chascun dire
> A Dieu et crier: 'Biaus douz sire,
> Gardez nos ames et noz cors;
> *Qui es in celis* haut là sus'.[10]

Poets found it easy to substitute jovial praise of drink for such devout glosses:

> *Pater noster,* biaus sire Dieus,
> Quant vins faudra ce ert granz deuls
> Toutes joies, toutes valors
> Seront en lermes et en plors.
> *Qui est in celis.* Clerc et lai
> Ne diront ja mès son ne lai.
> car en vin a trop de deduis.[11]

The popularity of such *Pater noster* parodies lasts into the sixteenth century, yielding Basochien tavern verse, prayers by syphilitics, and even political commentary in the *Patenostre du cummun peuple sellon le temps qui court* (after 1450).[12]

The nine thirteenth-century parodies edited by Ilvonen are a special group, for they represent an ongoing stream of thoughts expressed in colloquial speech and attributed to well-characterised individuals, poems in which the *saying* intrudes into the prayer.[13] The inner monologue in these parodies is completely worldly in content. The contrast between the prayer and such secular ruminations is supported, moreover, by the opposition between the fixed sequence of words in Latin, the language of lofty spirituality, and the unpredictable flow of

---

[9] See Evelyn Birge Vitz, 'The impact of Christian doctrine on medieval literature', in Denis Hollier (ed.), *A New History of French Literature* (Cambridge, MA: Harvard University Press, 1989), pp. 82–88.

[10] Ilvonen, *Parodies,* p. 146; copied in Paris, BnF, fr. 837 (fol. 274[r]).

[11] Ilvonen, *Parodies,* p. 118; copied in Paris, BnF, fr. 837 (fol. 177[r]).

[12] Ilvonen, *Parodies,* p. 38. On bilingual parodies generally, see Paul Zumthor, 'Un problème d'esthétique médiévale: l'utilisation poétique du bilinguisme', *Le Moyen Age* (1960), 301–36, 561–94 (pp. 310–11); and the works cited by Otto Müller, *Das lateinische Einschiebsel in der französischen Literatur des Mittelalters* (Zürich: Leemann, 1919), pp. 189 ff.

[13] There is no characterisation of the speaker in the satirical *Pater* studied by K. V. Sinclair, 'Le Dit des patenostres de Gieffroy: parodie d'un thème pieux', *Le Moyen Age*, 103 (1997), 561–70.

French words, the vernacular of everyday matters. This type of poem provides Villon with a literary model for the representation of a voice saying a prayer, and for the poetic expression of secularism.

Sermon *exempla* were a key source for these thirteenth-century poems showing a man at prayer distracted by temporal thoughts. One popular sermon story tells of a hermit trying *not* to think of his donkey while praying. It dramatises ecclesiastical condemnation of human preoccupation with worldly matters that divert men from salvation.

> Qui vult servire Deo et mundo, minor est utroque. Exemplum habemus de quodam eremita qui cum asino suo venit ad ecclesiam. Intravit in ecclesiam et demisit asinum suum ad ostium et incœpit dicere: 'Pater noster ...' et tunc cogitavit: 'Quid comedit asinus meus?' Secundo incœpit: 'Pater noster ...' et statim cogitavit: 'Latrones furabuntur asinum meum'. Et sic cogitans de asino, sollicitus de asino, non potuit perficere Pater noster. Exivit ecclesiam, accepit asinum, venit ad quemdam leprosum et dedit ei asinum et, reversus ad ecclesiam, dixit Pater noster et perfecit orationem suam.[14]

> [He who wishes to serve God and the world is diminished in both. Take the example of the hermit who came to church with his donkey. He entered into the church and left his donkey at the door, and began to say, 'Our Father ...' but then he thought, "What could my donkey be eating now?' Then he began again, 'Our Father...', and immediately he thought again, 'Thieves are going to steal my donkey!' and thus, since he kept thinking about the donkey, worrying about the donkey, he couldn't finish his prayer. So he went out of the church, took his donkey, went to a certain leper, and gave him the donkey, and, having returned to the church, he said his *Pater noster* and finished his prayer. (My translation)]

The *Patrenostre à l'userier* (cited in Appendix B) is an early thirteenth-century poem amplifying a sermon story like that of the hermit and the donkey.[15] Indeed, the author says he heard it told in a

---

[14] Ilvonen cites the version by Jean d'Orléans (d. 1306) of this anecdote first known in Pierre le Chantre's late twelfth-century commentary on Job (*Parodies*, pp. 54–55).

[15] Ilvonen edits the version copied in Paris, BnF, MS fr. 837, fols. 218ᵛ–19ᵛ, which contains six of the nine parodies he edits (*Parodies*, pp. 66–77); see the facsimile of BnF, MS fr. 837 published by Henri Omont, *Fabliaux, dits et contes en vers français du XIIIᵉ siècle* (1932; Geneva: Slatkine Reprints, 1973). I thank Olivier Collet for sending me transcriptions of seven glossed prayers from fr. 837, including *La patrenostre glosee* (fol. 172ᵛ) and *La patrenostre en françois* (fol. 226ᵛ). Collet observes that there are about as many parodies (some twenty) as serious adaptations of prayers in BnF, MS fr. 837; see 'Le manuscrit BnF, MS f. fr. 837 et le laboratoire poétique du XIIIᵉ siècle', in Milena

sermon by Robert de Courçon, papal legate to France from 1212–1219, who denounced usury and money-lending (vv. 6–10).[16] It describes the thoughts of a money-lender who prays on his way to church and during mass. The effect of alternation between the repetition of the Latin prayer and the obsessive mutterings of the money-lender as he leaves his house is comic (vv. 25–28); but the money-lender's soul is imperilled by his deafness to spiritual matters, which increases when he reaches the church. Hypocritically wetting his eyes with spittle so others will think he weeps from piety (vv. 108–12), he begins the 'Our Father' again. Distracted by thoughts of his money that continually intrude into his prayer, he cannot understand its spiritual message. '*Pater noster qui es in celis* / Qu'est-ce, sui je ore esbahis, / Qu'ore revueil commencier fable?' (vv. 115–17). He listens, uncomprehending, to the priest shouting at the altar: '*Nomen tuum*. Que senefie / Que nostre prestres si haut crie' (vv. 131–32). And he even grumbles about Robert de Courçon's trying to chase off money-lenders with his sermons (vv. 142–46).

If asked what the author probably intended, we would quickly answer, 'he directed his poem to laymen and wanted to condemn the spiritual bankruptcy, the secularism of money-lenders.' But as we read the poem, we may also detect a secularising tendency within the condemnation itself, for although the text may censure usury, it also gives considerable place to the lively talk of the miserly money-lender. What interests us as readers is not the familiar prayer, but the novel portrait of a human type: his desire to win first place in profit and hoarding (vv. 28–31); his thoughts of revenge against his wasteful maid, who gives all his money away 'a un pautonier qui la fout' (v. 130) by keeping her on a meagre diet of peas, watercress gruel, and a sliver of bacon. We look ahead, amused, interested, to see what the money-lender will say next: 'Nostre prestre veut orguener / Pour trer nostre argent de borse; / Mais ainçois avroit un pet d'orse / Qu'il ait du mien por tel abet / Tant ne chanteroit en fausset' (vv. 248–52). The didactic, spiritual intention is thus overtaken by the vivid, convincing characterisation of what goes on in a money-lender's mind. The durable popularity of such picturing of the state of mind of this unexemplary individual is confirmed by its appearance in four manuscripts and by a

---

Mikhaïlova (ed.), *Mouvances et jointures: du manuscrit au texte médiéval* (Orléans: Paradigme, 2005), pp. 172–92 (pp. 178–79).

[16] On Robert de Courçon and medieval attitudes to usury, see Ilvonen, *Parodies*, pp. 47–58.

parodic *Credo a l'userier* in which the usurer grabs at his money-bags on his deathbed.[17] Moreover, vv. 248–52 cited above from the *Patrenostre à l'userier* reappear virtually unchanged in the farce interpolated into the late fourteenth-century play *La Vie Monseigneur Saint Fiacre*, within the monologue of a peasant who complains about wasting his time at church.[18]

In these parodies, then, the interplay between religious and secular modes of discourse both reflects and enhances the process of secularisation. Although the authors may have intended to condemn secular concerns, juxtaposition of spiritual and secular themes tends to lend weight to worldly matters. As readers, we cannot 'give away the donkey', so to speak, for the money-lender cannot be dislodged from the poetic text. His mundane musings are locked safely into the prayer, which has become inseparable from its saying: the human voice of the speaker is more important than the devotional text.

Huitains [hereinafter 'H'] 80–84 of Villon's *Testament* are indebted to this literary tradition of works representing a prayer interrupted by the mutter of private thoughts. Within these stanzas, parenthetic comments mark or emphasise the presence of the human speaker, as in 'selon ma concepcion' (v. 807), or 'comme j'ay dit' (v. 825).[19] His drowsy clerk Fremin is summoned; the poetic text is defined as a will ('Car commencer vueil a tester'; v. 778); pen, paper, and ink are represented (vv. 789–90), as are the circumstances of dictation and promulgation (vv. 786, 791). Moreover, as in the *Patrenotre a l'userier*, the vicissitudes of the speaker's life are detailed: enfeebled by poverty, he is bedridden, his heart weakening; he can barely 'papier' (v. 786). The self portrait inserted at the very moment the speaker attempts to finish his prayer – 'Sans pechié soit parfait ce dit / Par moy, plus maigre que chimere' (vv. 827–28) – recalls the 'perfecit' of the hermit finishing off his prayer, while 'chimere' is a learned touch, characterising the poetic voice as that of a man of letters, menaced by the 'fievre eufumere' (v. 829), thought to be brought on by excessive thought.[20] Moreover, mention of this fever recalls the comic insult common in fifteenth-cent-

---

[17] Ilvonen, *Parodies*, pp. 58, 82, and similar parodies including those where a drunkard speaks (*La Patrenostre du vin*, pp. 115–21), an impoverished dice-player (*Le Credo au ribaut*, pp. 123–33), and a desperate lover (*La Patrenostre d'amours*, pp. 134–42).

[18] *La Vie Monseigneur Saint Fiacre*, eds James F. Burks, Barbara M. Craig, and Marion E. Porter (Lawrence: The University of Kansas Press, 1960), p. 29, vv. 726–30.

[19] I thank Alice Deakins for consultation about represented speech.

[20] Rychner-Henry, II, p. 124.

ury farce that recurs in the *Testament*: 'les fievres quartes' (v. 1101), appropriate to the persona of Villon as a 'bon follastre' (v. 1883).

Although the underlying structure is similar, the opposition between familiar talk and the formal language of prayer is more developed and complex in the *Testament* than in the *Patrenostre a l'userier*. In Villon, as in the *Patrenostre*, there is some roughening of rhythmic patterns in passages of familiar speech compared with the lofty smoothness of prayer. Villon makes no use of Latin to mark his prayer, but in H. 85 (vv. 833–40), which is entirely devoted to prayer, five out of the eight verses flow seamlessly, matching clauses to verse length without inner syntactic pause: 'La glorïeuse Trinité', 'Chambre de la divinité', 'Priant toute la charité / Des dignes neuf ordres des cieulx, / Devant le trosne precïeux.' In contrast with the even assertions of prayer, we hear the interrogative intonation of vv. 809–11 and the accusing exclamation of v. 812 – '"Qui vous fait mectre / Si tres avant ceste parolle, / Qui n'estes en theologie maistre? / A vous est presumpcïon folle"' – and the emphatic enjambment of vv. 814–15, 'Touchant du riche ensevely / en feu ...', as well as the fervent exclamation of vv. 823–24, 'Puisque boiture y est si chiere, / Dieu nous garde de la main mise!'[21]

Yet few patterns are simple in Villon! The initial shift from prayer to talk is so unmarked by any change in prosody or diction that editors Jean Rychner and Albert Henry, as well as translator Galway Kinnell, have added marks of ellipsis to clarify the shift in H. 80 from prayer to commentary: 'Qui sauva ce qu'Adam perit / Et du pery parre les cyeulx ... / Qui bien ce croit peu ne merite. / Gens mors estre faiz petitz dieux' (vv.798–99; Who saved those lost through Adam / And sets them all about heaven ... / No sensible person can believe / Dead people are made into little gods).[22] Typographic clarification, however, interferes with the effect of ironic undercutting resulting from the contrast between the shift in content and absence of rhythmic or lexical demarkation. The effect is enhanced by the similarities in rhythm and structure between vv.797 ('Qui sauva') and 799 ('Qui ce croit'), further smoothed by an extended pattern of alliterative '*p*'s ('perit, pery, pare, peu, petiz').

The parenthetic digression of personal commentary swells out in H. 81, developing the theme of death as the irreversible and universal destruction of body and soul, especially in v. 804, where 'De quell-

---

[21] Variant: 'bourde jus mise' ['all jokes aside'].

[22] *The Poems of François Villon*, trans. Galway Kinnell (Boston, MA: Houghton Mifflin, 1977).

conque condicïon' is identical to *Testament*, v. 310, where it rhymes with 'Mort saisit sans exceptïon'. Layers of embedded insertion erupt to thicken the intrusive personal commentary. Thus in the second half of H. 81, the speaker corrects himself, noting, in sharply familiar terms, an exception to the reign of death over body and soul: 'Touteffoiz fais excepcïon / Des patriarches et prophetes, / Car, selon ma concepcïon, / Onques grant chault n'eurent aux fesses.' In H. 82, where parenthetic speaking continues to hold centre stage, yet another voice chimes in, challenging the speaker's right to offer opinions: 'Qui me diroit: "Qui vous fai ct mectre / Si tres avant ceste parolle, / Qui n'estes en theologie maistre? / A vous est presumpcïon folle"' (vv. 809–12). Such dialogic exchange, marked by the inflections of informal speech, sustains the opposition between talk and the formal language of prayer, which is marked, not by Latin, as in the *Patrenostre a l'userier*, but by ponderous, polysyllabic Latinisms – 'perdicïon, condicïon, exepcïon, concepcïon, presumcïon' (H. 81–82). These give an appropriately stately (and ironic) effect when they are meshed with the trivial and even obscene terms of the inserted personal commentary, yielding what Vitz calls an 'unresolvable tension between Villon's prayers and his irreverent and mocking handling of them'.[23]

Formal and familiar discourses thus do not remain separate in Villon. They are fused again in the verses of H. 82–83, which tell the Gospel parable of the rich man and Lazarus (Luke 16:19–31), and in which there is a rich mixture of Latinisms with tavern talk. The Latin words for the rich man's plea that Lazarus cool his burning tongue are 'ut refrigerat linguam meam'. This image is both reiterated by the Latinising 'reffrigere' (v. 818) and undercut by 'raffreschir sa maschoüoire' (v. 820; literally, to refresh his jaw), an expression as colloquial as 'to wet his whistle'. Low talk of 'pyons' (v. 821) and 'boiture' (v. 823) describe the torments of Hell as a tough place where topers drink the shirts right off their backs.[24]

There is interesting evidence within the rhyme words of these *Testament* stanzas for phonetic support of the distinction between formal and informal speech. Villon enlivens his colloquial language with touches of a common, local accent. At v. 806, the word 'prophetes' takes

---

[23] Vitz, '"Bourde jus mise"', p. 175.

[24] This familiar slang for losing one's clothes to drink or dicing in the tavern hides a darker connotation of water torture, where a long cloth was stuffed into a victim's mouth and water poured down his throat forcing him to swallow the cloth.

a loose pronunciation to rhyme contemptuously with 'fesses',[25] in sneering mockery of the salvation promised Old Testament patriarchs and prophets. Another rhyme, 'ardre, aerdre' (vv. 817, 819), reflects the pronunciation typical of Parisian speech, often noted by Marot in the margins of his *Œuvres de François Villon*.[26] A Parisian pronunciation of these rhyme words, would, of course, be appropriate to Villon's poetic 'I', who describes himself as an 'enffant de Paris' (v. 1059). Indeed, Villon's interest in representing his themes through the very texture of his words is confirmed by similar phonetic, and lexical adaptations elsewhere: the archaising grammar of his 'Ballade en vieil langage françois' (vv. 385–512); the Occitan spellings that follow 'Se je parle ung poy poictevin' (v. 1060); the criminal jargon slipped into the verses addressed to the 'Enffans perduz' (vv. 1660–1727).

While the characterisation of the speaker and the effects of familiar speech opposed to formal prayer are thus more elaborated in the *Testament* than in the *Patrenostre a l'userier*, the inroads of secular thought are also far more profound in the *Testament*. Where the money-lender thought of business while praying, the speaker in the *Testament* questions the very beliefs expressed in the words of prayer he has just spoken: 'Qui bien ce croit peu ne merit" (v. 799) and contests the speaker's right to comment on theological questions – 'selon ma concepcïon' (v. 807) –, which is cast into doubt: 'A vous est presume-pcïon folle' (v. 812).

Villon's speaker answers as would a theologian, citing Gospel to confirm his views: 'C'est de Jhesus la parabolle / Touchant du riche ensevely / En feu, non pas en couche molle, / et du ladre de dessus ly' (vv. 813–16). But although Villon starts with an image taken from the parable, that of the rich man burning in Hell who begs relief from Lazarus in the bosom of Abraham, he then recasts Gospel, telling a new, hypothetical story, in which the fires of Hell consume Lazarus as well as the rich man: 'Se du ladre eust veu le doyz ardre' (v. 817). What dogma,

[25] Rychner-Henry, II, p. 301. Elsewhere in the *Testament*, 'prophetes' rhymes with '-estes' and '-etes' as in the ironic *Double Ballade* where 'prophetes' rhymes derisively with 'bestes, lunectes, amourectes, cuisses bien fetes, tartelettes, deshonnestes, sornettes', etc. (vv. 625–72); see Rychner-Henry, II, p. 288.

[26] Printed by Galiot du Pré (Paris, 1533). At *Testament* v. 42, Marot notes: 'Dyademe faut prononcer dyadame à l'antique ou à la Parisienne'; at v. 602, 'Fault dire appart, & non appert à l'usage de Paris'; at v. 750, 'Faut prononcer Robart, & non Robert au dit usage'; at v. 762, 'Fault prononcer tarre pour terre, & sarre, pour serre a cause du terrouer'; at v. 940, 'Ce qui se ryme en erre se doit prononcer en arre, comme dessus.'

indeed, is confirmed here? It is a terrible vision in which all bodies rot and all souls burn in the flames of Hell: 'Mors estoient et corps et ames, / En dampnee perdicïon, / Corps pourriz et ames en flasmes, / De quelconque condicïon' (vv. 801–04).

Here lies not only the expression but also the essence of Villon's secular vision. The speaker saying his prayers in these lines of the *Testament* has not merely substituted secular for spiritual concerns. By questioning the words of the prayer and the Gospel, by transforming their formal discourse into colloquial terms, he has shaken the foundations of belief, rewritten the sacred text, and challenged the Christian promise of salvation. Here indeed is the poetic expression of secularism.[27]

---

[27] On Villon's pessimistic denial of the possibility of spiritual knowledge, see Nancy Freeman Regalado, '*En l'an de mon trentiesme aage*: date, deixis and moral vision in Villon's *Testament*', in Emmanuèle Baumgartner and Christiane Marchello-Nizia (eds), *Le Nombre du temps. En hommage à Paul Zumthor* (Paris: Champion, 1988), pp. 237–46; and, by the same author, 'Villon's legacy from *Le Testament de Jean de Meun*: misquotation, memory, and the wisdom of fools', in Freeman and Taylor (eds), *Villon at Oxford*, pp. 282–311.

APPENDIX A: François Villon, *Testament*, ed. Rychner-Henry, I, pp. 73–76, trans. Galway Kinnell

H. 78	Somme, plus ne diray q'un mot,		Now I'll add just one more word
	Car commencer vueil a tester.		For I'm eager to start on the will
	Devant mon clerc Fremin qui m'ot,		Before my clerk Fremin who's listening
	S'il ne dort, je vueil protester	780	If not sleeping I want to state
	Que n'entens homme detester		I intend to cut off no one
	En ceste presente ordonnance,		In this present dispensation
	Et ne la vueil manifester .		But don't let word of this leak out
	Synom ou royaume de France.	784	Beyond the borders of France.

H. 79	Je sens mon cueur qui s'affoiblist		I can feel my heart getting weaker
	Et plus je ne puis papïer.		I must stop maundering on this way
	Fremin, siez toy pres de mon lit,		Fremin, sit here close by the bed
	Que l'en ne me viengne espïer.	788	So no one can enter and overhear
	Pren ancre tost, plume, pappier		Hurry, get ink, pen, paper
	Ce que nomme escriptz vistement,		Write down quickly what I dictate
	Puis fay le partout coppïer.		Then have a lot of copies made.
	Et vecy le commancement.	792	And here is the beginning.

H. 80	Ou nom de Dieu, Pere eternel,		In the name of God eternal Father
	Et du Filz que vierge parit,		And of the Son born of virgin
	Dieu au Pere coeternel		God co-eternal with the Father
	Ensemble et le Saint Esperit,	796	And with the Holy Ghost
	Qui sauva ce qu'Adam perit		Who saved those lost through Adam
	Et du pery parre les cyeulx . . .		And sets them all about heaven.
	Qui bien ce croit peu ne merit,		No sensible person can believe
	Gens mors estre faiz petiz dieux.	800	Dead people are made into little gods.

H. 81	Mors estoient et corps et ames,		For they were dead in body and soul
	En dampnee perdicïon,		And condemned to perdition

Corps pourriz et ames en
   flasmes,
De quelconque condicïon.   804
Touteffois fais excepcïon
Des patriarches et prophetes,
Car, selon ma concepcïon,
Oncques grant chault n'eurent 808
   aux fesses.

Bodies to rot and souls to burn

Regardless of their condition
Note I don't include
The patriarchs and prophets
According to my way of thinking
These never got their asses
   burned.

H. 82 Qui me diroit: 'Qui vous fait
      mectre
Si tres avant ceste parolle,
Qui n'estes en theologie maistre?

If someone should say 'How can
   you
Speak out so brashly
When you're not even master of
   theology?

A vous est presumpcïon folle', 812
C'est de Jhesus la parabolle
Touchant du riche ensevely
En feu, non pas en couche molle,
Et du ladre de dessus ly.   816

Your presumption is incredible'
The answer is Jesus' parable
Of the rich man who was laid out
In fire instead of a soft bed
And of Lazarus up above him.

H. 83 Se du ladre eust veu le doyz
      ardre,
Ja n'en eust requis reffrigere,

If he'd seen flames on Lazarus'
   finger
He'd not have asked it to cool
   him

N'au bout d'icelluy doiz aerdre
Pour raffreschir sa maschoüoire. 820
Pÿons y feront macte chierre,
Qui boyvent pourpoint et
   chemise!
Puis que boiture y est si chiere,

Or wanted water at that hand
To refresh his throat
Drunks will hate it down there
Who drink the shirt off their
   backs
Because of the high price of
   liquor

Dieux nous garde de la main 824
   mise!

God keep us from this, joking
   aside.

H. 84 Ou nom de Dieu, comme j'ay dit,
Et de sa glorïeuse Mere,
Sans pechié soit parfait ce dit

In the name of God as I said
And of his glorious Mother
May this task be done without
   sin

Par moy, plus maigre que 828
   chimere.
Se je n'ay eu fievre eufumere,

By me, skinnier than a madman

If I managed not to get the
   cholera

Ce m'a fait divine clemence;

It was by God's clemency

Mais d'autre dueil et perte amere   But of other sorrows and bitter
                                           loss

Je me tais, et ainsi commence.   832   I say nothing and so begin.

H. 85   Premier doue de ma povre ame   First I confer my pour soul
        La glorïeuse Trinité   On the glorious Trinity
        Et la commande a Nostre Dame,   And commend it to our Lady
        Chambre de la divinité,   836   Dwelling place of divinity
        Priant toute la charité   And petition all the charity
        Des dignes neuf ordres des cieulx   Of the nine Orders of Heaven
        Que par eulx soit ce don porté   That they may carry this gift
        Devant le trosne precïeux.   840   Before the precious throne.

APPENDIX B. *La Patrenostre a l'userier*, ed. Ilvonen, pp. 66–76; my translation)

Pour chastoier la riche gent		To catechise rich folk
Qui plus aiment or et argent		who love gold and silver
Qu'il ne font Dieu ne sainte Yglise,		more than they do God and Holy Church
Ai ci un poi m'entente mise	4	I've set myself to
A rimoier et a conter		rhyme and tell
Ice que j'oï raconter		what I heard
A mestre Robert de Chorson,		Master Robert de Courçon tell
A Paris, en un sien sermon	8	in his sermon in Paris:
Con fetement li userier		how the usurer
Va au moustier pour Dieu proier.		goes to pray in church
...		...
A tant s'en ist de sa meson,		As he leaves his house,
S'a commencïe s'oroison:		he has begun his prayer
'*Pater noster*, biaus sire Dieus,		'*Pater noster*, dear Lord God,
Donez moi que je soie tieus	28	make me so rich
Que je puisse par mon avoir		that I may win by my wealth
Et le los et le pris avoir		first place
De gaaignier et d'amasser		in profit and hoarding,
Tant que je puisse sormonter	32	let me outdo
Trestoz les riches useriers		all the rich usurers
Qui onques prestaissent deniers.		who ever lent a penny.
Qui es in celis. Mout me poise		*Qui est in celis*. Too bad
Que je n'i fui, quant la borgoise	36	I wasn't home when that townswoman
Vint çaienz emprunter deniers.		came to borrow money.
Mieus vousisse que li moustiers		I'd rather see the church
Et li prestres fussent fondu		in ruins, and the priest too,
Que g'i ëusse tant perdu.	40	than take such a loss.
...		...
Sanctificetur. Mout me grieve		*Sanctificetur*. What a pity
Que ma meschine est si esmievre	48	my servant is so quick
De mon argent issi gaster;		to spend my money so.
Mès ele me puet tant haster		But she can't push me around!

Qu'elle n'avra de tout cest mois		for she won't get this whole month long
Au feu c'un petitet de pois	52	in her pot more than a handful of peas
Ou porree de vieus cresson		or some old watercress slop
Et un petit de mon bacon		and a sliver of my salt pork.
Je despent trop, si faz folie;		I'm crazy to spend so much;
Mieus me vendroit mengier boillie	56	I'd do better to eat gruel
D'un poi de farine pilee		made with a little flour
Et avoir grosse borsse enflee'.		and have a big, fat moneybag.'
…		…
A tant est ou moustier venuz.	108	Finally he gets to church.
Puis se saine et entre dedenz		He crosses himself and goes in.
Et dist souef entre ses denz		Between clenched teeth, he hisses
Ses oroisons et s'agenoille;		his prayers and he kneels;
Ses ieus de sa salive moille	112	he moistens his eyes with saliva
Pour ce que on le cuit plorer.		so everyone will think he's weeping.
Lores recommence a orer:		Then he begins to pray again:
'Pater noster qui es in celis.*		'Pater noster qui es in celis.*
Qu'est-ce, sui je ore esbahis,	116	What's all this, have I lost my mind
Qu'ore revueil commencier fable?		beginning all this nonsense again?
Ce soit de par le vif deable		The Devil take me
Que or redi ce que j'ai dit.		if I say again what I just said.
…		…
Sanctificetur. Trop sui ci,		*Sanctificetur.* This is taking too long,
Ma fame fet son prest par li;	124	my wife is lending out my money;
J'i ai domage, je sais bien.		I'll be the loser, I know.
Car je i pert, si n'i gain rien.		For if I don't make a profit, I lose.
Ma meschine tout ensement		The same goes for my servant:
Represte par li mon argent	128	she lends my money out too,
Qu'ele despent et done tout		spending it and giving it all
A un pautonier qui la fout.		to some good-for-nothing who f–ks her.
Nomen tuum. Que senefie		*Nomen tuum.* What does all that mean
Que nostre prestres si haut crie?	132	that the priest is shouting about?
…		…
Adveniat regnum tuum.		*Adveniat regnum tuum.*
Qui est cil Robers de Corchon		Who's this Robert de Courçon, anyway,

Qui si va cest païs cerchant		who goes snooping around here
Et par ces mostiers preechant?	144	and preaching in our churches?
Cuide nous il si par sa guile		Does he think he can chase us
Escillier et chacier de vile?		Out of town by his tricks?
…		…
Amen. Je m'en vueil retorner,		*Amen.* I want to get out of here.
Nostre prestre veut orguener	248	Our priest wants to
Pour trere nostre argent de borse;		sing our money out of our pockets.
Mais ainçois avroit un pet d'orse		But he'll get a she-bear's fart
Qu'il ait du mien por tel abet–		before he gets anything of mine by tricks
Tant ne chanteroit en fausset'	252	no matter how much he sings in falsetto.'

5

'Le chapperon tousjours dure': the language of ageing desire in the *Debat de la damoiselle et de la bourgeoise* and *Debat du viel et du jeune*

Emma Cayley

– C'est d'umaine beaulté l'yssue! –
Les braz cours et les mains contra[i]ctes
Des espaulles toute(s) bossue(s),
Mamelles, quoy? toutes retraictes:
Telles les hanches que les tectes.
Du sadinet? Fy! Quant des cuisses,
Cuisses ne sont plus, mais cuissectes
Grivelées comme saulcisses![1]

The robust 'regrets' of Villon's once-Belle Heaulmière expressed here resonate throughout vernacular medieval literature. The initiated reader, à la Gruber,[2] will at once recognise not so distant intertextual echoes of La Vieille's speech to Bel Accueil in the *Roman de la Rose*,[3] or Jean le Fèvre's vernacular translation of the pseudo-Ovidian *De vetula*.[4] The

[1] François Villon, *Le Testament Villon*, eds Jean Rychner and Albert Henry, 2 vol. (Geneva: Droz, 1974), I, vv. 517–24.

[2] I refer to Jörn Gruber's exposition of the 'hermetische Lyrik' of the troubadours. See *Die Dialektik des Trobar: Untersuchungen zur Struktur und Entwicklung des occitanischen und französischen Minnesangs des 12. Jahrhunderts* (Tübingen: Niemeyer, 1983).

[3] Guillaume de Lorris and Jean de Meun, *Le Roman de la Rose*, ed. Armand Strubel (Paris: Librairie Générale Française, 1992), vv. 12559–4550.

[4] The original Latin text has been attributed to Richard de Fournival. See *Pseudo-Ovidius de vetula. Untersuchungen und Text*, ed. Paul Klopsch (Leiden: Brill, 1967) and

particularly alert initiated reader will also recognise in these lines a discussion of the topic by Jane H. M. Taylor in her magisterial 2001 monograph on Villon's poetry.[5] As Taylor meticulously demonstrates, Villon engages in an intertextual dialogue with his literary avatars; not content simply to 'lift' passages from the *Rose* or other sources, he self-consciously adapts and refracts the image of the Belle Heaulmière through what Taylor, following Burns, describes as 'a complex process of specularity'.[6]

The classical topoi of ageing female beauty and of ageing female desire – an arguably unpalatable yet inevitable pairing – elicit multiple fascinating questions about gender negotiations, the nature of the eroticised gaze, and the diegetic status of female, and feminised, speakers. These are questions which Jane Taylor has addressed over the course of an illustrious career.[7] Though I can hardly aspire to style myself a Villon, or indeed a Taylor, I too am engaged in an intertextual dialogue in this chapter with Taylor's work and, through her, with a collaborative community of medievalists. I might feel more inclined to draw a parallel between my interaction with Taylor and the young poets who aspired to engage with the fifteenth-century court poet and 'pere de l'eloquence françoyse', Alain Chartier.[8] It is to these earlier fifteenth-century circles of poetic influence, to Chartier and his emulators, that I wish to turn here, and to two poems in particular which capture the spirit of playful exchange that characterised later medieval poetic production: in Taylor's words, 'a poetics of engagement: debate, response, provocation, competition'.[9] I focus on two short amatory

---

The Pseudo-Ovidian de Vetula, ed. Dorothy Robathan (Amsterdam: Hakkert, 1968).

[5] See *The Poetry of François Villon: Text and Context* (Cambridge: Cambridge University Press, 2001), pp. 86–113.

[6] Taylor, *The Poetry of François Villon*, p. 89. See also E. Jane Burns, *Bodytalk: When Women Speak in Old French Literature* (Philadelphia: University of Pennsylvania Press, 1993).

[7] In addition to the Villon monograph, two articles to which I feel my work on poetic intertextual dialogue in the fifteenth century is particularly indebted are Jane H. M. Taylor, 'Inescapable rose: Jean Le Seneschal's *Cent Ballades* and the art of cheerful paradox', *Medium Ævum*, 67 (1998), 60–84, and her 'Embodying the rose: an intertextual reading of Alain Chartier's *La Belle Dame sans mercy*', in Barbara K. Altmann and Carleton W. Carroll (eds), *The Court Reconvenes: Courtly Literature Across the Disciplines* (Cambridge: D. S. Brewer, 2003), pp. 325–33.

[8] This distinction is granted to Chartier in 1521 by Pierre Fabri in *Le Grand et vrai art de pleine rhétorique*, 3 vol. (Rouen: Société des Bibliophiles Normands, 1889–90), I, p. 72.

[9] Taylor, *The Poetry of François Villon*, p. 7. On poetic competition in the late medieval

debates of the 1460s known as the *Debat de la damoiselle et de la bourgeoise* and the *Debat du viel et du jeune*.[10] Both poems have been attributed to Blosseville, a fifteenth-century poet attached to the cour de Blois, in the entourage of Charles d'Orléans.[11] In the former, the Damoiselle and the Bourgeoise appear before a 'cour d'Amours' to debate the merits of the head-covering each wears, the 'atour' (hennin or tall conical headdress) and the 'chapperon' (hood or bonnet) respectively, to which their distinct social ranks give them access. Implicitly, and later explicitly, the ladies argue about sexual predilection, experience, and *mores*.[12] The second of these debates stages a dispute between the Viel and the Jeune on the pains and pleasures of a life spent in the service of love. The Viel, in spite of his long experience of life, has found no happiness in love; the Jeune, by contrast, is idealistic, vigorous, and ready to serve.

Both debates stage a range of vexed questions about the effects of age, gender, and rank on homosocial and homoerotic desire. In particular here I want to think about the way in which the conflicts and oppositions represented by the debate form act as a motor of erotic arousal in which interlocutors, narrator, audience, and scribe/compiler are all implicated. As Valerie Traub puts it, 'erotic arousal is always imbricated with power differences – it functions by means of exchanges,

---

and early modern period see also Emma Cayley, *Debate and Dialogue: Alain Chartier in his Cultural Context* (Oxford: Oxford University Press, 2006), and Adrian Armstrong, *The Virtuoso Circle: Competition, Collaboration and Complexity in Late Medieval French Poetry* (Tempe: Arizona Center for Medieval and Renaissance Studies, forthcoming).

[10] All quotations from these two debates, the *Noire et Tannee*, the *Reveille Matin*, and the *Ambusche Vaillant* are from my forthcoming edition and translation of these and three further poems, *Sleepless Knights and Wanton Women*, vol. 1: *The Debate Poems* (Tempe: Arizona Center for Medieval and Renaissance Studies). Quotations will appear parenthetically in the body of the chapter by line number.

[11] The attribution of the *Damoiselle et Bourgeoise* to Blosseville is probably spurious, based as it is on erroneous information (Montaiglon reproduces the error of Abbé Gervais de la Rue). On the implications of attribution to Blosseville, see *Recueil de poésies françoises des XVe et XVIe siècles*, ed. Anatole de Montaiglon, 13 vol. (Paris: Jannet, 1855–78), IX (1865), pp. 216–20; Annie Angremy, 'Un nouveau recueil de poésies françaises du XVe siècle, le manuscrit B. N. nouv. acq. fr. 15771', *Romania*, 95 (1974), 1–53; and *Le Manuscrit B.N. nouv. acq. fr. 15771: une nouvelle collection de poésies lyriques et courtoises du XVe siècle*, ed. Barbara L. S. Inglis (Paris: Champion, 1985), pp. 174–86.

[12] This debate is one that Taylor, referring to Paris, Arsenal, 3523, discusses briefly in connection with Villon's *Lais* and the Bakhtinian 'polyphonic codex'. See Taylor, *The Poetry of François Villon*, pp. 27–30.

withholdings, struggles, negotiations.'[13] The debate is the conflictual form par excellence, in which two or more interlocutors proclaim their difference from one another by the very terms of their dispute. Age and experience, status, and gender provide further sets of power differentials which would appear to distance the speakers both from one another and from the narrator. However, as Simon Gaunt has observed, all forms of desire are predicated on the fundamental conflict between a desire for difference, and a contradictory instinct which tries to suppress difference (Lacan's 'désir d'être Un'), thus bringing about a potential implosion of dialectic structures in the courtly debate.[14] The late medieval French debate form, with its characteristic lack of conclusion identified by Adrian Armstrong, represents precisely this conflict.[15] The irresolution of a number of these debate texts can be read as demonstrating the incoherent nature of human communication and relationships within the medieval poetic form. These internal tensions or contradictions are at the heart of courtly texts, as Tony Hunt and Sarah Kay have demonstrated.[16]

The narrator as spectator of the debate is observed not only by the author of the text, but also by the scribe of the manuscript. Paris, BnF, MS fr. 1661, the large anthology I have chosen as the base manuscript for my editions of both the *Damoiselle et Bourgeoise* and the *Viel et Jeune*, presents some intriguing peculiarities in its transcription of the texts.[17] Thus there is a sense in which we are aware not just of the narrator/author observing and modifying/rewriting the characters' exchanges, but also of a further dialectic opened up by the scribe acting as author and editor of the texts. In other words, the workings of desire in the debate become more complex if we acknowledge the material

[13] See Valerie Traub, *Desire and Anxiety: Circulations of Sexuality in Shakespearean Drama* (London: Routledge, 1992), p. 104. See also Richard E. Zeikowitz, *Homoeroticism and Chivalry: Discourses of Male Same-Sex Desire in the 14th Century* (New York: Palgrave Macmillan, 2003), p. 11.

[14] See Simon Gaunt, *Love and Death in Medieval French and Occitan Courtly Literature* (Oxford: Oxford University Press, 2006), p. 170.

[15] See Adrian Armstrong, 'The deferred verdict: a topos in late-medieval poetic debates?', *French Studies Bulletin*, 64 (Autumn 1997), 12–14.

[16] See Tony Hunt, 'Aristotle, dialectic and courtly literature', *Viator*, 10 (1979), 95–129; and Sarah Kay, *Courtly Contradictions: The Emergence of a Literary Object in the Twelfth Century* (Stanford, CA: Stanford University Press, 2001).

[17] See my forthcoming edition and translation. For a description of this manuscript, see Alfred Jeanroy and Eugénie Droz, *Deux manuscrits de François Villon: Bibl. Nat. f.fr. 1661 et 20041* (Paris: E. Droz, 1932), pp. ix–xi.

circumstances of its inscription in manuscript context.[18] The power differentials I identified as characteristic of these two debate poems, as well as of others of the genre, may be illuminated through an investigation of the composition and circulation of the many fifteenth- and sixteenth-century French manuscript and early printed anthologies that transmit them. In this endeavour, I am again indebted to Taylor for her pioneering work on the composition of late medieval anthologies.[19]

The manuscript traditions of both the *Damoiselle et Bourgeoise* and the *Viel et Jeune* intersect with each other, with the tradition of the transmission of Chartier's French works, and also with the series of debate poems and texts collectively known as the *Querelle de la Belle Dame sans mercy*. My interest in what we might term 'codicological juxtapositions' here centres on Chartier as an authoritative mirror and a model for other poets composing in the debate genre. Within the physical space of the codex, then, Chartier has a magisterial role to play, and wields enviable poetic capital through this authoritative positioning.[20]

The *Damoiselle et Bourgeoise* survives in seven manuscripts and one early printed copy.[21] Six of the manuscripts are implicated in the *Querelle de la Belle Dame sans mercy*; four also contain other French works by Chartier. Paris, BnF, MS fr. 1661 is an anthology manuscript, dating to *c.* 1480, which Aubailly and Roy affirm 'a été pensé comme recueil homogène'.[22] Among its eighteen items, all apparently copied by

---

[18] For more on this see especially Elspeth Kennedy, 'The scribe as editor', in *Mélanges de langue et de littérature du moyen âge et de la Renaissance offerts à Jean Frappier*, 2 vol. (Geneva: Droz, 1970), I, pp. 523–31; see also Sylvia Huot, *The Romance of the Rose and its Medieval Readers: Interpretation, Reception, Manuscript Transmission* (Cambridge: Cambridge University Press, 1993).

[19] See Jane H. M. Taylor, *The Making of Poetry: Poetic Anthologies at the End of the Middle Ages* (Turnhout: Brepols, 2007).

[20] My use of 'capital' here derives from the theory developed by Pierre Bourdieu. See *The Logic of Practice*, trans. Richard Nice (Cambridge: Polity Press, 1990). For more on the application of Bourdieu's work to medieval literature, see Sarah Kay and Simon Gaunt (eds), *The Practice of Medieval Literature* [*Forum for Modern Language Studies*, 33 (1997)].

[21] These are: BnF, MS fr. 1661 (fols 2–12); BnF, n. a. fr. 4513 (fols 93–106ᵛ); Paris, Bibliothèque de l'Arsenal, 3523 (pp. 51–70); Bern, Bürgerbibliothek, MS 274 (a partial copy: fols 1–3ᵛ); The Hague, Koninklijke Bibliotheek, MS 71. E. 49 (fols 296–306); Vatican, Biblioteca Apostolica Vaticana, Reg. Lat. 1363 (fols 85–105); Vatican, Biblioteca Apostolica Vaticana, MS Reg. Lat. 1720 (fols 116–26); and *Le Debat de la damoiselle et de la bourgoise* (Paris: for Guillaume Bignaux, 1510; Chantilly, Musée Condé, III. F. 23).

[22] See *Deux Moralités de la fin du Moyen-Âge et du temps des guerres de Religion:*

the same scribal hand, it collects five debate poems which frequently appear in similar collections, as well as works by Chartier, works attached to the *Querelle de la Belle Dame sans mercy*, and Villon's *Lais*. Villon's *Lais* and *Testament* also appear alongside the *Damoiselle et Bourgeoise* in another manuscript copy, Paris, Arsenal, 3523. These codicological juxtapositions seem particularly coherent, as Taylor has suggested, in the light of Villon's graphic treatment of ageing and unfulfilled desire, in his depiction of the Belle Heaulmière, or Grosse Margot, as well as in the persona of 'amant martir' from the *Lais*, forced to languish at the whim of his lady.

The *Debat du viel et du jeune*, which appears with the *Damoiselle et Bourgeoise*, and Villon's poems, in BnF, MS fr. 1661, is one of three early debate poems on this popular theme with similar titles.[23] The only other manuscript source identified for our *Viel et Jeune* poem is BnF, n. a. fr. 15771, a collection of lyric pieces by poets from the circle of Charles d'Orléans, on which Barbara Inglis based her 1985 edition of the poem.[24] The majority of pieces are attributable to Blosseville, whom Inglis believes to be the compiler of this collection, and whom she identifies with one Jean Blosset, seigneur de Plessis-Pâté and de la Mote.[25] Like Chartier before him, Blosseville was secretary and notary at the court of Charles VII, and thus situated firmly in that particular poetic and intellectual milieu. The attribution of this poem to Blosseville is recorded both in the text itself, and in an explicit in BnF, MS fr. 1661.[26]

Excellence, Science, Paris et Peuple; Mars et Justice, eds Jean-Claude Aubailly and Bruno Roy (Geneva: Droz, 1990), pp. 17–20.

[23] The Institut de recherche et d'histoire des textes (IRHT) dossiers list Besançon, Bibliothèque municipale, MS 554 as a manuscript source for our *Viel et jeune*, but the poem copied here is a different debate on the *viel/jeune* theme known as the *Debat du saige et du fol*, fols 212ᵛ–14. A third poem, *Le Debat du jeune et du vieulx amoureulx*, was copied by Montaiglon (*Recueil*, VII (1857), pp. 211–24) from an edition printed in Paris by Silvestre, 1830. Andrew Pettegree, Malcolm Walsby and Alexander Wilkinson (eds), *French Vernacular Books: Books published in the French Language before 1601*, 2 vol. (Leiden: Brill, 2007), I, pp. 457–58, identifies six early editions of the *Debat*.

[24] See Inglis, *Le Manuscrit B. N. nouv. acq. fr. 15771*, pp. 174–86. There do not appear to be any early printed versions of our *viel/jeune* debate.

[25] *Ibid.*, pp. 19–24.

[26] At vv. 364–67, the narrator is identified: 'Car Blossevible me nommerent / Et doulcement me demanderent / Se le debat avoie ouÿ; / À coup, leur respondy "Ouÿ!"'; the explicit in BnF, MS fr. 1661 reads: 'Cy fine le debat du viel et du jeune fait par Blosemville à la requeste des dessus dits.'

I turn in what follows to a reading of the two debate poems which foregrounds the significance of power differentials between the interlocutors and the triangulation of desire via the male narrator figure, who in this case alleges that he is a literal voyeur of the scene played out in front of him. This voyeuristic scenario is further complicated by our awareness of a controlling scribal and authorial presence.[27]

The *Viel et Jeune* has 385 octosyllabic lines rhyming aabaab bbcbbc, arranged into 32 *douzains*,[28] usually with a change of speaker every other stanza. The *Damoiselle et Bourgeoise* is rather longer with 656 octosyllabic lines arranged into 82 *huitains*, with speakers alternating every stanza, and rhyming ababbcbc.[29] It is significant that the fifteenth-century debates which stage disputes between women tend to be longer than those between men. One can perhaps infer from this that greater pleasure was taken in the elaboration of poems staging debates between women for courtly audiences. Another attractive explanation is a residual misogyny at play here, which highlights and chastises female loquacity, one of two popular medieval stereotypes of women (passively silent or aggressively loquacious).[30] It is noticeable that the descriptions of the ladies' clothing in these debates are much more elaborate than those devoted to the men's dress, which seems simply to reflect their mood.[31] In the *Debat de la Noire et de la Tannee*, another similar fifteenth-century debate, the ladies are identified and distinguished from one another by means of their clothing: black and brown dress respectively. The violet-coloured 'doublures' of their dresses, their belts,

[27] I use the term triangulation here in reference not only to René Girard's account of the triangulation of desire, but also to Lacan's notion of the triangular nature of the gaze. See René Girard, *Deceit, Desire, and the Novel: Self and Other in Literary Structure*, trans. Yvonne Freccero (Baltimore: Johns Hopkins Press, 1972); Jacques Lacan, *Les Quatre Concepts fondamentaux de la psychanalyse: le séminaire XI* (Paris: Seuil Points, 1990); and Gaunt's discussion of Lacan in *Love and Death*, pp. 182–83.

[28] There is an extra line in both the manuscript sources.

[29] It inherits this pattern from many of the *Querelle de la Belle Dame sans mercy* debates.

[30] On the subject of women's responsive mode to male verbal attack and its inverse, see Helen Solterer, *The Master and Minerva: Disputing Women in French Medieval Culture* (Berkeley/London: University of California Press, 1995).

[31] For example, see Sophie Debeck (ed.), *Debat d'entre le gris et le noir* in *Édition critique du débat du gris et du noir. Édition complète basée sur le ms. 25421 du f. fr. de la BnF* (unpublished *mémoire de licence*, Université catholique de Louvain, Louvain-la-Neuve, 2004)). I am working on a new edition of this poem with Olivier Delsaux.

their hose, the way their 'robbes' cling to their 'tetins', and so on, are lovingly – indeed rather lasciviously – described at length before the start of the debate. The hidden narrator takes his time to record his lingering visual impressions of the ladies, and when he finally begins to listen to what they are saying, over a fifth of the poem has already elapsed.

In the *Damoiselle et Bourgeoise*, just as in the *Noire et Tannee*, then, clothes serve to direct the male desiring gaze at female objects; but they also establish the social position of the women who wear them, and may, as Burns suggests, reflect the women's own sexuality, subjectivity and desire.[32] Clothes for the Damoiselle and Bourgeoise symbolise not gender but primarily rank. The difference in the ladies' rank here serves the power differential which, as mentioned above, is a trigger for erotic arousal. The narrator/author delights in reinforcing this imbalance of power by suggesting that the difference in status accompanies a difference in sexual *mores* and experience.

Most of the dispute between the Damoiselle and the Bourgeoise centres on their respective ranks; the clothes and assorted adornments to which these ranks give them access. Initially this is reflected in the 'atour' worn by the Damoiselle and the 'chapperon' worn by the Bourgeoise. The action is played out in a traditional 'cour d'Amours' setting, to which the narrator is transported in a dream. By the time he arrives, unusually coming face to face with the two women, the pair are already engaged in dispute, and initially are described together, 'elles', rather than by their respective appellations. There is mutual sympathy in their common desire to have their case heard:

> Si advint, ainsi que j(e) entré
> Dedans le parc de l'auditoire,
> Que, fronc à fronc, je rencontré
> Deux femmes dignes de memoire,
> Commamçans si treshault à braire
> Que on leur imposa scilence;
> Mais oncques ne se vouldrent taire,
> Jusques elles eurent audience. (*Damoiselle et Bourgeoise*, vv. 33–40)

The nobility of the Damoiselle is associated by the Bourgeoise with frigidity; the Bourgeoise's lowlier rank is, conversely, associated by the

---

[32] On this question as illustrated by the *chanson de toile*, see E. Jane Burns, *Courtly Love Undressed: Reading Through Clothes in Medieval French Literature* (Philadelphia: University of Pennsylvania Press, 2003), pp. 88–118.

Damoiselle with sexual excess. The clothes themselves seem intimately connected to the ladies' sexuality, and the Bourgeoise in particular uses an ostensibly innocuous conversation about headdresses to attack the sexual capacity of the Damoiselle:

> Celle qui le chapperon delaisse
> Pour couvrechief et atour prendre
> Cuide monter mais elle abesse
> Car ilz sont de toille trop tendre
> Les vent les fait voller et fendre
> Mais le chapperon tousjours dure
> Ne la pluye ne s'i peut estandre
> Car il a double couverture. (vv. 185–92)

The 'chapperon' and the 'atour' may be understood here to represent the female genitalia, and this is certainly the author's intention. Further contemporary instances of the comparison of hats and genitals are found in the medieval French proverb recorded by Rose Bidler, 'Les hommes saluent du chapeau, et les femmes du cul', or the 'atour d'honneur', used in Gautier de Coincy's *Miracles* to refer to a woman's virginity.[33] The use of the verbs 'voller' and 'fendre' in v. 189 here reveals a certain sexual aggressivity which, the Bourgeoise intimates, the Damoiselle is not used to, and could not sustain.[34] On her side, the Damoiselle rejects the brand of sexual availability advocated by the Bourgeoise for, as she cautions, 'du chapperon (il) n'y que meschef' (v. 195). The Bourgeoise, on the other hand, is experienced, and suggests that her 'chapperon' can survive the ravages of time and heavy onslaught.

References to dress abound in the debate, and always seem to veil discussion of the sexual act just as they drape the female body. The Damoiselle argues that the Bourgeoise does not possess a fine wardrobe, though we suspect what she is really saying is that the Bourgeoise does not attract or entertain men sexually as well as she does. The references

---

[33] See Rose M. Bidler, *Dictionnaire érotique: ancien français, moyen français, Renaissance* (Montreal: CERES, 2002), p. 185 For the reference to *Les Miracles de Nostre Dame*, see Bidler, p. 40.

[34] I am grateful for illuminating comments on an early version of this chapter from members of the Cambridge Medieval French Seminar, sponsored by the AHRC-funded project 'Poetic Knowledge in Late Medieval France', in October 2006. In particular it was suggested that the 'atour', and the 'queue' of v. 337 quoted below, could in fact represent male genitalia, deliberately obscuring the gender question.

to 'velours' and 'soye' seem to have a particular resonance in this connection:

> Vous n'avez habits ne joyaulx
> Pour cueurs à amans esmouvoir,
> Chesnes d'or, coliers, ne camaulx,
> Ne velours à les recevoir;
> Aussi n'oseriez vous avoir
> Robes, ne cornetes de soye,
> Ne gorgias dont on peut veoir
> Le tetin, qui donne grant joie. (vv. 449–56)

The Bourgeoise retorts that softness is not necessarily all-important. She may not have the 'satin' or 'soye' of the Damoiselle, but she can entertain men just as well; and, unlike the Damoiselle, she does not keep her lovers dangling, but is always sexually available:[35]

> Se n'avons robbes de satin
> Pour faire monstrë ou estandart
> Nous portons le petit patin
> Et la bote faulve à couvert
> Et pensez qu(e) ung beau corset vert
> Ou une chausse bien tiree
> Vault bien ung tetin descouvert
> Ou robe de soye figuree. (vv. 457–64)

As the debate progresses, the women move from this 'veiled' metaphor to open discussion of sexual practice. We could read here a mounting desire on the part of the narrator/spectator whose growing excitement engineers a mental ripping-off of clothing, leaving the women and their discourse exposed to the naked eye. In the following passage the Damoiselle's language is surprisingly explicit for one described by the narrator as 'parlant en tresbelle maniere'(v. 47):

> Aussi voz queues[36] sont trop petites
> A les assëoir et tenir
> Mais les nostre sont pieça duites
> Pour tous amans entretenir
> Que vous ne pourrez soustenir
> En voz girons non pas voz haulses

---

[35] Taylor makes a similar, though differently focused, point in her discussion of the *Damoiselle et Bourgeoise* in *The Poetry of François Villon*, pp. 28–30.

[36] Montaiglon sanitises this reading to 'cuisses' from the early printed edition, but all manuscript versions have 'queues'.

Aussi garde n'ont d'y (ve)venir
Car ilz gasteroient [là] leurs chausses. (vv. 337–44)

In the general excitement, any differentiation between the refined
language of the Damoiselle, and the coarser language of the Bourgeoise
(described in the first few stanzas by the narrator as 'treshardie et aspre
en langaige / Pour ung homme à ses piez confondre', vv. 52–53), has
become blurred. The narrator's voyeuristic excitement finally climaxes
at the height of the ladies' argument with his distinctly post-orgasmic
awakening from slumber:

Alors comme tout esblouÿ
Tremblant [me] prins esmerveillier
Et du debat plus riens n'ouÿ
Si commamcé à m'esveiller
Et à dressier mon oreillier
Qui avoit lors beaucop affaire
Et diz pour une nuyt veiller
Que je reveleroye l'istoire. (vv. 641–48)

The use of the verbs 'esblouir', 'trembler', and 'esmerveillier' in vv. 641–
42 are suggestive of recent and intense sexual activity; 'm'esveiller' (v.
644) may be read in its erotic sense. The phrase 'dressier mon oreillier'
in v. 645 is similar to the medieval expression 'faire dresser l'oreille': to
become aroused or have an erection.[37] Furthermore, in two of the seven
manuscripts of this poem, the narrator does not so much wake up ('Si
commamcé à m'esveiller', v. 644), as hastily throw his clothes back on:
'(Si) commençay a moy/me habiller' (v. 644, Vatican, MS Reg. Lat. 1363;
Paris, Bibliothèque de l'Arsenal, MS 3523).

The similarity of the women's language towards the height of the
debate, with the textile and textual masks of social decency cast aside, is
suggestive of an erosion of the power differential between them, and of
a certain *rapprochement*. On some level each emulates the speech
patterns of the other, in apparent accord with Lacan's notion of 'le désir
d'être Un'. Through the interchanges of the debate, a homosocial
relationship develops between the women, which is suggestive of an
erotic friendship.[38] Although opposed in outlook and status, in desiring

---

[37] See Bidler, *op cit.* See my forthcoming monograph, *Sleepless Knights and Wanton
Women, vol. 2: Gender and Voice in Late Medieval French Debate Poetry* (Tempe: Arizona
Center for Medieval and Renaissance Texts Studies) for further discussion of the erotic
expression 'avoir puce à l'oreille' and its context.

[38] On homosociality, see Eve Kosofsky Sedgwick, *Between Men: English Literature and*

victory over the other, each must also end up desiring that other. So competition leads to erotic arousal, not just for the narrator/spectator of the debate, but for the interlocutors engaged in conflictual discourse.

The use of coarse language to reveal a rampant female sexuality is a topos much rehearsed in the golden age Latin love poetry of Horace and Ovid. Models of ageing and repulsive female desire are stock-in-trade for both poets. Horace's *Epodes* and *Odes* introduce a range of women whose appearance and sexual antics inspire little more than revulsion and pity in the poet.[39] Here, as in Ovid's later texts, we find a firm emphasis on social appropriateness. These women are to be censured mainly for desiring when they ought not, for inappropriately attempting to prolong their youth. Horace's *carpe diem* topos goes hand in hand with a swift condemnation for trying to hold on to the day when it is over.

It is this emphasis on appropriateness and timeliness that links our *Damoiselle* et *Bourgeoise* with debates where age is the major power differential. It is significant that in the *Viel et Jeune* the men are of similar social rank and are only differentiated by age. The Damoiselle and Bourgeoise are of differing ages, but it is predominantly their divergent social ranks that motivate debate. The Bourgeoise refers to this difference in a *huitain* that recalls the *Viel et Jeune*:

> Messeigneurs il est verité
> Que j'ay servy ung temps Amours,
> En froit, chault, yver et esté,
> Où j'ay souffert maintes douleurs;
> Et combien que, d'ans et de jours
> Je suis plus ainsnee, jus et sus,
> Neantmoins, pour ses grans atours,
> Elle veult aller audessus. (vv. 105–12)

Here the Bourgeoise argues that age and experience should, in theory, command greater respect than social rank. In the course of the debate, though, it becomes clear that this is not the case: '[c]ar', as the

---

Male Homosocial Desire (New York: Columbia University Press, 1985).

[39] Lydia of Book 1, Ode 25 must leave romance to younger women, as she mourns for the days her door moved smoothly on its hinges, with the comings and goings of young men, rather than sticking on its jamb as it now does, with increasingly rare incursions, while Chloris of Book 3, Ode 15 is advised to stop acting like her daughter, cut back on the red wine, and leave young men alone. Lyce of Book 4, Ode 13 is also overly fond of alcohol, but she cannot solicit young men as she used to when merry, since Cupid and Venus have abandoned her for a younger disciple.

Damoiselle declares, 'icy n'a lieu droit de aisnesse' (v. 152). The younger, nobler of the two seems to secure the respect of the court (if only because the Bourgeoise has been seen running round flirting with the jurors, and attempting to sway the decision in her favour), and it is likely that the verdict will eventually swing in the Damoiselle's favour, though the debate is left unconcluded.[40]

The greater emphasis on social propriety for women here is perhaps not surprising, and it underpins the eroticism of the debate for an audience of any gender. The *Viel et Jeune* again rehearses the notion of appropriateness, but here it is time that governs action. The trio of actors in this debate are all male. Unlike in the *Damoiselle et Bourgeoise*, the narrator is not asleep but merely hidden, and specifically refers to his pleasure at *listening* to the debate. We do not have the same sense of spectacle here, and therefore the debate appears less erotically charged. This is also reflected in the use of language which is more straightforwardly antagonistic. It is the veil of metaphor, gradually removed, in the women's debate which exposes the erotic subtext of the *Damoiselle et Bourgeoise*; here, in the *Viel et Jeune*, the men's language is naked from the start. Like the Bourgeoise, the Viel's age and experience is reflected in his language: he speaks first, 'en terme bien fort sauvaige' (v. 35).

The two interlocutors argue bitterly, though we have the sense that they are in fact rather similar characters. This very similarity is ultimately at the heart of their dispute. The Viel has never found any pleasure in love, and condemns Amours with a mixture of bitterness and nostalgia. The Viel openly identifies with his interlocutor, and advises him to avoid following the same course:

> J'ay veu le temps que je disoie
> Comme vous, car point ne pensoye
> Qu'en amours y eust tant de maulx;
> De lui tousjours je devisoie,
> Ou plaisans propos advisoie,
> Pour faire chançons et rondeaux;
> Parmy les villes et chasteaux
> Faisoie en l'air bondir chevaulx;
> En moy n'avoit raison ne sens;
> Au gré des autres jouvenceaulx,

---

[40] A preliminary sentence is delivered, though the case is set to continue, '(Et) pour le cas qui est incertain / Chascunne de vous produira / Quatre tesmoings dedans demain / Mais jusques ordonné en sera / La damoiselle joïra / Par manïere de recrëance / Et au dessus de vous ira / Nous le vous dison [sic] par sentence' (vv. 625–32).

> J'ay fait des luctes et des saulx,
> Dont à present bien fort me sens. (*Viel et Jeune*, vv. 159–70)[41]

The Jeune, though, is idealistic and headstrong – the mirror image of the man his interlocutor once was – and he serves Amours, accepting the bad with the good, and rejecting the Viel's advice in no uncertain terms.

> Par Leaulté, las, n'est ce mie;
> Fortune vous est ennemye
> Qui vous a fait mal gouverner
> Au gré de vostre belle amye,
> Par quoy Pitié est endormie,
> Qui ne vous veult mercy donner,
> Et brief, à vous ouïr parler
> Car je ne me puis adonner,[42]
> Je n'entens rime ne raison;
> Icy ne vueil plus sejourner;
> Là dehors m'en voys pourmener
> Vostre fait n'est que abusïon. (vv. 279–90)

The dispute between the Viel and the Jeune, although heated, never turns into a character assassination in the same way as does the barbed sparring of the Bourgeoise and Damoiselle. Here we have the impression, as in so much medieval debate poetry, that men are the aggressed not the aggressors, that men's suffering is brought about not through character defects, but via external agencies, and in particular at women's hands. In his opening remarks, the Viel invokes the sinister female figure of 'Paillarde Vieillesse':

> Sans avoir ne bien ne plaisir
> En langueur et en desplaisir
> J'ay vesqu toute ma jeunesse,
> Et maintenant me vient saisir,
> Dont me convient à dueil gesir,
> La faulce, Paillarde Viellesse. (vv. 38–43)

---

[41] We note also the mutual sympathy, frequently underlined in courtly debates, between the male narrator and an interlocutor in whom he recognises a kindred spirit. See, in particular, Alain Chartier, *La Belle Dame sans mercy* – 'Autel fusmes comme vous estes' (v. 120) –, in David Hult and Joan E. McRae (eds), *Le Cycle de 'La Belle Dame sans mercy'* (Paris: Champion, 2003), pp. 15–83 (p. 24).

[42] This line is missing in our base copy; I have corrected it from Paris, BnF, n. a. fr. 15771.

His description gives us an almost visceral sense of a man forced to lie in the embrace of a repulsive old woman, with the use of the verbs 'gesir', and 'saisir'. There are correspondences here between the libidinous 'Paillarde Viellesse' and Vetula from the pseudo-Ovidian *De vetula* text (with whom Ovid sleeps by mistake), as well, of course, as the celebrated 'entremetteuse' of the *Rose*, La Vieille.[43]

The mutual 'suffering' of the men at the hands of women and feminised personifications creates bonds of friendship and identity between the two interlocutors, which the author exploits at the end of his debate. In appointing judges, the men make appeal to others who are 'gens de nostre sorte' (v. 300), and agree to elect two male judges, 'par bon accord ensemble' (v. 303), who will pass sentence in an extra-textual future. The narrator too identifies with the interlocutors, and he comes forward to offer his advice on hearing the closing words of the Jeune, who condemns the Viel's rejection of Amours:

> 'Mais vous (en) avez tant fort mesdit
> Que vous serez d'Amours mauldit
> Et en mourrez de dueil et d'ire'.
> Par quoy me prins bien hault à rire
> En disant: 'Vous devez escripre
> Tout vostre debat, si me semble,
> Et puis leur envoierez pour lire'. (vv. 354–60)

The narrator's laughter has the dual narrative function of interrupting the interlocutors to signal his presence, while also underlining the light-heartedness of the debate to the audience. The Viel and Jeune may curse each other as part of their playful sparring, but we know that their bond of friendship remains strong. Competition merely reinforces their mutual appreciation. The women's sparring in comparison is more troubling, more consciously eroticised. The narrator of the *Damoiselle et Bourgeoise* is excited by the conflict of the two women in a voyeuristic and ostensibly heterosexual way; he does not wish to involve himself in their dispute or appointment of judges, though he is represented as physically present with them in his dream. The hidden narrator of the *Viel et Jeune* enjoys the spectacle of debate, but desires social intercourse with the interlocutors, offering to record the debate 'pour

---

[43] For the repulsive, sagging Vetula with whom Ovid sleeps, and her comparison with La Vieille and Villon's La Belle Heaulmière, see Jane Taylor's discussion in *The Poetry of François Villon*, pp. 88–89, with quotations from Jean le Fèvre's translation of the *De vetula*.

mieulx estre de leur butin', to quote from the narrator of another debate.[44] The conclusion to the *Noire et Tannee* demonstrates the same narratorial reticence in the presence of women. The narrator here prefers to stay in his 'embusche' rather than approach the speakers at the end of their debate.[45] A gendered language of desire begins to emerge from a closer examination of these debate poems. It is evident that male narrators spend a significant proportion of their time looking at the women rather than recording their actual words, but remain socially and spatially distanced from them – a distance which increases the 'spectacular' eroticism of the debate both for the narrator and for the audience. The women's language, too, is noticeably more explicit.

However, I am not sure that we can read this quite so straight-forwardly, merely as male enjoyment of female spectacle. As Gaunt suggests, in courtly literature there may occur a feminisation of the gaze, in which the gaze becomes aligned with its female object rather than its male subject.[46] This in its turn, following the dominance of and assertion of female *franchise* by the *Belle Dame sans mercy*, has implications for a discussion of men in late medieval debate culture not as the aggressors but rather as the aggressed victims, assaulted by a range of merciless 'amies' and ill-disposed female personifications.[47] The topos of the hidden male narrator also suggests his feminised and passive position as observer rather than actor in the debate. Male-male debates with male narrators are also shot through with sexual tension, but this tends to be externalised and directed at extradiegetic female objects in the courtly tradition, while homoerotic tension is exploited

---

[44] The debate in question is Chartier's *Debat Reveille matin*, v. 366. For this text, see Hult's edition in *Le Cycle de 'La Belle Dame sans mercy'*, pp. 439–71, and *Alain Chartier, The Poetical Works*, ed. James C. Laidlaw (Cambridge: Cambridge University Press, 1974), pp. 305–19, as well as my forthcoming edition.

[45] 'En mon embusche me laisserent / Et allerent vers le jardin / Depuys par ung couvert chemin / Vins, où faisoië menssïon / Là trouvay ancre et parchemin / Pour mectre mon intencïon' (*Noire et Tannee*, vv. 887–92). The narrator of the *Ambusche Vaillant* is discovered in hilarious fashion when his shoe falls off as he tries to make a getaway: '(Et) en saillant lors je trebuschay / Par le sommeil lors que j'avoye / Puis aussi clerté je n'avoye / D'aultre part mon patin me cheut / Qui fist grant bruyt en my la voye / Descouvert fu trop me mescheut' (vv. 963–68).

[46] See Gaunt, *Love and Death*, especially pp. 168–204.

[47] See Helen Solterer, 'The freedoms of fiction for gender in premodern France', in Thelma S. Fenster and Clare A. Lees (eds), *Gender in Debate from the Early Middle Ages to the Renaissance* (New York: Palgrave, 2002), pp. 135–63; also Cayley, *Debate and Dialogue*, pp. 116–17.

diegetically through the bonds established through conflict between the speakers and narrator. Perpetuation of desire is ensured by the characteristically unconcluded debate form.

This study of single-sex debating in the fifteenth century has obvious resonances with earlier troubadour lyric, and work on voice and gender, while an investigation of the material context of the debates has wide-reaching implications for fifteenth-century poetic composition and transmission. I hope to have shown how power differentials such as age, experience, status and gender are addressed in both the *Damoiselle et Bourgeoise*, and the *Viel et Jeune*, as in many other similar triangulated debates of the period. These debates can help us to understand how these differentials may impact more widely on the terms of erotic arousal in late medieval poetry, and how poetic language may be manipulated to emphasise, confuse, or suppress difference.

Part II: Coming after

6

Fictio personæ and subtle rewriting in later medieval French poetry

Douglas Kelly

> Se vous demandez: 'Et qu'esse?'
> N'enquerez plus; elle est mussee.[1]

Fictio personæ, or fictional representation of the person and his or her actions – what late medieval authors refer to as *faindre*[2] – is prominent and obvious in medieval literature. Such fictional inventions illustrate subtle poetics.[3] For example, nearing the end of the *Voir Dit* Machaut announces in a letter to Toute Belle that 'ores vient le fort, et les beles et subtives fictions dont je le pense a parfaire'.[4] For Christine de Pizan they represent 'le stille a moy naturel'; she delights 'en leurs soubtilles couvertures et belles matieres mucees soubz fictions delictables et morales'.[5] Yet the interest and uses of that fictionality on its own terms have often proven difficult to assess.

---

[1] Charles d'Orléans, *Ballades et rondeaux*, ed. Jean-Claude Mühlethaler (Paris: Librairie Générale Française, 1992), *rondeau* 28.

[2] Heinrich Lausberg, *Handbuch der literarischen Rhetorik: eine Grundlegung der Literaturwissenschaft*, rev. ed. (Munich: Hueber, 1973), §§826–29; Marc-René Jung, 'Poetria: zur Dichtungstheorie des ausgehenden Mittelalters in Frankreich', *Vox Romanica*, 30 (1971), 44–64; Didier Lechat, *'Dire par fiction': metamorphoses du 'je' chez Guillaume de Machaut, Jean Froissart et Christine de Pizan* (Paris: Champion, 2005) (the last title reached me too late to be referenced more extensively in this chapter).

[3] Jacqueline Cerquiglini, *'Un engin si soutil': Guillaume de Machaut et l'écriture au XIVe siècle* (Paris: Champion, 1985), pp. 7–11, 211–21.

[4] *Le Livre du Voir Dit*, eds Paul Imbs and Jacqueline Cerquiglini-Toulet (Paris: Librairie Générale Française, 1999; hereinafter *VD*). References are hereinafter given in parentheses in the body of this chapter.

[5] Christine de Pizan, *Le Livre de l'advision Cristine*, eds Christine Reno and Liliane Dulac (Paris: Champion, 2001), p. 110.

The difficulty is two-fold: appreciating the unusual modes of fictional representation and the subtlety with which they are drawn. Such fictions and their hidden *matières* include various kinds of personifications, exemplary and mythological figures, bestiaries, and other images that populate late medieval poetry. Traditional since Antiquity, they mingle in poetry and prose such that, for example, Machaut may encounter a personified Esperance while anxiously travelling the dangerous roads of the Hundred Years War (*VD*, v. 4258), a variant of his similar encounter with the same personification in the more peaceful Parc de Hesdin in the *Remede de Fortune*.[6] In another passage, Honneur holds Toute Belle's stirrup while Sens guides her, Raison serves her, and Estableté neither falters nor metamorphoses into inconstancy or fickleness; Toute Belle is a goddess served by the goddesses Venus, Pallas, and Juno (*VD*, vv. 6130–39). One notices here a seemingly effortless amalgamation of different fictional modes in diverse narrative environments.[7] Virtual visions,[8] they are so casual as to be almost commonplace, even ordinary, in fiction. Moreover, these scenes leave out the conventional dream motif that lends a certain verisimilitude to such encounters in, for example, the *Roman de la Rose*. Machaut's meetings with Esperance in the waking world are true fictions and Esperance, as well as Machaut himself, illustrate *fictio personæ*. Anomalies like these are standard sources of poetic subtlety and originality.

Two figures in the *Roman de la Rose* exemplify the subtle anomalies *fictio personæ* may produce: the gender change of Malebouche and the specialised meaning assigned to Dangier. Why do Guillaume de Lorris and Jean de Meun give Malebouche a male persona? Personifications customarily acquire the gender of the noun they personify; *bouche* is a feminine noun. Why is Dangier, who personifies an aristocratic prerogative, described as a 'villein'? Such 'expérience de l'insolite'[9] invites subtle reading.

---

[6] Guillaume de Machaut, *'Le Jugement du roy de Behaigne' and 'Remede de Fortune'*, eds James I. Wimsatt, William W. Kibler and Rebecca A. Baltzer (Athens: University of Georgia Press, 1988), vv. 786 and 2286 of the *Remede*.

[7] See Isabelle Bétemps, *L'Imaginaire dans l'œuvre de Guillaume de Machaut* (Paris: Champion, 1998), pp. 199–206.

[8] Pierre-Yves Badel, *Le Roman de la rose au XIVe siècle: étude de la réception de l'œuvre* (Geneva: Droz, 1980), pp. 338–40.

[9] Armand Strubel, *'Grant senefiance a': allégorie et littérature au moyen âge* (Paris: Champion, 2002), p. 44.

Before the thirteenth century, William of Conches notes that gender change does not refer to literal sexual gender.[10] Rather, such fictions signify a moral gender based on commonplace misogynist stereotypes. Women acting in conformity with male stereotypes illustrate an allegorical change into a man like that described by Christine de Pizan in the *Mutacion de Fortune*, whereas men whose acts correspond to those of commonplace women become moral women. By the same token, bestial conduct does not make of a bestiary image a literal beast but an example of immoral bestiality.

Gender change on the literal level is an ambiguous term because it may refer to grammatical gender and/or sexual gender.[11] For example, a feminine noun may describe a man, as when, for example, *la victime* refers to a man, just as a masculine noun may designate a woman, as in *Madame le professeur*. In current usage, with audiences aware of the masculine/feminine distinction, there have been attempts to make grammatical gender correspond to sexual gender, as in *Madame la professeure* or *Christine de Pizan l'écrivaine*. Uneducated audiences in the Middle Ages may not have been aware of the gender principle, although they may well have noticed that something unusual takes place when the feminine noun Malebouche is treated as a male figure who 'tot le mal qu'*il* set retret'.[12] Similarly, Chrétien de Troyes makes the personification of the feminine noun *amor* into a male figure.[13] Soredamors exclaims, in grammatically correct language, 'Ja ne soit amors si *vilainne* / Que je pri cestui premeraine' (vv. 1009–10), shortly after noting of the personification 'Molt m'a donc Amors enoree, / Quant *il de lui* m'a sororee' (vv. 983–84) (my emphasis in each example). She may have the god of love in mind. However, *Yvain* names the god of love, but the personification is feminine-female.[14] The

[10] Paule Demats, *Fabula: trois études de mythographie antique et médiévale* (Geneva: Droz, 1973), p. 147.

[11] See my *Internal Difference and Meanings in the 'Roman de la rose'* (Madison: University of Wisconsin Press, 1995), pp. 108–10, 122.

[12] Guillaume de Lorris and Jean de Meun, *Le Roman de la rose*, ed. Félix Lecoy, 3 vol. (Paris: Champion, 1965–70), v. 3495; my emphasis (hereinafter *Rose*). The issue was first discussed critically by David F. Hult, *Self-Fulfilling Prophecies: Readership and Authority in the First 'Roman de la rose'* (Cambridge: Cambridge University Press, 1986), p. 244, n. 80.

[13] See Chrétien de Troyes, *Cligés*, eds Stewart Gregory and Claude Luttrell (Cambridge: D.S. Brewer, 1993), p. 321. One exception, 'Et la fins Amors me recorde…' (v. 974), may refer to the abstraction, not the personification.

[14] *Le Chevalier au Lion ou le Roman d'Yvain*, ed. David F. Hult (Paris: Librairie

Roman de la Rose identifies the personification of the feminine *amor* as the 'dieu d'amour' in the Jardin de Deduit (v. 864). Christine does the same in the *Epistre au dieu d'amour*. Not so Machaut, whose Amour in the *Voir Dit* is feminine and female, as in 'tresfine Amour que je honnour' (v. 2) and 'Veuil tresbonne Amour mercier' (v. 227).[15] The gender of Amour deserves further study.

The other anomaly referred to above, the villein Dangier, is a specialisation.[16] Conventionally *dangier* is not a negative attribute, as when the beloved 'Me tient et joliement / En son dangier' (*VD*, vv. 980–81). In the *Rose* Amant evokes the noble sense of this figure by asking to be imprisoned with Bel Accueil. 'Dangiers, fis je, biau gentis hon, / franc de queur et vaillanz de cors, / piteus plus que je ne recors' (vv. 14926–28). Dangier's attributes here link the personification to Franchise and the noble prerogatives of power and dominion. But in this passage the praise is patently ironic, because elsewhere in the *Rose* Dangier is a villein[17] armed with a club (vv. 3141, 3739). To Amant the lady's dominion seems harsh and ignoble.

Guillaume de Lorris's description of Dangier has tended to obscure the subtlety and originality of the *Rose*'s portrayal of this personification. A perusal of Godefroy's careful analysis of the word *dangier*[18] illuminates its primarily aristocratic and, therefore, noble connotations: 'puissance, pouvoir, droit, empire, domination, jouissance, discrétion', including more concretely those of 'captivité, prison' evoked by Amant in the foregoing quotation from Jean de Meun's

---

Générale Française, 1994), v. 5373 and p. 600 (some instances may refer only to the abstraction).

[15] See also *VD*, vv. 235–338, 254–56, 7292–7302, 8771–72. Amour, although a 'jouvencel' (v. 7242), is still feminine and/or female (vv. 7301, 7344). Toute Belle mixes the genders in a letter (p. 674c); Machaut is not always consistent either (vv. 8328–32). Double gender, as in Old French nouns like *amor*, *sort*, *art*, etc, may betray no special significance when oscillation occurs; see Mildred K. Pope, *From Latin to Modern French with Especial Consideration of Anglo-Norman: Phonology and Morphology* (Manchester: Manchester University Press, 1952), §§ 776–77.

[16] On 'spécialité' and 'généralité' in medieval descriptions, see my 'La Spécialité dans l'invention des topiques', in Lucie Brind'Amour and Eugene Vance (eds), *Archéologie du signe* (Toronto: Pontifical Institute of Medieval Studies, 1983), pp. 101–25.

[17] *Rose*, v. 2809, vv. 2904–34, 3713, cf. v. 3653: 'le peïsant'.

[18] Frédéric Godefroy, *Dictionnaire de l'ancienne langue française*, 10 vol. (Paris: Vieweg 1881–1902), II, pp. 419–21; see my *Medieval Imagination: Rhetoric and the Poetry of Courtly Love* (Madison: University of Wisconsin Press, 1978), pp. 85–90.

Rose.[19] Dangier exercises the right to punish when assuming the worst after Amant kisses the rose. Lovers conventionally submit to their lady's *dangier*[20] or, as in the *Rose*, to Franchise when Dangier is lulled to sleep (vv. 3651–57).[21] In the tournament in Jean's part, Dangier defeats Franchise (v. 15337), but 'l'ort vilain' is overcome in turn by Pitié (v. 15375–76).

In the *Rose* Dangier serves his lady, the damsel Amant is courting (as in Guillaume) or seducing (as in Jean). In this subordinate role he guards her castle like a *sergent de guet* (*Rose*, vv. 3849–55), not, for example, as a knight. The ignoble personification[22] is analogous, *mutatis mutandis*, to the husband who exercises excessive power in a medieval marriage or any similar authority, such as that of overly restrictive parents over a daughter. More broadly, the 'dangier de Fortune' (*Remede*, vv. 2783–84; *VD*, p. 780b) is mutable whereas God's stable *dangier* (*Poire*, vv. 119–20) connotes the power to reward in heaven and punish in hell. The slippage of the word towards its modern sense of 'danger' is evident in the description and qualification of Dangier as 'mauves dangier' or 'faulx dangier'. The need to qualify the word with negative attributes attests to its evolution from legitimate power towards danger and illegitimate acts like rape.[23]

In another instance Toute Belle assures Machaut that she has a firm hold on Dangier and Malebouche and that she has put Argus to sleep (*VD*, p. 604b).[24] She does so not to keep her beloved poet at a distance, as in the *Rose*, but to facilitate their meeting despite impediments. Toute Belle's Dangier and Malebouche know when, respectively, to guard against intruders and to keep silent. Argus is the culprit. It follows that the *Voir Dit* lovers, after their first kiss, need not fear reliving the *Roman de la Rose* where Malebouche begins to prattle and Honte and

[19] Cf. *VD*, v. 6455: 'la belle qui m'a en sa prison'.

[20] Nicole de Margival, *Le Dit de la Panthère*, ed. Bernard Ribémont (Paris: Champion, 2000), vv. 2217–21 (hereinafter *Panthère*).

[21] See also Franchise in Tibaut, *Le Roman de la Poire*, ed. Christiane Marchello-Nizia (Paris: Picard, 1984), vv. 1054–58 (hereinafter *Poire*).

[22] Richard Glasser, 'Abstractum agens und Allegorie im älteren Französisch', *Zeitschrift für romanische Philologie*, 69 (1953), 43–122 (61).

[23] Adolf Tobler and Erhard Lommatzsch, *Altfranzösisches Wörterbuch*, 11 vol. (Berlin: Wiedmann, 1925), II, pp. 1193–94; Godefroy, *Dictionnaire de l'ancienne langue française*, II, pp. 420, 421.

[24] Cf. *VD*, pp. 570e, 576d, vv. 6521–31, p. 680c. Machaut's 'Anemi-qui-ne-dort' is Desire (*VD*, vv. 5162–63).

Peur arouse the sleeping Dangier.[25] Toute Belle's Malebouche is in her power and she is in love. Unlike the *Rose*, Machaut personifies the noun as a female: 'elle n'aroit jamais envie / Se nous meniens joieuse vie' (*VD*, vv. 6526–27). However, another Malebouche in the guise of male *mesdisans* has been bad-mouthing Toute Belle to the poet – 'Ves la celle qui se fourfist' (*VD*, v. 3177) – because they suspect her of infidelity or fickleness. Without admitting directly his suspicions, Machaut urges her to keep her Dangier and Malebouche alert if temptations arise (*VD*, p. 680c). Comparison with the same personifications in the *Rose* shows how connotation of personifications adapts thematically and semantically to persons, circumstances, and points of view. Malebouche and Dangier show how diverse and subtle personifications may be in different contexts, even when the word personified is the same.

Although personification is a relatively modern term in the grammatical and rhetorical tradition,[26] the trope is common in literary and other writing from early Antiquity into modern times.[27] The phenomenon prior to the term is treated as metaphor[28] and, by extension, as allegory in which the *figura personæ* personifies another, veiled meaning. Personification is, therefore, a variety of *abstractum agens*. Such abstract agents include exemplary or legendary, historical or pseudo-historical, and mythological figures, bestiaries, etc. – figures that, in descriptions and narratives, permit the writer to refine and clarify obvious or veiled meanings.[29] All fit well into the *fictio personæ* context when they represent a persona or his or her attributes. Verbs and other parts of speech that qualify the noun figures further delineate their significance.[30] That medieval authors do not make sharp distinctions among *abstracta agentia* suggests that such distinctions are less important in their minds than the stylistic demands and imaginative subtlety of specific passages.

[25] Machaut's own Honte, Dangier and Peur are not so docile (see, for example, *VD*, vv. 2082–294).

[26] *Dictionnaire historique de la langue française*, eds Alain Rey [*et al.*], 2 vol. (Paris: Dictionnaires Le Robert, 1992), II, p. 1488. There is no Latin equivalent (Lausberg, *Handbuch der literarischen Rhetorik*, p. 932).

[27] See Strubel, '*Grant senefiance a*', pp. 47–51, and Glasser, 'Abstractum agens', pp. 105–21.

[28] Lausberg, *Handbuch der literarischen Rhetorik*, §559c.

[29] Glasser, 'Abstractum agens', pp. 58–60.

[30] *Ibid.*, pp. 87, 90, 93.

An example of specialisation like that for Dangier occurs in Jean Froissart's *Joli buisson de jonece*. There Froissart confronts Philosophie and Jonece, personifications who give him conflicting counsel; moreover, their advice seems to be inconsistent with the notion each personifies. Philosophie does not show forth the scope of the noun we might expect, especially after reading the description of Philosophy in Boethius's *Consolation of Philosophy* or in Christine de Pizan's *Advision Cristine*. Yet Boethius's description offers a clue to Froissart's treatment of the figure. In the *Consolation* Philosophy has been mistreated by diverse philosophies that have torn pieces from her robe, violence that separates thought and action. Froissart's Philosophie also has, implicitly, rent Philosophy's robe to expand on a *carpe diem* morality especially appealing to the young. She encourages Froissart to look to the past, to relive his youth as poet and lover rather than dwell on his present age or the life that lies ahead as he grows older.[31] Philosophie addresses only Froissart's newly acquired youth. But that youth is a fiction that masks an ageing persona.

When Jonece appears the medieval reader encounters another feature in the invention of personifications. Jonece teaches what we might have initially expected from Philosophie: an all-encompassing philosophy of life, of which she is merely a part. As the *puella senex* variety of the commonplace *puer senex*,[32] Jonece reunites thought and action. The specialisation we observed in Dangier and Philosophie becomes a generalisation with Jonece, made possible by another commonplace, the *gradus ætatum* or ages of life script. Jonece is fully aware of the whole of which she is a part and, accordingly, she teaches a *modus vivendi* consistent with that knowledge and the broader perspective it offers. 'Chils mondes n'est q'uns trespas' (*JB*, v. 1684), she exclaims. Conscious of the passage of time and life, her lesson diverges sharply from that offered by Philosophie who, like the *Rose*'s Jeunesse, seems 'Niceite' because she 'ne s'esmaie / fors de jouer' (*Rose*, vv. 1261, 1264–65). Like them, the fictional Froissart rejects Jonece's advice on approaching age and death. 'C'est mieulz mes hes / A moi deduire et resjoïr / Que ce ne soit a vous oïr' (*JB*, vv. 1721–23), words that echo Amant's rejection of Reason's lessons in the *Roman de la Rose*: 'des

---

[31] Jean Froissart, *Le Joli buisson de jonece*, ed. Anthime Fourrier (Geneva: Droz, 1975), vv. 460–547 (hereinafter *JB*).

[32] See Ernst Robert Curtius, *Europäische Literatur und lateinisches Mittelalter*, 2nd rev. ed. (Bern: Francke, 1954), pp. 108–15.

poetes les santences, / les fables et les methaphores / ne bé je pas a gloser ores' (*Rose*, vv. 7160–62). Perhaps some other time, each allows (*JB*, vv. 1732–38; *Rose*, vv. 7163–68). Although picturing himself as young in his dream,[33] Froissart has in fact reached a time in life when Philosophie's youthful lessons are invalid (*JB*, vv. 5156–66). Awakened (*JB*, v. 5081), he discovers, not his ongoing youthful love, but his relatively advanced age. Youth lies behind him and a new persona emerges to depict the change. I return to his reawakening below.

Jonece's lessons in Froissart's *dit* offer a blueprint for the poet's metamorphosis and for that of the bush metaphor that the *Joli buisson* adapts from its predecessor, the *Espinette amoureuse*. The *espinette*, or amorous 'bush', grows into the Tree of Life in the *Joli buisson*, its branches illustrating the ages in life. In the dénouement, the tree metamorphoses anew as the Burning Bush, a biblical image that brings the now mid-life Froissart to wisdom and a new lady – Our Lady, the Virgin Mary, to whom he dedicates a lyric lay.[34]

These metamorphoses of *espinette* – bush, Tree of Life, Burning Bush – and beloved – damsel, lady, Virgin Mary – are analogous to Christine de Pizan's metamorphosis in the *Mutacion de Fortune*, although Froissart's is based on the age common place rather than the gender common place.[35] It resembles even more closely Machaut's oscillation between love as desire and love as hope in the *Voir Dit*. Christine's 'historical' change derives from a syllepsis when she refers to herself as *fils*, or son, of her father: 'Filz de noble homme et renommé / Fus.'[36] Further on in the poem she links her male persona to Tiresias and Yplis (*MF*, vv. 1060–158), Ovidian examples of gender change. But she also compares it to the metamorphosis of Ulysses's men into swine (*MF*, vv. 1043–54), in which mythography borders on the bestiary. Gender change may link to the *natura* common places: age, name, nationality,

---

[33] Machaut too speaks of his rejuvenation (*VD*, vv. 5080–5123).

[34] See also Sylvia Huot, *From Song to Book: The Poetics of Writing in Old French Lyric and Lyrical Narrative Poetry* (Ithaca, NY: Cornell University Press, 1987), pp. 321–23.

[35] On the distinction between commonplace as a common, even hackneyed, topic and common place as a feature common to persons or things that an author defines or describes in an original way, see Rita Copeland, *Rhetoric, Hermeneutics, and Translation in the Middle Ages: Academic Traditions and Vernacular Texts* (Cambridge: Cambridge University Press, 1991), pp. 64–76, and my *Christine de Pizan's Changing Opinion: A Quest for Certainty in the Midst of Chaos* (Cambridge: D. S. Brewer, 2007), pp. 49–64.

[36] Christine de Pizan, *Le Livre de la Mutacion de Fortune*, ed. Suzanne Solente (Paris: Picard, 1959-66), vv. 171–72 (hereinafter *MF*).

language, etc., just as, according to William of Conches, it may be the allegory of a moral transformation.

The 'name' common place is prominent in *fictio personæ*. Perceval's mother tells her son that 'Par le sornon connoist on l'ome'.[37] This reading occurs in only one manuscript; the others use 'non' rather than 'sornon', as 'Car par le non connoist on l'ome'.[38] The latter reading is more common.[39] But the editing problem in the *Perceval* is not a problem here, as either reading – *non* or *sornon* – fits the name common place. Audiences hearing the surname would note an evaluation of action or inaction by the person it designates, whereas the proper name's significance would grow as the designated individual becomes, for example, a Lancelot or an Yvain, a Guenevere or an Enide, as their plots unfold. An analogous evolution occurs when the name Renart is associated with 'le goupil' in the Renart cycle. The proper name designates both a red-haired person as a type and the treacherous fox, while 'goupil' drops from currency. A similar development occurs with the phoenix-like Fenice. On the other hand, Soredamors is a virtual surname that foreshadows and qualifies her subsequent actions and sentiments. 'Por neant n'ai ge pas cest non / Que Soredamors sui clamee. / Amer doi, si doi estre amee' (*Cligés*, vv. 962–64). Therefore, she concludes, 'je metrai en ce ma cure / Que de lui soie doreüre' (vv. 9853–86). Thought leads to action.

Multiple names suggested by the *non/sornon* occur for personifications too. [40] Just as Boethius ascribes various heights to Philosophy in order to suggest her range and different competencies, Alain de Lille's Prudence in the *Anticlaudianus* suggests a similar range of activities that her different names evoke: Phronesis, Sapientia and Sophia. Similarly, in Christine de Pizan's *Advision Cristine* Philosophie is also named Sapience, Serenité and Theologie. Does not Penthesilea acquire a new name, description and narrative as Othea in her *Epistre Othea*?

Enclinpostair is an example of renaming. In Froissart's *Paradis d'amour*, Morpheus, the 'noble dieu dormant',[41] sends his son Enclinpostair (v. 28) to Froissart. The invention is not unlike the poet's other

---

[37] Chrétien de Troyes, *Le Roman de Perceval ou le Conte du Graal*, ed. Keith Busby (Tübingen: Niemeyer, 1993), v. 562 (hereinafter *Perceval*).

[38] *Perceval*, ed. Busby, p. 430, n. 561–62.

[39] *Poire*, vv. 139–40.

[40] On what follows, see my *Christine de Pizan's Changing Opinion*, p. 47.

[41] Jean Froissart, *Le Paradis d'amour – L'Orloge amoureus*, ed. Peter F. Dembowski (Geneva: Droz, 1986), v. 25.

pseudo-Ovidian inventions, in which he recycles Ovidian material in new fictions.[42] But Froissart has two models: Ovid and Machaut. In the *Fontaine amoureuse* the god of sleep has a son named Morpheus,[43] a figure Machaut seems to identify with (*FA*, vv. 786–88).[44] Like Morpheus, he describes his lord so that the lord's lady will recognise him in this *dit*. The model is the Ovidian fable of Ceyx and Alcyone, in which a similar revelation occurs. Such renaming conforms to a truth veiled, or *mussee* as Charles d'Orléans and Christine put it, beneath the fable. Froissart illustrates such renaming of the Machaut model for Architelés and Orphane:[45] 'le faux se mélange au vrai, devient vrai.'[46]

Name and gender come together in the feigned metamorphosis of Machaut into a woman at the end of the *Voir Dit*. Male characters in the role of Malebouche, which can also be translated as 'male mouth' in the fourteenth century, bad mouth Toute Belle, likening her to Fortune because both are women. Machaut's feminine personification of Amour permits him to add her to the allegory of the *donna mobile* (*VD*, v. 8171). The commonplace mutability of all three supports the *mes-disans'* argument that Machaut terminate his relationship with Toute Belle.

But another interpretation emerges: the mutable figure in the *Voir Dit* is Machaut. A cleric who is also Toute Belle's confessor reinterprets the preceding link between Fortune, Amour and Toute Belle. Retaining the mutability attribute that links Fortune and Amour, he revises the comparison by emphasising commonplace conduct rather than gender, implicitly rehearsing interpretations like those advocated by Guillaume de Conches when dealing with gender change. Machaut's own changeableness – he vacillates between positive hope and self-defeating desire – makes him an exemplar of the commonplace woman of misogyny: 'Vous avés maniere de fame: / Trop souvent mue vos courages' (*VD*, vv. 8697–98). As allegory, the issue is mutability, not

---

[42] Kelly, *Medieval Imagination*, chap. 7; see also Kelly, 'Les Inventions ovidiennes de Froissart: réflexions intertextuelles comme imagination', *Littérature*, 41 (1981), 82–92, and 'Imitation, metamorphosis, and Froissart's use of the exemplary *Modus tractandi*', in Donald Maddox and Sara Sturm-Maddox (eds), *Froissart Across the Genres* (Gainesville: University Press of Florida, 1998), pp. 101–18; Lechat, *Dire par fiction*, pp. 315–16.

[43] Guillaume de Machaut, *Œuvres*, ed. Ernest Hoepffner, 3 vol. (Paris: Champion, 1921), III, vv. 651–52 (hereinafter *FA*).

[44] On Machaut as Morphée and Orphée, see Lechat, *Dire par fiction*, pp. 148–49.

[45] *Ibid.*, pp. 339–30.

[46] *Ibid.*, p. 343.

gender: which, Toute Belle or Machaut, is mutable and therefore the exemplar of the *donna mobile*?[47]

A subtle poetics is at work here. To understand it we come to Fulgentius (*VD*, v. 8185). Machaut refers to Fulgentius's alleged adaptation of Livy's depiction of Fortune to define, first, Toute Belle's alleged inconstancy and, then, by her cleric confessor and Toute Belle herself, Machaut's own 'womanly' mutability (*VD*, vv. 8186–88).[48] Fulgentius was an authority on euhemerism in medieval commentary and poetics.[49] According to him, the gods and goddesses were once extraordinary human beings who were honoured after their death and eventually deified and worshipped. Machaut mentions the deification of Julius Cæsar and Hercules (*VD*, vv. 6146–56), Caneus (vv. 6710–13) and Æneas (vv. 6881–83). These transformations justify deifying Toute Belle, who, he opines, deserves a place among the gods (v. 6157) and in the stars.

> Li dieu de vous aussi feront
> Une estoille et vous metteront
> Ou firmament, delés l'estoille
> Qui a fait retourner maint voile,
> Si qu'a vous bon avis penra
> Qui a bon port venir volra. (vv. 6189–94)[50]

Machaut anticipates her deification by the way he addresses Toute Belle in the early part of his *Dit*: 'C'est mon dieu souverain en terre' (*VD*, v. 565) and 'deesse' (v. 816). He models his Fulgentian adaptation on the courtly love commonplace: the lady as goddess – and as god.

The anagram that reveals Toute Belle's name, 'Peron', is a masculine name not incompatible with her desire to have been a man in order to be with Machaut more often.[51] Subsequent analysis confirms Cerquiglini's suggestion[52] that Peron/Peronne is a name invented and

---

[47] See Cerquiglini, *'Un engin si soutil'*, p. 143.

[48] Personification is not unrelated to mythography. Many abstractions were deified in Rome (Glasser, 'Abstractum agens', p. 82; *VD*, vv. 8191–93).

[49] Demats, *Fabula*, pp. 55–60. Ovid's *Metamorphoses* and its medieval glosses like the *Ovide moralisé* were Machaut's sources (*VD*, vv. 5551–53, 5606–07). Note also a tendency to recycle frequently used exemplary material – Narcissus, Pygmalion, the judgment of Paris, etc. – that would facilitate non-clerical audiences' appreciation of significant variations; see also Badel, *Le Roman de la rose au XIVe siècle*, pp. 90–91.

[50] See also *VD*, vv. 6195–6202, 6223–30.

[51] *VD*, pp. 122b, 138b, 160a, 286c; cf. vv. 169–76.

[52] See Cerquiglini, *'Un engin si soutil'*, pp. 228–29.

deified as Machaut's bisexual, terrestrial god and goddess. Like Froissart's Enclinpostair, she too is a *fictio personæ*. Recapitulating the Fulgentian view of how the gods emerged to explain the poet's adoration of his lady, Machaut applies himself

> En ma douce dame honnourer,
> Servir, amer et *aourer*;
> Et, par Dieu, faire le devoie
> Dou cuer et dou sens que j'avoie,
> Com a ma dame et *ma deesse*
> Et ma souveraine maistresse. (vv. 812–17; emphasis mine)[53]

Fulgentius's script by which honour leads to deification patterns Toute Belle's. As Machaut's goddess, or god, she performs miracles.

> Car unques mais je ne vi certes
> Faire *miracles si apertes*
> Com elle fist a ma personne;
> Et ce si bon renon li donne
> Qu'on dit, quant elle finera,
> Qu'en *paradis sainte* sera,
> Car bien puis dire en verité
> Que .II. fois m'a *ressuscité*. (vv. 818–25; emphasis mine).[54]

Miracles reveal saints – and goddesses.

Machaut's depiction of himself as a woman reflects allegorically the distinction he makes between two kinds of love: love as desire and love as hope.[55] The distinction dates from the *Jugement dou roy de Navarre* and, more importantly, the *Remede de Fortune*. The latter grounds the distinction on the Boethian notion of virtue that does not require the sexual intercourse stage in a conventional *gradus amoris* like that in the *Roman de la Rose*. Hope for love supplants desire, making love a virtue not subject to Fortune. The *Voir Dit* ends in hope, although the hope-desire cycle may continue[56] since the *Voir Dit* is a tale of such cyclic tribulations.[57]

---

[53] Toute Belle's countrymen make a statue or portrait in her honour, the first step to deification in the Fulgentian model that Machaut illustrates with Semiramis (vv. 4925–36).

[54] See also vv. 870–71, 927–33, 1690, and so on.

[55] See my *Medieval Imagination*, chap. 6.

[56] *Remede*, vv. 3053–180, 3381–400; see also Cerquiglini, pp. 51–89.

[57] *VD*, vv. 1261–64, p. 150c, vv. 1568–85, 2873–76, 3341–44, 3521–50, 4620–39, pp. 554–56a.

Now, the Machaut figure in the *Voir Dit*, like his counterpart in the *Jugement Navarre*, evinces comic features.[58] There is mockery[59] when his January May love becomes widely known. Of course, Toute Belle insists on revealing their innocent, honourable relation.

> Je veus bien c'on voie
> Nos amours par rue et par voie,
> Car puis qu'il n'i ha que tout bien,
> Il me plaist et se le veul bien. (*VD*, vv. 2753–56)[60]

Indeed, the *Voir Dit* was put together 'ainsi comme il est et sans glose' (v. 2077) at her command (vv. 497–520), a point Machaut makes often.[61]

Their public love seems at first to excite curiosity and even some admiration.[62] Toute Belle's brother and sister know and apparently approve of her 'affair' with Machaut.[63] She asserts that 'onques en ma vie je ne trouvai personne qui me blamast de chose que je feysse pour vous'; but she also admits that not everyone may understand their love: 'les gens la ou nous sommes a hostel sont simples gens et ne vous congnoissent, si y porroient penser autre chose qu'il n'i ha' (*VD*, p. 538d)[64] and that hardly anyone understands it perfectly (p. 780d). In fact, even those who know Machaut become 'mesdisans' (vv. 7714).[65] Doubts and suspicions eventually arise as to the 'purity' of their love[66] and Toute Belle's constancy. The issue is still debatable in modern scholarship in the context of 'did they or didn't they?' In the context of this chapter the issue is *fictio personæ*. That is, does the love of Machaut and Toute Belle represent, in one or the other, or in both, the virtuous love as hope that Machaut promotes and idealises in his other writings, a love that is pure in the sense of chaste?[67]

---

[58] On Machaut's different personas, see Kevin Brownlee, *Poetic Identity in Guillaume de Machaut* (Madison: University of Wisconsin Press, 1984).

[59] *VD*, vv. 7368–69, 7394–96.

[60] *VD*, vv. 7546–57, 8430–34, p. 730b.

[61] *VD*, vv. 347–49, 490–98, 2078–81, 2691–94, 3237–40, 4142–53.

[62] *VD*, pp. 422b–24d, 426i, 432b, 434–36e, 448c, 450h.

[63] *VD*, pp. 96g, 124b, vv. 3572–82, 3830–32, pp. 426l, 434e, 452i, 456a, 462h, 516a, 536b. But p. 508e she suggests circumspection in speaking to her brother (compare p. 520e).

[64] See also pp. 510g, 672–74b, 780–82d.

[65] See also vv. 7365–75, 7546–57, pp. 672–74b.

[66] On 'amour pure', see *VD*, vv. 6502, 7308, 8798.

[67] Christine de Pizan extols platonic love in her early writings (Kelly, *Christine de*

Part of the problem is the definition of hope. Although Machaut's ideal love may be modelled on Boethius's notion of virtue as a good, hope itself may reflect not Boethian virtue but the theological one. Alain Chartier's *Livre de l'Esperance* defines the theological virtue hope as follows: 'Et qu'est esperance, si non certaine attente de la beneureté future par grace de Dieu et par prevention de ses saintz merites?'[68] We need only paraphrase this definition of hope to appreciate the adaptation in the *Remede de Fortune*: 'Et qu'est esperance, si non certaine attente de la beneureté future par grace d'Amour et par prevention de ses gracieus merites?' In Esperance's words,

> Je t'ay dit ce que tu feras
> Et qu'en verité trouveras;
> Se tu le fais, bien t'en venra;
> Et se non, il t'en mescherra. (*Remede*, vv. 2813–16)

In the *Voir Dit* too, 'douce Esperance / . . . m'affermoit que sans doubtance / Elle [Toute Belle] m'amoit de cuer parfait' (vv. 595–97) and that 'Escondis tu ja ne seras!' (*VD*, vv. 2262). Such certain love is 'parfaite souffisance' and 'mercy n'est autre chose que souffisance' (*VD*, p. 150b).[69]

The debate in modern scholarship on 'what happened' after Venus enclosed the lovers in an impenetrable cloud is a conundrum. One must remember that Toute Belle's 'pucellette' is in bed with her, and Machaut is outside her 'fenestrelle', or small window (vv. 3899–915).[70] Whatever activity one thinks happened in that cloud, 'elle est mussee' in Charles d'Orléans's words – the *dit*'s fiction reveals nothing. There emerges from the cloud a *chanson baladée* (vv. 4028–31), then a *rondeau* by Toute Belle (p. 372d), and, finally, the *Voir Dit* itself.[71] Interpretation depends on whether the union satisfied the poet's and Toute Belle's desire or their hope. Such 'irresolution' is common in late medieval French writing.[72]

Pizan's Changing Opinion, pp. 108–11).

[68] *Le Livre de l'espérance*, ed. François Rouy (Paris: Champion, 1989), p. 87.

[69] See *VD*, p. 154e, vv. 3712–26, 3757–68, 3819–22, 4050, 4745–56, 8637–41, p. 780b.

[70] Shortly before they bed with Toute Belle's sister and cousin (vv. 3656–75), he desires a kind of rape, exclaiming: 'On m'efforce!'. This is a curious variant of the misogynist commonplace that women want to be raped: 'N'autres pastés de desiroie, / D'autre avaine ne hanissoie' (vv. 3676–82).

[71] Cequiglini, *'Un engin si soutil'*, p. 223.

[72] See Emma Cayley, *Debate and Dialogue: Alain Chartier in his Cultural Context* (Oxford: Oxford University Press, 2006).

The future of Machaut's and Toute Belle's love after the conclusion of the *Voir Dit* depends on the same issue that clouded their union at St-Denis and at La Chapelle. Is their love based on virtuous hope or is it a love based on sexual desire? The issue is the same as that raised by the two judgment poems: which, love as desire in the *Jugement Behaigne* or love as hope in the *Jugement Navarre*, should prevail? The veiled answer is rendered more complex and perhaps more troubling, depending as it does on how each individual member of the poems' audiences perceives and evaluates the issue. Indeed, audiences may contemplate multiple denouements or continuations. Machaut stops wavering by adopting a strict view of love as hope like that set out in the *Remede*, a choice that meets Toute Belle's unwavering devotion on the same terms. But if the Malebouches are right and one of them opts for love as hope, whereas the other surrenders to love as desire and even envisions inconstancy and duplicity, then different denouements must be entertained and the poem, as allegory, draws nearer to the context of Jean's *Rose*.

The *fictio personæ* has, therefore, multiple scripts, a not unusual feature of allegory. Nicole de Margival's *Panthère* is an example. But there are important differences. The *Rose* concludes abruptly: 'Ainsint oi la rose vermeille. / Atant fu jorz, et je m'esveille' (*Rose*, vv. 21749–50). Not so the *Panthère* or Froissart's *Joli buisson*, discussed above. After the analogous awakening in the *Panthère* –'A tant la guete, sans sejor, / Qui assez prés ert de m'oreille, / Corne le jour, et je m'esveille' (vv. 2186–88) – there follow nearly 500 lines of waking reflections. Uncertain and pessimistic, the would-be lover determines not to 'grow up' like Froissart but to persevere in pursuit of Venus's promise of happiness despite the opposing nightmare of failure, demonstrated in two separate dreams, the latter inserted in the former.[73] The reader is confronted not by the actual experiences of a particular individual we might identify with the author of the *Dit*, but rather by the diverse *gradus amoris* scripts in the imbedded *insomnia*. Macrobius defines such dreams as false depictions of the joys or sorrows of love. Waking reality reverts to an open-ended script that relates a new *fictio personæ*.

---

[73] Cerquiglini, pp. 29–30; Douglas Kelly, 'Matière, sens et *compilacion* dans le *Dit de la panthère* de Nicole de Margival', in Anne Amend-Söchting [*et al.*] (eds), *Das Schöne im Wirklichen – Das Wirkliche im Schönen: Festschrift für Dietmar Rieger* (Heidelberg: Winter, 2002), pp. 125–34. Dreams followed by waking experiences also occur in the *Voir Dit* (vv. 5731–33, 8107–10). The latter passage refers to the *Fontaine amoureuse*, where a waking sequence also follows an inserted dream.

The *fictio personæ* device suggests fiction, but presumes significant meaning hidden beneath the fiction on the allegorical level. The fiction brings together the heterogeneous modes that define its fictionality but that also conform to the more fundamental purpose of uncovering subtle truths, not by a moral imposed on the text, but by the ways authors and, then, audiences construe their fictions and their truths. Such diversity and originality in the deployment of these modes defines a major literature from the thirteenth into the fifteenth century. They raise multiple questions but the answers, as in Charles d'Orléans, are *mussees* beneath fictions that mask perhaps highly subjective and individual responses. We find them scattered through the medieval anthologies and miscellanies that manuscripts transmit to us. Jane Taylor's recent publications show how important it is to study such diversity.[74] I hope that this chapter, written to honour her life and scholarship, will contribute in its small way to the impetus she has given to the study of such late medieval poetic subtlety.

[74] See Jane H. M. Taylor, *The Making of Poetry: Poetic Anthologies at the End of the Middle Ages* (Turnhout: Brepols, 2007); see also Taylor, 'Courtly gatherings and poetic games: "coterie" anthologies in the late Middle Ages in France', in Adrian Armstrong and Malcolm Quainton (eds), *Book and Text in France, 1400–1600: Poetry on the Page* (Aldershot: Ashgate, 2007), pp. 13–29.

7

Editing, e-Science and exhibitions

Peter Ainsworth

Notwithstanding the Herculean labours of the Société de l'Histoire de France and the Académie royale de Belgique, editorial work on Jean Froissart's formidably prolix *Chroniques* continues unabated. This chapter charts recent progress relating to Book III of the *Chroniques* before engaging with several developments that have 'come after' the initial phases of the work: an online edition, a range of associated e-Science tools, an international Grid collaboratory, and a national exhibition mounted at the Royal Armouries Museum in Leeds.

Most readers familiar with Book III of Froissart's *Chroniques* will have gained their acquaintance via the edition published between 1931 and 1975 by the Société de l'Histoire de France.[1] Its four volumes provide scholars with a (largely) reliable text derived from Paris, BnF, MS fr. 2650, deemed by its editors to be the sole complete witness for what they decided (though with scant evidence adduced, since the critical Introduction was never published) was a 'second redaction' of Book III.[2] This would naturally lead one to surmise that the remaining manuscripts, of which there are over twenty, must belong to a 'first' or subsequent redaction or redactions. Scholars wishing to test the hypothesis will soon have at their disposal a new edition of a complete 'first redaction' manuscript witness, Besançon, Bibliothèque municipale, MS 865. Tome 1 of the new edition appeared in December 2007 in Droz's 'Textes Littéraires Français' collection, the choice of publisher and series

---

[1] *Jean Froissart, Chroniques*, eds. S. Luce, G. Raynaud, Léon Mirot and Albert Mirot, 15 vol. (Paris: Société dl'Histoire de France, 1869–1975). Book III takes up volumes XII–XV (eds L. and A. Mirot).

[2] The Belgian Academy edition published the text of the so-called 'Breslau' (Rehdiger) MS transcribed in 1468, but is unduly interventionist and modernises many of the original spellings: *Chroniques*, ed. baron Kervyn de Lettenhove, 26 vol. (Brussels: V. Devaux, 1867–77).

reflecting the ambiguous generic status of the Book III text.[3] Comprising around a third of the total narrative and incorporating a substantial critical apparatus, it will be completed by two further volumes scheduled by Droz to reach the press in 2008–9.

A first observation in this context is that the opening third of the Besançon, MS 865 Book III text (which in total occupies folios 201[r]–451[v] of that manuscript, the opening two hundred being devoted to a text for Book II) is in many respects identical to the equivalent section of the so-called 'second redaction' as represented by Paris, BnF, MS fr. 2650. Collation against two other complete 'first redaction' witnesses for Book III, British Library, MS Arundel 67 and BnF, MS fr. 6475, again shows up what appear to be only very minor differences, usually involving words, short phrases or three- to four-line variants. However, a recent selective collation of the entire corpus of extant Book III manuscript witnesses by our collaborator Godfried Croenen,[4] using an approach developed by Alberto Várvaro for Book IV manuscripts,[5] has put the entire 'two redactions' hypothesis into question. BnF, MS fr. 2650 emerges from this collation as distinctive to the extent that Croenen believes it to derive from a different (lost) source to that (also lost) from which all other Book III witnesses derive. Besançon, MS 865, meanwhile, emerges convincingly from this analysis as one of the earliest witnesses indirectly derived from the latter source, *O1*, via a lost, intermediate copy or exemplar labelled α (from which stems also what remains of its 'close relation' Bibliothèque royale de Belgique, MS II 88, ff. 16–23 only). From *O1* stems also a second sub-class comprising this time British Library, MS Arundel 67.iii and a fragment now at Cambridge University Library (MS Hh.3.16), and a third, Paris, BnF, fr. 6475, from which descends in turn Paris, BnF, n. a. fr. 9605. Compared to (what little remains of its near neighbour) Bibliothèque royale de

---

[3] Jean Froissart, *Chroniques. Troisième Livre. MS 865 de la Bibliothèque Municipale de Besançon*, ed. Peter Ainsworth (Geneva: Droz, 2007). Part of the Besançon MS 865 text was published by A. H. Diverres as *Froissart, Voyage en Béarn* (Manchester: Manchester University Press, 1953); there are several translations of the *Voyage* sequence into modern French.

[4] Godfried Croenen, 'La Tradition manuscrite du Troisième Livre des *Chroniques* de Froissart', in V. Fasseur (ed.), *Froissart à la cour de Béarn: l'écrivain, les arts et le pouvoir* (Turnhout: Brepols, forthcoming).

[5] Alberto Várvaro, 'Problèmes philologiques du Livre IV des Chroniques de Jean Froissart', in Godfried Croenen and Peter Ainsworth (eds), *Patrons, Authors and Workshops: Books and Book Production in Paris Around 1400* (Leuven: Peeters, 2006), pp. 255–77.

Belgique, MS II 88, and to the Cambridge fragment, Besançon, MS 865 has the merit of being part of a 'complete set' of Books I–III; unlike the otherwise excellent British Library, MS Arundel 67.iii, it is complete and undamaged by the miniature thieves who, in the act of excising MS Arundel 67's miniatures, took with them chunks of text on the verso of each of these. It is certainly one of the best witnesses amongst this particular group of Book III manuscripts; but at time of writing it would be injudicious to assign to it, or indeed to either of the other, early and complete witnesses, BnF fr. 6475 or BnF n. a. fr. 9605, a description quite so categorical as 'first redaction'. Our edition for Droz of Besançon, MS 865 remains perforce more 'bédiériste' than critical in the fullest sense, though the *Online Froissart* that we are preparing (on which more below) will provide a more comprehensive collation of our base manuscript against those referred to immediately above.

What we can say with some confidence at this juncture, in light of the evidence so far adduced and with particular reference to Croenen's most recent work, is that there would appear to be at least two major extant recensions (if not *redactions*) of Book III, deriving respectively from *O1* and *O2*. Only one of the latter survives; each, however, merits scholarly attention, especially with regard to the *filiation* of the twenty or so witnesses and sub-witnesses deriving from *O1*.[6] A second observation that can be made with equal confidence is that an edition of the text from at least one of the complete witnesses derived from *O1* (the so-called 'first redaction') is urgently needed. Our edition of the entire Besançon, MS 865 text will provide scholars with just such a benchmark, against which to collate not only BnF, MS fr. 2650, but also other complete and early 'first redaction' witnesses for Book III, such as BnF, fr. 6475 and BnF, n. a. fr. 9605.

The editorial project based on Besançon, Bibliothèque municipale, MS 865 has in any case already spawned a not inconsiderable *Nachleben*. Work on the base manuscript began in the usual way with on-site scrutiny of the manuscript, supplemented by later recourse to a black and white microfilm for transcription purposes. Technology has since moved on; an opportunity arose in 2002–3 to negotiate special arrangements at the Bibliothèque d'Étude et de Conservation in Besançon, allowing the author to photograph the whole of MS 865. The first photo-shoot was undertaken by David Cooper, sometime Fellow

---

[6] See Croenen, 'La Tradition manuscrite du Troisième Livre', which contains a proposed *stemma* for the Book III manuscripts.

Librarian of Corpus Christi College, Oxford, in association with Colin Dunn (subsequently of Scriptura Ltd). Having worked on a number of early digitisation projects at the Bodleian Library and at Trinity College Library, Dublin, Dunn had developed a concurrent interest in the use of representational technologies for the generation of CD-based viewing systems. An early example of his work using Flash software was a viewing tool devised to enable scholars to explore digitised folios of the Stowe Missel. These skills were soon applied, at the invitation of the author of this chapter, to the development of a viewer for Besançon, MS 865 (comprising Books II–III of the *Chroniques*). A particular appeal of this spin-off project was the fruitful dialogue it opened up between scholar, photographer/programmer and curator. Dunn being also a graphic designer of no mean talent as well as a skilled calligrapher, there was scope for interplay across a fairly broad range of complementary skills. Not the least interested partner in the process was the Bibliothèque municipale in Besançon: rather than hedge the project round with what would have been understandably draconian strictures, on grounds of copyright and protection of their intellectual property, the Bibliothèque d'Étude et de Conservation offered its undiminished support throughout the digitisation project and on to the consequential developments described later in this chapter.

In 2005 the award of a Leverhulme Research Fellowship provided opportunity and resource to extend the digitisation programme. The objective this time was to photograph the first of the two Besançon Froissart manuscripts, MS 864 (containing a complete text for the *première rédaction proprement dite* of Book I).[7] The overall plan was to produce a digital surrogate of a 'complete set' of the *Chroniques* as constituted *c.* 1392, that is to say, comprising Books I–III inclusive. Copied in Paris between *c.* 1412 and *c.* 1418, the Besançon Froissart had already been the object of an extensive study by Auguste Castan, published in 1865.[8] An article part-authored by Godfried Croenen (with Mary Rouse and Richard Rouse) has more recently explored the context of production underlying the Besançon codices.[9] Croenen and the Rouses have shown how the Saint-Vincent Froissart volumes evince a

---

[7] Edition by Valentina Mazzei (unpublished PhD thesis, University of Sheffield, 2008).

[8] 'Étude sur le Froissart de Saint-Vincent de Besançon', *Bibliothèque de l'École des Chartes*, 26 (1865), 114–48.

[9] Godfried Croenen, Mary A. Rouse and Richard H. Rouse, 'Pierre de Liffol and the manuscripts of Froissart's *Chronicles*', *Viator*, 33 (2002), 261-93.

close relationship with BnF, MSS fr. 2663–64, which contain texts (respectively) for Books I and II. The Paris and Besançon manuscripts appear to have been produced concurrently as *manuscrits jumeaux*, Croenen's hypothesis being that the scribal and artistic 'teams' responsible for preparing BnF, MS fr. 2663 (Book I) would have been set to work thereafter on what is now known as Besançon, Bibliothèque municipale, MS 865 (Books II and III), whilst the 'teams' responsible for Besançon, Bibliothèque municipale, 864 would have subsequently moved on to the production of BnF, MS fr. 2664. Two artist masters were engaged on this project: the Giac and Boethius Masters, the former often associated with the Master of the Rohan Hours, the second generally considered by art historians to have been a follower or associate of the Master of the Berry Apocalypse (named after New York, Pierpont Morgan Library, MS M.133).[10] The copyists involved must have moved from one codex to another; or rather, the quires would have moved in each case from one group of copyists to another. From behind this activity emerges the shadowy figure of Pierre de Liffol. Already known to the Rouses as a Parisian *librarius* active during the first quarter of the fifteenth century, his involvement with the production of manuscripts of Froissart's *Chroniques* was established for the first time in 2002 by Croenen's discovery of an almost totally erased *quittance* on the flyleaf of BnF, MS fr. 2663, only partially visible under UV light. This revealed the name of the *librarius* responsible for overseeing the preparation and decoration of BnF, MS fr. 2663, and therefore very plausibly of the Saint-Vincent Froissart also (or at least of Books II–III as found in MS 865): Pierre de Liffol. Still tantalisingly illegible because partially obscured by a later *ex-libris* was the name of the client for whom the book was made. We hope to reveal the identity of this person in the not-too-distant future, by means of image-enhancing techniques such as multispectral analysis.

The high-resolution digital surrogate derived from Besançon, Bibliothèque municipale, MSS 864–865 is currently seeing service in the context of an AHRC Resource Enhancement award to Ainsworth and Croenen for an *Online Froissart* (Sheffield and Liverpool, October 2007

---

[10] For a recent reassessment by Inès Villela-Petit, see her essay in the forthcoming Catalogue for the Armouries exhibition; a preliminary version is published along with essays by Godfried Croenen, Anne Curry, Valentina Mazzei, Katariina Närä and the author on the exhibition DVD (available from the Department of French, University of Sheffield, Western Bank, Sheffield S10 2TN).

to September 2009). The Book I text has been transcribed from Besançon, MS 864 by Valentina Mazzei; Books II and III are being transcribed from Besançon, MS 865 respectively by Croenen and Ainsworth. Collation of these against transcriptions by Hartley Miller (Liverpool) of other manuscript witnesses will be managed with the assistance of Peter Robinson's *Collate* software. Historical, political and cultural annotation will be prepared by Katariina Närä (Sheffield) and Natasha Romanova (Liverpool). New translations into modern English by Keira Borrill (Sheffield) will provide anglophone historians having little or no Middle French with reliable access to sections of the *Chroniques* that are amongst the most important narrative sources for the Hundred Years' War period. A concordance, glossary and index will also be provided.

The *Online Froissart* will allow users to consult the image files as well as the edited texts, concordance and content database (accessed via a search engine). To explain how this is to be achieved using an approach that we believe to be quite innovative, we return for a moment to the topic of digitisation. Funding from the Yorkshire Universities' Gift Aid scheme in 2004 helped to support further rounds of digital photography, including a project undertaken at Stonyhurst College Library near Clitheroe in Lancashire. Originally a Jesuit foundation, Stonyhurst is today a flourishing co-educational Roman Catholic secondary school. Its founders and subsequent benefactors endowed it with what is today a prodigiously rich collection of rare books, so extensive and varied that the College Library is faced with a major conservation challenge which never diminishes in urgency. MS 1 is a magnificent copy of Book I of Froissart's *Chroniques* thought to have been brought over from France by Sir John Arundell shortly after the battle of Agincourt in 1415, in which he was a combatant, and during or after which he may have looted it. Like Besançon, MS 864, Stonyhurst, MS 1 is illustrated with miniatures in which can be detected the hand of the Giac Master (and possibly of his or her associates). In contrast to Besançon, MS 864, however (whose miniatures highlight the achievements of Edward III and his captains), Stonyhurst, MS 1 was almost certainly destined for a client with strong French sympathies or allegiance: its predominant palette of blue and gold, and the largely gallocentric subjects featuring in the miniatures, redound to the glory of the Valois monarchy of France, rather than to that of its Plantagenet rival.

Having had sight of Dunn's photographic work on the Stonyhurst and Besançon volumes, two other major libraries owning manuscripts copied and decorated by the same scribes and painters (namely the Bibliothèque d'étude et du patrimoine in Toulouse, and the Bibliothèque royale in Brussels) expressed their wish to become involved in the project. Toulouse, MS 511 was successfully photographed on site in July 2006 by Colin Dunn; once again the Library was supportive and keen to help take the project forward a step further. The Toulouse MS is one of several Book I witnesses (like New York, Pierpont Morgan Library, MS M.804, produced for Pierre de Fontenay, seigneur de Rance) which emphasise the role of key military leaders in the Hundred Years' War. It is noteworthy for the consistently accurate heraldic blazon featuring on the armorial surcoats and banners of the French and English protagonists represented in the miniatures. At Brussels two manuscripts were photographed early in 2007, once again to identical standards and requirements as those deployed elsewhere, and with excellent support facilities provided. Brussels, Bibliothèque royale, MS II 88 (produced, perhaps, for a member of the Luxembourg family) is a compendium of fragments made up of leaves from Books I and III. Brussels, Bibliothèque royale, MS IV 251, on the other hand, is a complete two-volume copy of Book I produced for an identifiable patron: Michel de Laillier, *conseiller à la Chambre des Comptes*. The digital surrogates created at Brussels will contribute in due course to the Bibliothèque royale's forthcoming permanent exhibition on the History of the Book.

During the Brussels photo-shoot, the Bibliothèque royale was coincidentally visited by M. Thierry Delcourt, Head of Manuscripts at the Bibliothèque nationale de France. Offered the opportunity to watch Colin Dunn at work, he subsequently invited the Sheffield team to extend the project to Paris.[11] Funding from the Worldwide Universities Network made the Brussels visit possible; it has since provided an additional tranche of funding for photographic capture of BnF, MS fr. 2664. Matched funding to support the capture of BnF, MS fr. 2663 has been promised by M. Delcourt. The final phase of the photo-shoot will take place, fittingly enough, just a morning's stroll from the quarter in

---

[11] The quality of Dunn's work is matched by his ability to work sympathetically with partner librarians, curators and conservators. Many years of experience with manuscript material at the Bodleian in Oxford and at Trinity College Library in Dublin have contributed to his ability to convince librarians and conservators that the volumes photographed will invariably be handled with extreme care and sensitivity.

which Pierre de Liffol once identified, briefed and employed his preferred copyists and artists. It will provide the modern team with a digital copy of two manuscripts enjoying, as noted above, a very close codicological, art-historical and palaeographical relationship with Besançon, MSS 864–865.

Software development has followed hard on the heels of the digital photography, inspired in part by the aims of the *Online Froissart*. A first inspection of the 900 images processed from the raw TIFF data files captured from Besançon, MS 865 convinced us early on that the editorial project would benefit immeasurably from a tool allowing us to scan through the data at speed, reliably and efficiently. It also became clear that advantages were to be gained from developing a viewer equipped with a powerful zooming tool, together with a facility for opening up more than one image at once. A 'multiple viewing pane' interface would permit us to look at juxtaposed images from different folios from the same or from different manuscripts, or at several areas selected from the same folio. Art historians and iconographers, so we reasoned, would also surely welcome a viewing environment permitting these kinds of associations, whilst editors collating a text from several sources could not possibly fail to derive benefit from being able to juxtapose (for example) three witnesses for the same fragment of text. In particular, the opportunity to develop a viewer that would allow us to look at two or more closely related manuscript witnesses for Books I, II or III, copied by the same scribes and decorated by the same artists (though perhaps employing different associates or apprentices, we surmised) was very appealing. The originals were of course housed in libraries across the world, whereas the project team had, in theory at least, the possibility of bringing some or most of them together, marshalled for viewing within the same software environment. Such a viewing tool did not as yet exist; nor were proprietary tools such as Adobe Photoshop or Microsoft PowerPoint fit for the specific purposes we had in mind. It occurred to the team that the kind of tool under review might be even more useful to scholars if it could be designed for use on a laptop (for research, editing, workshops and lectures) and/or over the Internet. We began to explore the way forward, starting with a prototype designed by Colin Dunn, using Flash, which is illustrated in Figure 1.

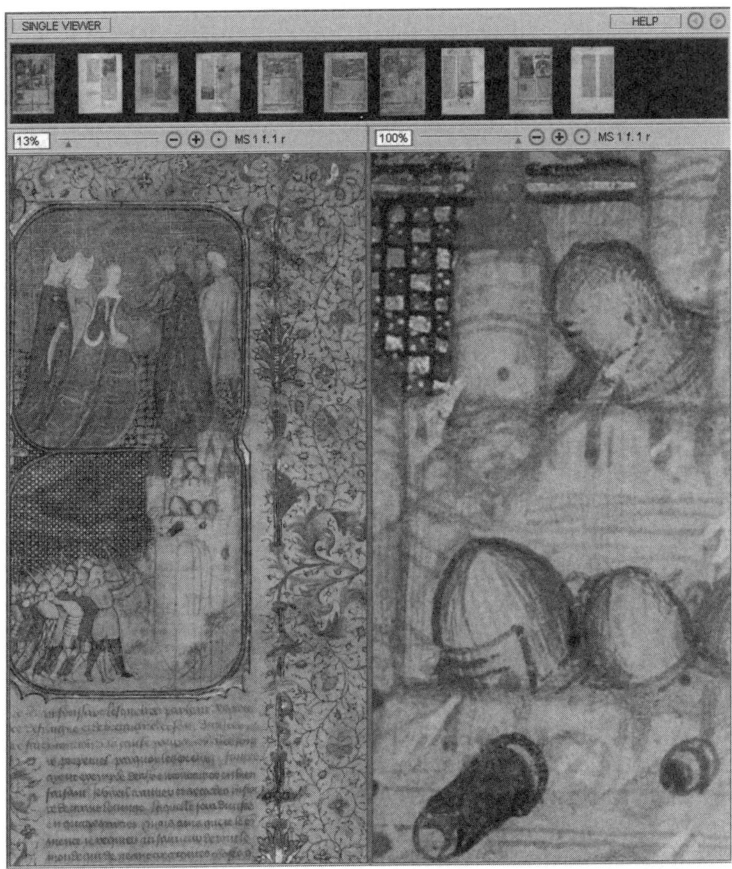

FIGURE 1: Illustration of the Flash-based prototype image viewer showing two folios from Stonyhurst MS 1 side-by-side. Images © Stonyhurst College, Lancashire, and Scriptura Ltd (digitiser of all the manuscript images).

***

During the academic year 2005–06 a 'one-off' funding initiative co-sponsored by the Arts and Humanities ICT Methods Network, the Engineering and Physical Sciences Research Council, the JISC and the UK e-Science core programme was announced, calling for 'innovative e-Science demonstrator projects'. It offered us an unforeseen opportunity to request funds to develop Dunn's Flash-based viewing tool. A bid was therefore submitted to support research and development for a platform-independent, open source and open access tool of the kind described above, but using Java version 1.2 and the JPEG 2000 image file standard rather than (respectively) Flash and the JPEG standard. The proposal was positively received and duly funded, work being undertaken between July and December 2006 consequent upon the appointment of Dr Michael Meredith (of the University of Sheffield's Department of Computer Sciences) as Technician Associate and Programmer. With additional support from the University's Humanities Research Institute, a demonstrator of the new viewer (named *Virtual Vellum*) was built incorporating a range of additional tools and functionalities. The product was demonstrated at several UK e-Science events and has since proved popular with our partner libraries and with at least one other UK editorial project.

Put simply, *Virtual Vellum* allows users to access at high speed, from a laptop, PC or hard drive, over the Internet or a network grid, images downloaded from collections of high-resolution data files. It has potential applicability for any discipline involving images: manuscript studies, art history, iconography, theatre, film and cinema studies, museums and galleries studies, pamphlet studies and *bande dessinée* are just a few that come to mind. Scholars presenting papers live at conferences or delivering seminars online that incorporate reference to the image (typically involving side-by-side comparison of two slides) have hitherto been largely dependent on 35mm slide projectors or on PowerPoint. Good as these are, they are far from ideal for such presentations; what they lack in particular, in our view at least, is the active involvement of scholar-users in the design process. A more flexible, robust viewing environment was clearly needed that would allow scholars to present papers with confidence, and to manipulate their associated image files quickly and efficiently. The availability of such a versatile 'show-and-tell' environment might, we thought, have the additional benefit of encouraging scholars to use otherwise dormant or little-used datasets. The objective, then, was to devise a robust, customisable software environment for desktop work entailing the use of high-resolution image files, configurable to address the particular needs of Arts and Humanities researchers, and compatible with different kinds of platform. The following few lines provide a more technical account of what is actually 'inside the tin'.

Virtual Vellum enhances techniques currently employed to display high-resolution images in real-time, where image sizes are typically greater than 8K x 6K pixels. Areas of specific interest include the use of the JPEG 2000 image file standard, platform independence, and the potential use of both Access and Data Grids. JPEG image compression is currently the predominant technique used for viewing high-resolution images in real-time. This is partly due to its affording a noticeably smaller file size as compared to that of a raw (TIFF) image file. However, high-resolution images still take a considerable time to download over the Internet, and in addition require a large amount of processing to convert them into a state allowing them to be displayed to best advantage. Image-viewing tools currently available resort to splitting the complete image into smaller fragments (a process known as 'tiling'). This produces smaller JPEG file sizes, but at the cost of requiring many JPEG files to display a single high-resolution image. When a user views an image in this way, the software retrieves only the relevant JPEG sub-images for the portion of the main image being displayed. The technique of fragmenting a single image into multiple JPEG files is, however, redundant with respect to pre-processing of the data and storage of it. JPEG 2000 presents an attractive alternative, since it achieves the segmentation desired by using a single file without any redundancy. Furthermore, at similar compression ratios the JPEG 2000 compression technique achieves better visual results than its JPEG counterpart. Thus, compared to the original compression quality and ratios, we can have either smaller file sizes or higher-quality encodings.

Virtual Vellum embraces the enhancements that JPEG 2000 offers over its JPEG predecessor, and facilitates the viewing of images that are encoded in the new format (although it is backwards-compatible for viewing image datasets encoded using the older, JPEG tiling approach). Like its JPEG predecessor, the JPEG 2000 viewer can be used to manipulate the display of high-resolution images in real time (as illustrated in Figures 2 and 3). Platform independence is another characteristic of the demonstrator. Since *Virtual Vellum* is written entirely in Java version 1.2, there is no need to download extra plug-ins (e.g. Flash) before the software can be run. Application of 'pre-fetching' algorithms maximises performance and speed of access, whilst the addition of several complementary tools (including a TIFF > JPEG file converter) has enriched the product's overall versatility. *Virtual Vellum* is now in regular use for seminar and conference presentations, and is an integral part of the *Online Froissart* text editing project. As a platform-independent application, the software has been developed as open source and open access. It is anticipated that this will allow Arts and Humanities scholars to develop *Virtual Vellum* further in directions that meet their specific needs. As the software is completely self-contained it can be easily transferred between different computers.

FIGURE 2. Using *Virtual Vellum* to compare the frontispiece from four different manuscripts that are located at 3 different physical locations. Images © Bibliothèque royale Albert 1er, Brussels (left- and right-most images), Stonyhurst College, Lancashire (second from the left), Bibliothèque municipale de Besançon (second from the right) and Scriptura Ltd.

The AHRC-funded *Online Froissart* project provided the experimental dataset of no fewer than six complete digitised manuscript surrogates, generating ~1.5 TB of uncompressed image data. The raw TIFF data is stored on a server; the processed JPEG 2000 files are stored on and retrievable from a local hard drive; and they can also be accessed over the Internet or via a Data Grid using Storage Resource Broker (SRB) middleware developed at the University of California at San Diego. *Virtual Vellum* is as adept at facilitating stand-alone presentations of images to conference or lecture audiences as it is at streaming data from a non-local source, and again in real time. The demonstrator application is therefore ideally suited to Access Grid environments where scholars in locations remote from one another wish to discuss the iconographic or art-historical details of an image or image collection (see below, *Pegasus* project). Access and Data Grids offer the ideal framework and computing power for the efficient and rapid handling of large-scale collections of high-resolution files, permitting real-time, close-up scrutiny of single or juxtaposed images, with independent zooming control and other function-alities.

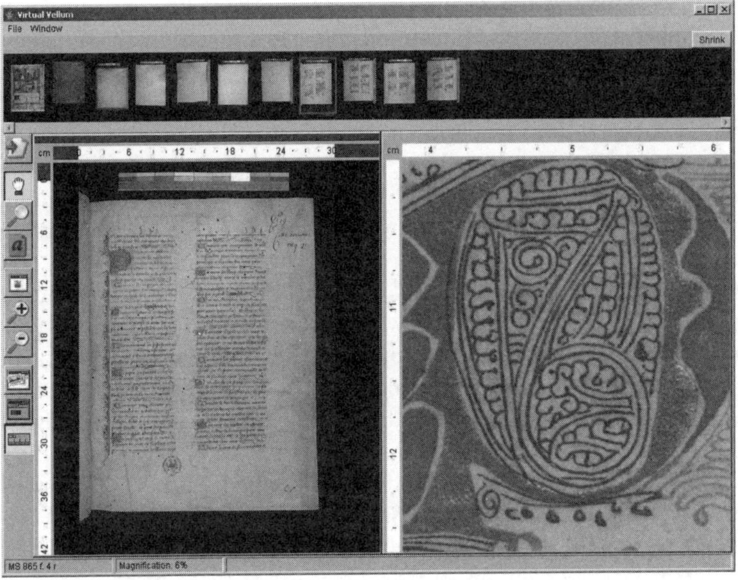

FIGURE 3. Two different views of the same folio from Besançon, MS 865. The left window shows the folio in full with the right window magnifying into it. Images © Bibliothèque municipale de Besançon and Scriptura Ltd.

The White Rose Grid and Worldwide Universities Network's WUN Grid are providing the primary grid networks to be used during the initial phases of development. The retrieval of images not held locally but housed elsewhere on a grid network further justifies the need for the comparatively better JPEG 2000 compression technique, since band-width is in such instances inevitably at more of a premium. Annotation tools still to be developed for *Virtual Vellum* will allow scholars to annotate data online individually, collaboratively and in real time.

Virtual Vellum was the inspiration for another significant development undertaken in 2005–7 with funding provided this time under the auspices of the Knowledge Transfer Partnerships scheme (overseen by what used to be known as the Department of Trade and Industry). The objective this time was to develop a form of viewing software to allow museum visitors to explore flexibly and interactively a set of surrogate manuscripts forming part of a public exhibition at the Royal Armouries Museum, Leeds. Entitled 'The Chronicles of Froissart: From Conflict to Co-operation', this free exhibition opened to the public on Saturday 8 December 2007 for a four-month run. It featured the Stonyhurst College manuscript, displayed in a high-security sealed case. Visitors were able to view a single spread (verso and recto) from the codex, but not of course to turn its pages and explore it as they might wish to do. The British Library's excellent 'Turning the Pages' software is one solution to such a challenge. But it expends a great deal of computing power on generating an almost lifelike facsimile in something approaching 3D. Simulating the turning by hand of each folio, and mimicking the characteristic 'fall' of the vellum as the folios are turned over, 'Turning the Pages' allows museum visitors to explore pre-programmed pathways and to appreciate the beauty of the artefact. In addition to the Stonyhurst College manuscript in its case, the Leeds exhibition deployed no fewer than half a dozen full-length digital surrogates of cognate manuscripts, from the early fifteenth-century corpus described above. The Knowledge Transfer Partnership referred to, involving the University of Sheffield's French Department and e-Learning specialists Tribal (Sheffield) led to the development of a rather different viewing solution to the one achieved (with great success, it must be acknowledged) by the British Library. Called *Kiosque*, it provides an arguably more flexible approach and visitor experience. Not the least original of its features is that it allows visitors to compare and contrast different manuscript witnesses for the 'same' text, and (like its progenitor, *Virtual Vellum*) to set one manuscript alongside one or more of its 'cousins', for comparison and evaluation (see Figure 4). Several image views of the same folio can be juxtaposed, or the visitor can opt for a synchronous view of the ways in which, say, four of the manuscripts illustrate the battle of Poitiers in their respective miniatures. Figure 5 illustrates how Kiosque can be used to guide a user through a narrative, supported by the manuscript images. A key aim of the Royal Armouries exhibition was to educate and entertain (*plaire et instruire encore et toujours*); but the exhibition itself arose in part as the result of conversations about the surrogates' role in helping to secure the long-term conservation of the original manuscripts of Froissart's *Chroniques*.

As noted above, the *real* manuscript on display in the exhibition's Treasury was Stonyhurst, MS 1, kindly loaned to the Royal Armouries for the whole run by Stonyhurst College. Complementing the Stony-hurst original were six closely related *digitised* manuscripts from the corpus already described. The originals were of course housed in libraries across Europe, their contents never before having been assembled in a single location. This underscores further the advantages of simultaneous display of all six in digital format.

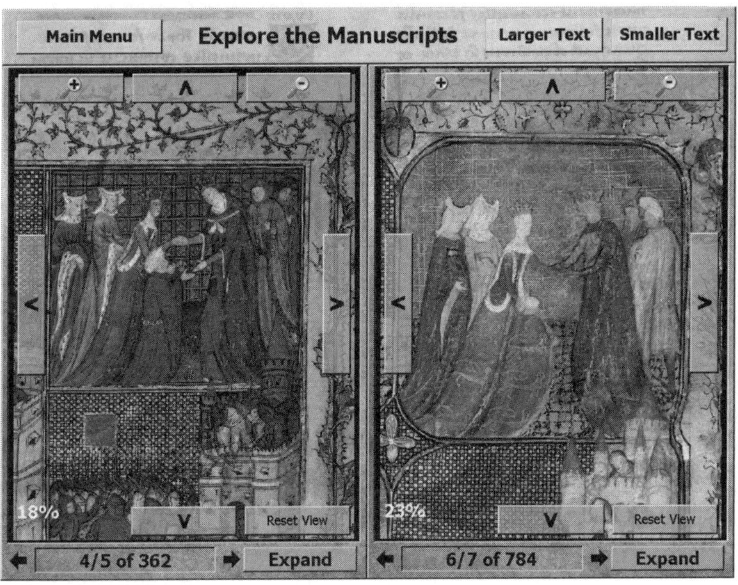

FIGURE 4. Using *Kiosque* to choose and compare folios from any of the 6 digitised manuscripts. The left window shows a folio from Brussels, IV 251, whereas the image in the right window is from Stonyhurst MS 1.

Images © Bibliothèque royale Albert 1ᵉʳ, Brussels, Stonyhurst College and Scriptura Ltd.

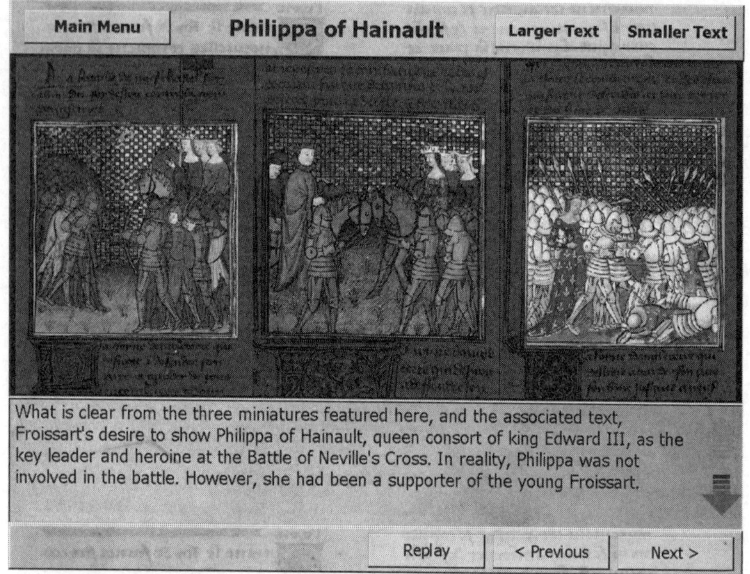

FIGURE 5. Describing Philippa of Hainault's depiction at the Battle of Neville's Cross within *Kiosque*. Images © Bibliothèque royale Albert 1ᵉʳ, Brussels, Stonyhurst College, Bibliothèque municipale de Besançon and Scriptura Ltd.

Composed between *c.* 1356 and *c.* 1400, Froissart's *Chroniques* remain one of the most significant works of later medieval French literature; even today they remain a prime source for historians of society, politics, culture, warfare, costume, heraldry and narrative. Widely regarded as the most important prose chronicle arising from the Anglo-French conflict, the *Chroniques* are a blend of historical record, memoir, autobiography, journalism and 'war reporting'. Using our *Kiosque* software, visitors to the exhibition were able to access more than just the digital manuscripts; maps, genealogies and narratives from the *Chroniques* were combined with interactive tours of the manuscripts and their contents.

Younger visitors to the Museum had the opportunity to try out an interactive computer game called *Castle Siege*, devised in association with ZOOtech Interactive DVD and Video (Sheffield) by Genesys

Solutions Ltd, a student-run company based at the University of Sheffield. The Royal Armouries' contribution to the exhibition was two-fold: a stunning design (the work of Graham Moores) and a selection of contemporary arms and armour specially chosen by Senior Curator Dr Karen Watts from the Armouries' world-famous collection. The items were thoughtfully identified and arranged to match and 'meet up with' objects depicted in the real and virtual manuscript miniatures. Music, educational events, enactments, swordfights, demonstrations of calligraphy and a DVD (including *Kiosque* and a selection of contemporary music specially recorded by Paul Bracken) completed the exhibition experience.

In addition to the support it gave to the Royal Armouries exhibition, the English-language version of *Kiosque* is currently available over the intranet at Stonyhurst College, for students and scholars to consult. A French-language version of *Kiosque* is in use at the Ceccano Library in Avignon, the Cité du Livre in Aix-en-Provence's Bibliothèque Méjanes, the Alcazar Library in Marseilles, and at our partner libraries in Besançon and Toulouse and Brussels (an illustration of the software is given in Figure 6).

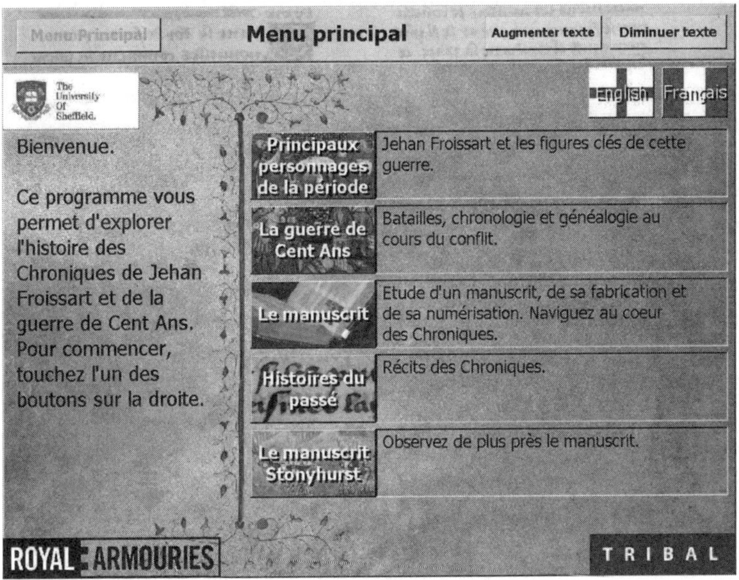

FIGURE 6. The *Kiosque* main menu, illustrating the different facets of the

software, using the French-language side.

Discussions are under way with a view to mounting a French event on a scale similar to the Leeds exhibition at the Musée de l'Armée (Hôtel des Invalides) in partnership with the Department of Manuscripts, Bibliothèque nationale de France. The *Kiosque* software will live on, we trust, provided that platform changes do not shorten its life in ways as yet unanticipated. *Kiosque* and *Virtual Vellum* are both generic and designed to be adaptable for other exhibitions or image-based research projects. *Virtual Vellum* is freely available to researchers or museums, downloadable from the project website together with a user-friendly instruction manual.[12]

The most recent avatar of the Froissart projects' afterlife is another demonstrator, funded this time by the Engineering and Physical Sciences Research Council in association with the National Science Foundation of America. We had always envisaged *Virtual Vellum* (or something incorporating it) would prove to be of interest to research teams, rather than just to individual users. Arts and Humanities scholars working on international collaborative research projects involving large-scale image collections held on local or distributed databases may from time to time wish to consult one another to explore questions of mutual interest (e.g. aspects of iconography, sundry art-historical features, definitions and descriptions of image content, real-time comparisons of related images). As mentioned above, the Access and Data Grids afford the ideal framework (and computing power) for rapid and efficient handling of large-scale collections of high-resolution images, permitting real-time, close-up scrutiny of single or (two or more) juxtaposed images, with independent zooming controls and functions such as hot-spotting, highlighting and blogging. Such tools were not yet available in 2007; the prospect of having the resource and expertise to develop them presented an appealing challenge.

The *Pegasus* project was inaugurated in January 2008 at Sheffield in partnership with the National Center for Supercomputing Applications based at the University of Illinois at Urbana-Champaign. *Pegasus* aims to promote, demonstrate and run experiments in grid technologies and digitised media applied to research and museum experiences in the Arts and Humanities. In particular, *Pegasus* seeks to develop a grid-enabled

---

[12] See www.shef.ac.uk/hri/projects/projectpages/virtualvellum.html (accessed 17 June 2009).

interface incorporating *Virtual Vellum* and *Kiosque* (once again using the Storage Resource Broker clientware) to support a programme for sharing and displaying in real time selected virtual reality exhibition materials of mutual interest to participating institutions on either side of the Atlantic Ocean, drawing on high-volume, high-resolution digital image datasets held on and managed via compatible Solaris SUN servers. Robust protocols will permit real-time access to, and shared distribution of, exhibition packages and toolsets, and will in turn give access to other kinds of museum experience such as those developed at the Armouries' sister institution in the United States, the Frazier Gallery (at Louisville, KY). During 2008, *Pegasus* will aim to establish a secure infrastructure to allow each partner museum or library to create, share and exchange such materials with the other's audiences and researchers. There is potential also for more ambitious international Data Grid projects involving the controlled sharing of large-scale image collections, such as those held by regional French libraries or even by national institutions, over a robust, high-speed network such as WUN Grid, which could make these items available to scholars all over the world – together with the *Virtual Vellum* and *Kiosque* toolsets.

Public exhibitions and e-Science applications for the Arts and Humanities (e-Science being understood here as the combining of computer science solutions with high-resolution digital photography to achieve objectives not otherwise attainable) are just two of the strands to the *Nachleben* enjoyed by the Froissart project team. They have allowed exciting new pathways to open up and unexpected forms of interdisciplinary partnership to germinate. Built on traditional modes of scholarship including the skills of the editor-medievalist, they have fostered the widening of our potential audience, and the creation of new ways of articulating to a broader public the riches of the texts and artefacts on which we have the privilege to work.

8

Did Ronsard really read Coquillart?

† Michael Freeman

In his biography of Pierre de Ronsard, first published in 1586, Claude Binet claims that in his youth Ronsard had been a close friend of 'un Gentil-homme Piemontois nommé le seigneur Paul', who had

> fort bien estudié les Poëtes Latins, et mesmes, lors qu'il estoit page, avoit aussi souvent un Virgile en la main qu'une baguette, interpretant aucunesfois à Ronsard quelques beaux traits de ce grand Poëte, et Ronsard au contraire ayant tousjours en main quelque Poëte François, qu'il lisoit avec jugement, et principalement, comme luy mesmes m'a maintesfois raconté, un Jean le Maire de Belges, un Romant de la Rose et les œuvres de Coquillart, et de Clement Marot, lesquels il a depuis appelé, comme on lit que Virgile disoit d'Ennie, les immondices, dont il tiroit de belles limures d'or. Fust donc par la lecture de ces livres, fust par la hantise de ce docte Gentil-homme, qui luy donna entierement le goust de la Poësie, et le premier jetta en son esprit la semence de tant de beaux fruicts, qu'il a enfanté depuis à l'honneur de nostre France.[1]

This would appear to be, on Ronsard's part, damning the French poets referred to with faint praise, the implication being, insofar as Binet's account of these discussions is in any way coherent, that the poet, under the influence of the somewhat shadowy seigneur Paul, of whom we know little, soon put behind him his youthful tastes, moving quickly on to greater – namely, Latin, Greek and Italian – things. French poetry, in this version, would appear to have been little more than a passing fancy. The tone is implicitly but umistakably patronising even if, in characterising them as 'les immondices', he is referring the reader back to Virgil. The role of the 'docte Gentil-homme' was to have widened the

---

[1] See *La Vie de P. de Ronsard de Claude Binet*, ed. Paul Laumonier (Paris: Hachette, 1910), p. 10.

young Ronsard's poetic horizons by encouraging him to read classical (*ergo* superior) authors.

The – at first sight surprising – assertion that Ronsard's first love was French poetry has never been fully investigated, especially with regard to Guillaume Coquillart, who cannot be spoken of as a major figure in the same breath as a Guillaume de Lorris, Jean de Meun, Jean Lemaire de Belges, or Clément Marot. Given that the Pléiade poets were almost without exception haughtily dismissive of previous generations of French poets, and sometimes (as with François Villon) did not deign to mention them at all, one might assume that Claude Binet was simply mistaken. Binet is not always a very reliable witness, it has to be said. There is little doubt that he knew Ronsard well, but not nearly as well as he would have his readers believe. Not quite Ronsard's Boswell, he was perhaps kept at something of a distance by an older (by some thirty years) and justly famous man. One cannot avoid suspecting that where there were awkward gaps in his knowledge of Ronsard's life, habits and intellectual preferences, he gratefully filled them. And perhaps he consciously set out to prove to contemporaries that he had been closer to the great man than he really had: 'luy mesmes m'a maintesfois raconté' suggests an intimacy that may have been more apparent than real. In the notes to his authoritative edition of Binet's life of Ronsard, Paul Laumonier is of the opinion, however, that, although Binet is the only contemporary to have said anything along these lines, 'ce propos est vraisemblable' and 'malgré son excessif dédain' less contemptuous than the poet's description in the *Odes* of 1550 of the works of his French predecessors as a 'monstrueuse erreur' which he rejected completely.[2] By the time he came to discuss his tastes and literary influences with Binet, whom he appears to have met for the first time around 1570, Ronsard may well have mellowed, and been more forgiving of those who had gone before him.

The fact remains, nevertheless, that Ronsard and those of his generation who shared his likes and dislikes had taken French poetry in new directions, breaking with the past and seeking to render their predecessors unreadable in the eyes of a new public. The choice of books Binet mentions is a curiously mixed one. One might expect the *Roman de la Rose* to be on any budding poet's reading list at the time, even if it belonged to a world long gone, while Lemaire de Belges's style and content were recognisably 'modern'. As for Clément Marot,

---

[2] *Ibid.*, p. 87.

Ronsard could not help but be an admirer *malgré lui*, anxiety of influence notwithstanding.[3] The one name that does seem incongruous is that of Coquillart, and it is interesting to note that he is left out of the third and last edition (1597) of *La Vie*.[4]

Of the names on Binet's list, Guillaume Coquillart is the least well known. He was born in Reims around 1452 and died in his native city in 1510. As a romantically inclined critic once remarked, he thus had his cradle in the Middle Ages and his grave in the Renaissance! For more recent literary critics who have studied the Age of Ronsard, he might be thought to be decidedly old hat. But this would to be to take the Pléiade generation at its own word and assume that a clean break with the past really had taken place. We shall see that things are not quite so clear. As with the other works mentioned by Binet, Coquillart's were frequently reprinted in the first half of the sixteenth century. They effectively come to a halt, however, after the mid-1550s. This is no surprise; times and tastes had changed.[5] Alain Chartier, François Villon, Pierre Meschinot, Jean Molinet *et al.* had all drifted into semi-oblivion.

But is this the whole story? In recent years the conventional doxa of a permanent and radical break with the literary past has been questioned. While there is no doubt that the reading public of the late sixteenth century did not always have at its disposal new editions of the works of the past, recent and not so recent, this should not lead us to the conclusion that what we now call 'medieval' authors were not read at all. Robert Peckham has made the case for Villon being read and admired by cognoscenti at least well into the seventeenth and eighteenth centuries.[6] As for Coquillart, he is quoted approvingly by Clément

---

[3] Gérard Defaux makes much (and rightly so) of Ronsard's apparent need to do the 'Marot generation' down in 'Facing the Marot generation: Ronsard's *giovenili errori*', *Modern Language Notes*, 119, Supplement (2004), 299–326. He mentions Binet's reference to Coquillart, but only in passing, and draws no conclusions from it.

[4] This may simply be a printer's error, as Laumonier, *La Vie de P. de Ronsard*, p. 87, points out.

[5] We know of at least twenty editions of Coquillart's complete works before 1553, the date of Ronsard's *Livret de Folastries* and also the year in which an edition of Coquillart's works was published in Paris, 'reueuës & corrigées' by Ronsard's friend, Claude Colet. For the early history of Coquillart's printed works, see M. J. Freeman, 'Les Éditions anciennes de Coquillart', *Bibliothèque d'Humanisme et Renaissance*, 36 (1974), 87–104. After the 1550s editions of his works are few in number. This is the case for most other fifteenth-century authors.

[6] See Robert Peckham, 'À la recherche d'un Villon perdu. Pour une histoire de sa réception au XVIIIe siècle', in Jean Dufournet, Michael Freeman et Jean Dérens (eds),

Marot, Estienne Pasquier, Charles Estienne, among others, and copies of his works are frequently found in *inventaires après décès* of the period. The situation may well have been that men of letters enjoyed fifteenth-century texts, even if they sometimes had to be read in quaintly (and no doubt dog-eared) old-fashioned editions passed down from father to son, or among bookish friends with antiquarian tastes. Things were very different, of course, for the writings of earlier periods, which presented insurmountable linguistic challenges to all but the very few. But many of the great works of the distant past had, of course, been conveniently modernised.

Guillaume Coquillart is something of a special case. His works date from the end of the fifteenth century and were not apparently collected in their entirety until the beginning of the sixteenth. He was also widely read throughout the first half of the sixteenth century, having received (like Villon) the imprimatur of a careful edition by the Parisian publisher and bookseller, Galliot du Pré.[7] It would not be entirely surprising, therefore, to find his works figuring on the bookshelves of the young Pierre de Ronsard – but not so much as a poet in the higher style as a writer of witty and linguistically sparkling (and frequently coarse) satires on the Parisian *beau monde* of his day. We know that Ronsard read and enjoyed Rabelais, alluding memorably to his celebration of the pleasures of flesh and table. There is every reason, therefore, to believe that he did indeed find enjoyment in reading another representative of the *tradition gauloise*, namely Guillaume Coquillart. To speak of there being any direct influence is another matter; more a case perhaps of a community of taste, a fondness for ribaldry and an amused tolerance of the silliness of things. The Ronsard who felt obliged to defend himself against censorious Protestants in later years (in 1563 during the first Wars of Religion) was reaffirming his commitment to pleasure and to fun:

Villon et ses lecteurs (Paris: Champion, 2005), pp. 71–88.

[7] The first complete edition of Coquillart's works would appear to be the one published by the veuve Trepperel in Paris around 1513. The gothic editions which follow at regular intervals for the next twenty years derive from it for the most part. In 1532 the well-known publisher Galliot du Pré brought out a new edition of Coquillart's works which became in its turn the template for successive editions. On Galliot du Pré, see Jean Balsamo, 'Galliot du Pré, éditeur de Guillaume Coquillart', in Jean-Frédéric Chevalier (ed.), *Les Mondes théâtraux autour de Guillaume Coquillart (XVe siècle)* (Langres: Dominique Guéniot, 2005), pp. 95–112. Balsamo reminds us that Coquillart 'avait été célébré par Marot et placé au rang des grands poètes français' (p. 112).

J'ayme à faire l'amour, j'ayme à parler aux femmes,
A mettre par escrit mes amoureuses flames,
J'ayme le bal, la dance et les masques aussi,
La musicque et le luth, ennemis du souci.[8]

The world described and lampooned by Coquillart is the Paris of the early 1480s. Dizzy with a new-found prosperity and political security, the Parisian bourgeoisie (lawyers, wealthy dealers and tradesmen, prosperous and frequently lax churchmen), happily gave themselves over to the delights of 'les plaisirs mondains'. Moralists thundered, university dramatists sharpened their pens and mocked them in their *farces* and *sotties*. Coquillart laughed good-humouredly, while pricking their pretensions, in what one might call 'affectionate satire'.[9] His language is often crude, and the scenes and situations he describes immoral, involving scurrilous and cynical individuals, both male and female. It is very close to the humour of the Basoche, the corporation of lawyers and their clerks, law students and writers connected in some way to the world of the Châtelet and the Palais de Justice. They put on short plays, called 'causes grasses', which used the language and procedure of the law to deride conventional customs and the hypocrisies of the times. Plays such as the *Farce du Cuvier*, the *Farce du Pet* and, of course, the *Farce de Maistre Pierre Pathelin*, clearly show their links to this world and to its mind-set. As do the works of François Villon. But none more so than those of Guillaume Coquillart. It is hard to believe Ronsard did not know them.

Written for the most part in a few years either side of 1480, Coquillart's gentle satires are in some ways very traditional, cast in the same mould as the *fabliaux* and the *farces*. Wives are capricious and unfaithful, and men of the church grasping and unscrupulous, as are merchants and the inevitable *voisin*: in the comic theatre of the time, one must always beware of the man next door. The *voisine*, of course, is fair game. Young men about town are also made fun of as they go around Paris, bent on impressing bourgeoises and demoiselles. Coquil-

<hr>

[8] See Ronsard, *Discours des misères de ce temps*, ed. Malcolm Smith (Geneva: Droz, 1979), p. 181, vv. 551–54.

[9] See M. J. Freeman, 'La Satire affectueuse dans les *Droitz nouveaulx* de Guillaume Coquillart', *Réforme Humanisme Renaissance*, 11 (1980), 92–99. While claiming to satirise contemporary mores, Coquillart is in fact implicitly celebrating them, in a world turned upside down. For a fuller discussion of this point, see Michael Freeman, 'Guillaume Coquillart ou l'envers de la sagesse', in Chevalier (ed.), *Les Mondes théâtraux autour de Guillaume Coquillart (XVᵉ siècle)*, pp. 11–26.

lart's world is very much an urban landscape, indeed a specifically Parisian one, and the few peasants who venture on to its streets are soon routinely found out. It is a world in which there are few friends, and some clearly defined enemies: crafty, scheming women, jealous husbands, untrustworthy servants, pretentious snobs, hypocrites and poseurs, men and women who work against the common good (Coquillart calls it 'la chose publicque') of harmless fun. A particular target, as with Villon, Marot and many others, is the ubiquitous *macquerelle*.

His first known work is *Le Plaidoié d'entre la Simple et la Rusee*, which can be dated from 1479. It is continued in the following year by *L'Enqueste d'entre la Simple et la Rusee*. Each is under a thousand verses long, and would presumably have been read out or acted out in similar circumstances, that is to say before a Basoche audience in Paris on the occasion of one of their 'jours de feste'. Essentially, it is the story of two young women who squabble over their right to possess the body of a young man ('Le Mignon') and who bring their case to court, complete with judge, counsel, and witnesses. It is not hard to imagine the turn the events take, inevitably accompanied by clever word-play and sexual innuendo. The language, a mixture of legal jargon and street slang, is predictably coarse, with a sly, knowing tinge. It is also a valuable tool for anyone today wishing to catch the flavour of the spoken French of the time.

Coquillart then moves on to a slightly more ambitious work, the *Droitz nouveaulx*. Since the world has changed, and all values have been turned on their heads by the new prosperity, a new morality is in place, which needs to be regulated by new laws, the *droitz nouveaulx*. These laws are based on Justinian but in a very idiosyncratic and topical manner. They deal with such cases as whether a woman has the right to take a lover if she is neglected by her husband for more than eight nights, whether a young mother has the right to refuse to breast-feed if she feels it will spoil her figure, whether a cuckolded husband should be 'cocu et content' if his wife's lover is providing them with valuable goods. Legal precedents and examples from the appropriate authorities in Roman law are brought to bear on these weighty issues.

In one such case a *macquerelle* takes under her wing a scruffy and promiscuous young country girl and turns her into a prostitute, decked out with fine clothes and jewellery:

> Tant que devant pour trois festuz
> Vous l'eussiez eue, ou pour du pain,
> Maintenant la couple d'escuz
> Ou le noble luy pend au sain.[10]

The jocular implication of all this is that she has now been priced out of the range of the sort of young men, students, young lawyers and their clerks, who made up Coquillart's primary audience. The fault lies with the woman who put her up to it:

> Or l'inventeur de tout le mal
> A esté ceste macquerelle.
> Je demande comment doit elle
> Estre pugnye, veu qu'elle s'applicque
> De bailler si lourde marelle
> Et tromper la chose publicque? (vv. 1921–26)

In law and in theory, the author points out, she should be severely punished. In practice, what happens nowadays, he claims in tones of scandal and mock indignation, is that she is made to pay a fine which soon finds its way into the pocket of some policeman, and the whole affair is quickly hushed up. This is the way of the world, he implies. With a wry smile he confirms his audience in their belief that the greatest enemy of a young man who wishes to sow his wild oats on the cheap is an evil *macquerelle*. These are feelings which Ronsard will share in his *Livret de Folastries*, as we shall see.

Nevertheless, all this might seem to some to be a long way from the world of Pierre de Ronsard as he is frequently portrayed. This might be because, encouraged by the poets and dramatists of the mid-sixteenth century themselves, we have erected an artificial barrier between the so-called Middle Ages and the Renaissance. When did the one end and the other begin? Both are visible in the works of Rabelais (born 1484), as they are in Noël du Fail and Bonaventure des Périers. The first French regular comedy, Etienne Jodelle's *L'Eugène*, written and performed in 1552, may have a prologue, be written in five acts, have the sort of felicitous tying-up of loose ends which is typical of classical comedy, but it remains very close in inspiration and world-view to those of the 'medieval' *farces* it sets out to supplant. In fact, it is far from innocent,

---

[10] All quotations of Coquillart are taken from Guillaume Coquillart, *Œuvres*, ed. M. J. Freeman (Geneva: Droz, 1975). Here, vv. 1907–10 (p. 225). References to the text are hereinafter given in parentheses in the body of the chapter.

given that no young couple provides us with a regulation happy ending in which love triumphs over adversity. The happy couple who invite the audience to join them in their celebration of the good life at the close of this play is made up of a corrupt churchman, Eugène, and Alix, a promiscuous wife. So much for the new sanitised morality. 'Medieval' farces, which in many cases could still be seen on the streets of Paris and other big towns in Jodelle's day, had a similar take on the realities of life. Some of them seem to date from the 1520s and 1530s. The hey-day of 'medieval' comic theatre in France would appear to be the first half of the sixteenth century. Where does that leave our neat periodisations?

It would be pointless to attempt to suggest that Ronsard closely imitated, or was greatly influenced by, Coquillart. In his notes to his edition of Binet, Laumonier judiciously remarks: 'Quant à Coquillart, je ne le vois cité et imité nulle part chez eux [Ronsard, Du Bellay and Baïf], si ce n'est dans les *Folastries* de Ronsard, et encore l'imitation serait-elle très lointaine.'[11] But the point at issue here for me is not whether he ever consciously imitated Coquillart, but whether he might have enjoyed them in his youth, at a time when Coquillart's works were freely available and clearly still popular. I can easily imagine a conversation some time in the 1570s when, asked by his future biographer (who was perhaps already taking discreet notes) which French authors he had read in his early years, he mentioned some of those he had found amusing or pleasing. Like many of his generation, he would have had a natural affinity, as did Rabelais, with the deliberate trivialisation of legal rigour and pomposity which is the hallmark of Coquillart's satires. He would no doubt have appreciated the wit, the sheer verbal dexterity, of the fifteenth-century writer which had lost nothing of their freshness. Playful humour is an aspect of Ronsard's genius which is often overlooked. He sometimes gives free rein to it in his love poetry but also, and above all, in the *Livret de Folastries*.

The *Livret de Folastries* appeared (anonymously) in April 1553. Ronsard was not yet thirty. He had, of course, achieved critical acclaim and more with his odes in the classical style and his sonnets to Cassandre in the Petrarchist mode. He now turned his attention to the 'beau style bas' which was to be the defining feature of his poems, the *Continuation des Amours* (first published in 1555), in praise of the charms of a young French woman, Marie Dupin, supposedly encountered by chance in Bourgueil and who is presented as having

---

[11] *La Vie de P. de Ronsard*, p. 87.

both turned his head and inspired him to write in a more down-to-earth and less ornate register. In the preface to his new collection he famously announces that he is no longer a slave to Petrarch and the Italians, preferring to find sources for his style and subject-matter elsewhere. He is referring, among others, to Catullus; significantly, Catullus is specifically invoked and named on the title page of the *Livret de Folastries*:

> Nam castum esse decet pium poëtam
> Ipsum; versiculos nihil necesse est.[12]

This suggests a certain defensiveness on the part of the young poet, hiding behind an illustrious predecessor, as well as choosing not to put his own name to the collection on the title page. There can be little doubt Ronsard had widened his reading in the early 1550s, allowing other influences to shape his writing. Ronsard tells us that he wrote these frivolous pieces when a 'jeune garson' but, as Laumonier points out, 'il se peut au reste qu'une ou deux de ces pièces datent de sa prime jeunesse, mais la plupart ne remontent pas au delà de juin 1552 et quelques-unes sont probablement du début de 1553.'[13] The same critic notes that in these years Ronsard reminded himself of 'la manière "gauloise" qu'il lui plut d'adopter, par l'entremise des Anciens et des Italiens, en 1552 et les années suivantes'.[14] This is a conversion, then, to the style and manner of Catullus but also a reconversion in part at least to the style and subject-matter of Clément Marot ... and others. Laumonier remarks that, while Ronsard follows Catullus, he grafts them on to 'des sujets français, tels que le Robin et la Marion des pastourelles, la Margot de Villon, l'Alix et la Catin de Marot, le Roger et la Marion de Saint-Gelais, le Thenot des farces, type traditionnel du soldat poltron et ivrogne'.[15] The only name missing from this list is (inexplicably?) that of Coquillart. This omission is especially surprising when one reads the 'Premiere Folastrie', in which the poet compares the rival attractions of 'une pucelette grasselette' and of a 'pucelette maigrelette' in a style very reminiscent of the author of *Le Plaidoié et l'Enqueste d'entre la Simple et*

---

[12] Pierre de Ronsard, *Œuvres complètes*, ed. Paul Laumonier, 20 vol. (Paris: Didier, STFM, 1968), V (*Livret de Folastries (1553)*), p. 1. All references to Ronsard are from this edition.

[13] *Ibid.*, p. viii.

[14] *Ibid.*, p. xvi.

[15] *Ibid.*, p. x.

la Rusee. Ronsard is drawn to the plumper of the 'deux belles' because of her physical attributes:

> Un grasselet embonpoint,
> Une fesse rebondie,
> Une poitrine arondie
> En deux monteletz bossus,
> Où l'on dormiroit dessus,
> Comme entre cent fleurs décloses,
> Ou dessus un lit de roses. (vv. 86–92)

The 'maigrelette', on the other hand, seems more intellectually inclined, as well as more demure. She sings beautifully, dances divinely, is the very image of discreet charm as she plays music for him:

> Une douce mignardise,
> Un doux languir de ses yeux,
> Un doux souspir gratieux,
> Quand sa douce main manie
> La douceur d'une armonie. (vv. 120–24)

There are echoes in the description which follows of the 'maigrelette' and of her feminine virtues (what Coquillart calls 'la façon feminine') which are reminiscent of Coquillart's praise of ladies' 'doulx entretien', and 'gracieux accueil' in his *Debat des dames et des armes*, written to be performed before either Charles VIII in 1484 or Louis XII in 1498. In a debate which weighs up the relative merits of the military and the courtly virtues, the poet had concluded – diplomatically and predictably – that both were equally desirable in a monarch. Ronsard's 'folastrie' has no such pseudo-political ambitions. Unable to choose between the two 'pucelettes' who, through fear perhaps of gossip, have been less willing to allow him to enjoy their favours, he closes with a show of imaginary bravado, advertising his determination to continue to love them both. In a final flourish, he berates the usual kill-joys who make life difficult for a lover and his lass or, in this case, lasses:

> Ny le temps, ny son effort,
> Ny violence de mort,
> Ny les mutines injures,
> Ny les mesdisans parjures,
> Ny les trop sales broquards
> De nos voisins babillars,
> Ny la trop songneuse garde
> D'une cousine bavarde,

Ny le soupson des passans,
Ny les maris menaçans,
Ny les audaces des freres,
Ny les préchemens des meres,
Ny les oncles sourcilleux.
Ny les dangers perilleux
Qui l'amour peuvent defaire,
N'auront puissance de faire
Que tousjours je n'ayme mieux
Que mon cœur, ny que mes yeux,
L'une & l'autre pucelette,
Grasselette, & maigrelette. (vv. 203–22)

There is nothing particularly 'gaulois' about this first 'folastrie', with its restrained and amused eroticism. The cast of characters who stand in the way of lovers could be taken from the newly popular comedies of Plautus or Terence, who were in the process of being rediscovered. They are also remarkably similar to the troublesome figures who upset the plans of the 'galants' to be found in dramatic monologues (of which Coquillart was the recognised master), in farces and contemporary *contes*. There are links, too, in the fourth 'folastrie' to both the classical and 'medieval' worlds. At once an imitation of a poem by Catullus and a parody of a pastourelle, it introduces us to Jaquet and 'sa Robine' and to a description of their idyllic mutual fulfilment. This use of archetypal lovers' names would not have been lost on Ronsard's readers. Similarly, the use of expressions drawn from popular literature sets the tone: Jaquet

        a veu,
Guignant par le travers du feu,
De sa Robine recourssée
La grosse motte retroussée,
Et son petit cas barbelu
D'un or jaunement crespelu,
Dont le fond sembloit une rose
Non encor' à demy déclose. (vv. 59–66)

Those who remembered their Villon or the 'blasons anatomiques' would feel immediately at home with both the style and the sentiments of this 'folastrie'. Unlike the haughty Cassandre or any other fashionably Petrarchan lady, Robine invites Jaquet to put 'le grand pau que je voy / Dedans le rond de ma fossette' (vv. 82–83). The poem ends with 'le bon Jaquet qui l'embroche' (another metaphor familiar to readers of the *contes* and Coquillart) in a bucolic setting which owes something to Virgil and even more to those who were still popular with the public and who still had a lot to teach the young poets of the early 1550s, who were now bent on forgetting the art of 'pétrarchizer' and wished to relearn the art of speaking of love 'franchement', in other words, freely, frankly, and 'Frenchly'.[16] The conclusion is a *faux-naïf* praise of the joys of requited love:

> O Robine bien fortunée
> De s'estre au bon Jaquet donnée,
> O bon Jaquet bien fortuné
> De s'estre à Robine donné,
> O doucelettes amourettes,
> O amoureuses doucelettes. (vv. 103–08)

In Ronsard's third 'folastrie', however, the tone is much harsher. It charts in 174 quite scabrous verses the decline and fall of Catin, a young and blissfully amoral young woman who once joyfully offered her 'rougnons paillars' to all:

>   à gauche & à dextre,
> Jamais ny à Clerc ny à Prestre,
> Moine, Chanoine, ou Cordelier
> N'a refusé son hatelier. (vv. 4–8)

So delightfully naïve was she that

>   autant le pauvre luy plaisoit
> Comme le riche, & ne faisoit
> Le soubresaut pour l'avarice,
> Mais ell'disoit que c'estoit vice
> De prendre ou cheine, ou diamant,
> De pauvre, ny de riche amant,
> Pourveu qu'il servist bien en chambre
> Et qu'il eust plus d'un pié de membre.
> Autant le beau, comme le laid,
> Et le maistre, que le valet,
> Estoient receus de la doucette
> A la luitte de la fossette. (vv. 19–30)

---

[16] In 1553 also, du Bellay attacked his previous attachment to the high-flown Petrarchist manner of writing about love in his poem 'Contre les Pétrarquistes': 'J'ay oublié l'art de pétrarquizer / Je veulx d'Amour franchement deviser.' See Joachim du Bellay, *Divers Jeux Rustiques*, ed. V. L. Saulnier (Geneva: Droz, 1965), p. 70.

Sadly, and inevitably, old age creeps up on the carefree Catin, who turns to religion, or at least to hypocrisy. This is a scenario which readers of Villon and Coquillart knew well. The 'Belle Heaulmière' springs to mind. Like her, this 'insensée' takes to preaching, and to issuing awful warnings. 'Amour affolle le plus sage', she says ('Folles amours font les gens bestes' according to Villon)[17] in a long litany of complaint which ends with the thought that 'toujours d'aymer on se repent.' The worst of it is that she has managed, by means of 'mille bigotations', to convert Ronsard's sweetheart to her joyless philosophy. She succeeds in persuading her to avoid 'les banquetz, & les dances', to eschew jewellery and pretty clothes. So much so that,

> quand baiser je la veux,
> Elle me tire les cheveux:
> Si je veux tater sa cuissette,
> Ou fesser sa fesse grossette,
> Ou si je mez la main dedans
> Ses tetins, elle à coups de dens
> Me dechire tout le visage,
> Comme un singe émeu contre un page. (vv. 125–32)

The remainder of the poem consists of bitter recrimination. Ronsard describes the young woman's new-found prudishness and his own sexual frustration, and ends with a diatribe against Catin, the cause of his woes:

> Qu'à cent diables soit la prestresse
> Qui a bigotté ma maistresse. (vv. 155–56)

The picture that emerges from the *Livret de Folastries* is that of a poet who is not insensitive to the manner in which French poets of previous generations dealt with themes which they perhaps shared with the authors of Antiquity. It may well be that he viewed them rather in the way Virgil did Ennius. But he clearly read them none the less and learned from them. In a typically challenging article, David Mus reminds us of the links that existed between the writers of the fifteenth century and those who came to literature a century later.[18] Critics have

---

[17] François Villon, *Le Testament Villon*, eds. Jean Rychner and Albert Henry, 2 vol. (Geneva: Droz, 1974), I, v. 628.

[18] David Mus, 'François Villon: le drame du texte', in Michael Freeman and Jane H. M. Taylor (eds), *Villon at Oxford. The Drama of the Text* (Amsterdam: Rodopi, 1999), pp. 1–34.

understandably tracked down (in many ways encouraged to do so by the authors themselves, it must be said) classical references in the works of sixteenth-century writers. This has inevitably been the case with Ronsard and his *Livret de Folastries*. David Dorais ably shows how in this collection Ronsard moves away from Petrarchist idealisation towards a more down-to-earth expression of sexual desire.[19] Sophistication – and a consciously artificial style – is thus replaced by the search for an 'authentic' note. However, it is still principally Catullus who is credited by Dorais with being responsible for this change of tack:

> Ainsi, ce que Ronsard a transmis aux poètes 'païens' qui l'ont suivi, c'est un ton poétique – et non un modèle – plus libre, plus franc, lui-même inspiré de la poésie latine et néo-latine et incorporant des éléments des *realia* de l'époque.[20]

For Catharine Randall, the *Livret de Folastries* represented for Ronsard a chance to break free: 'a private, playful space in which to express interests, and to explore themes, at variance with official speech', seeing 'a fascinating tension between public and private poetic personae'. In this version of events, the veneer of Petrarchism cracks to reveal briefly (but significantly) a poet yearning to give voice to his 'frivolous, erotic sensibility'.[21] But there is no mention of where he might have looked to find inspiration for this bawdy work. There is some discussion of classical allusions but no reference to the 'gaulois' tradition. It is as if the poems appeared *ex nihilo* from Ronsard's fevered imagination. In a more substantial piece, Lance K. Donaldson-Evans analyses 'Ronsard's most anti-Petrarchan text' but, while noting in the fourth *folastrie* 'the

---

[19] See David Dorais, '"Les Païens de la Pléiade": l'érotisme dans les *Folastries* de Ronsard et dans les *Gayetez* d'Olivier de Magny', *Renaissance and Reformation/ Renaissance et Réforme*, 23 (1999), 65–79: 'Tout différent de l'adoration pétrarquiste qui se voulait idéalisée et contemplative, l'amour exprimé dans les *Folastries* s'apparente plutôt à un désir charnel criant' (p. 66).

[20] *Ibid.*, pp. 76–77. Curiously, while recognising the role of the *realia* which help to create the 'effet de réel' in the *Folastries*, Dorais does not pursue his insight into the fact that, of all the poets of his group, Ronsard 'est celui qui est allé le plus loin dans l'expression de la gauloiserie' (p. 77). Reality was all around, as were copies of those French authors of yester-year who had spoken of love 'franchement'. For Dorais, Ronsard's sources were 'la poésie latine hendécasyllabique inspirée de Catulle' (p. 68).

[21] Catharine Randall, 'Poetic license, censorship and the unrestrained self: Ronsard's *Livret de folastries*', *Papers in French Seventeenth-Century Literature*, 23 (1996), 449–62 (p. 450).

direct sensuality of the *gauloise* tradition, in contradistinction to the refinement and sublimated desire of Petrarch', does not dwell on the point. Ronsard's poetic heroes are evidently 'Catullus, Tibullus and Marullus'. In his conclusion, he stresses that

> whether the style of the individual poems in this collection be high or low, each marks its distance from the Petrarchan tradition. By their suppression of the Petrarchan intertext, the *Folastries* express Ronsard's fundamental rebellion both against the title 'French Petrarch' which was bestowed upon him, and against the tyranny of the Petrarchan mode in general. Boldly proclaiming the pre-eminence of Greek and Latin poetry as the appropriate models for the rejuvenation of French poetry, the *Folastries* may well be Ronsard's most subversive collection, calling into question the prevailing poetic practice of his contemporaries.[22]

It is a moot point, perhaps, and one which forces an apparently light-weight volume to carry a heavy burden on its slim shoulders. The implied message is, nevertheless, clear. The road to the future, even in the realm of erotica, involved a diversion via the ancient world.

Knowledge of classical culture has long been seen as the demarcation line between the Old World and the New, between the Middle Ages and the Renaissance. It was frequently felt in any case to be more rewarding to discover influences drawn from an author's reading of ancient texts than to plumb the depths of the submerged continent of popular culture: a culture which often appeared trivial and of limited interest, to boot. *Enfin Bakhtine vint*, of course, with his reappraisal of Rabelais, but that is another story, and it was always conceded that Rabelais was a case apart. What Mus usefully points out is that 'les poètes de la Pléiade, aussi, malgré leur parti pris et leur recherche stylistique, malgré l'apprentissage du grec et la pratique assidue des auteurs latins, parlaient, quand ils ne l'écrivaient plus, la langue de Villon'.[23]

A continuity, therefore, at the level of everyday communication and discourse which is not always immediately obvious to modern-day scholars. Comparing Villon and du Bellay, Mus rightly states that 'malgré les bouleversements survenus entre la composition du *Testament* en 1461 et la mort de Du Bellay en 1560, malgré l'évolution des mœurs et de la langue, les deux poètes sont de la même époque

---

[22] Lance K. Donaldson-Evans, 'Ronsard's *Folies Bergères*: the *Livret des Folastries* [sic] and Petrarch', *Neophilologus*, 91 (2007), 1–17. The above quotations are from pp. 2, 10, and 16.

[23] Mus, 'François Villon: le drame du texte', p. 12.

linguistique et de la même aire culturelle, le moyen français de l'Ile de France.'[24] This continuity was not restricted to language. Nor was it just a question of 'l'héritage oral'. It stretches credulity to believe that young poets of the generation of 1550 had not read the works of their predecessors, most of whom were still in print at that time. The author of *L'Eugène*, for example, would have read (and no doubt seen) farces. The author of the *Livret de Folastries* had read his Coquillart. What they read, of course, was not pale imitations of classical texts but lively, irreverent pieces meant often to move but above all to amuse, or both at once. It is what Mus calls 'l'esprit burlesque', close to what is still part of the French tradition, namely 'l'esprit gaulois': 'le style burlesque atteint son apogée avec Villon, Pathelin, Coquillart; mais il ne meurt pas avec eux, il reste bien vivant jusqu'aux œuvres de Mathurin Régnier, de Scarron et [...] jusqu'à Marivaux.'[25] This 'esprit burlesque' relied upon puns, innuendo, recourse to popular maxims and expressions. One late sixteenth-century author, Estienne Tabourot, himself steeped in that tradition, called it 'l'esprit lascif' in the 'folastre livre' he published in 1588, *Les Bigarrures*. The flame of scurrilous vulgarity had not been entirely extinguished. As we have seen, Ronsard had not been above writing in this vein.[26] It is what the author of the *Livret de Folastries* would have appreciated in the deliberately frivolous works of Guillaume Coquillart. Claude Binet was probably right: Ronsard had read and enjoyed as a young man 'les œuvres de Coquillart', and was happy to say so. Whether, as a poet of the Renaissance, he would have identified Guillaume Coquillart as a typical product of the as yet undiscovered Late Middle Ages is open to question.

[24] *Ibid.*, p. 17.

[25] *Ibid.*, p. 10.

[26] In his splendidly idiosyncratic *Le Ton Beau de Marot: In Praise of the Music of Language* (New York: Basic Books,1997), Douglas R. Hofstadter, an unconditional admirer of Villon and Marot, rebukes the Pléiade poets for being 'an aristocratic bunch' who 'recoiled from gutteral [sic] language' (p. 184). I hope to have shown at least that this was not the case.

9

Printing and metrical naturalisation: Jean Molinet's *Neuf Preux de Gourmandise*

Adrian Armstrong

> De la musique avant toute chose,
> Et pour cela préfère l'Impair
> Plus vague et plus soluble dans l'air,
> Sans rien en lui qui pèse ou qui pose.[1]

The notion famously expressed by Verlaine, that imparisyllabic lines in French verse have a tantalising instability, is not at all peculiar to the late nineteenth century. In what follows I demonstrate that the metrical theory and practice of late medieval France evince the same attitude, an attitude exemplified in the reception of a light-hearted poem, *Les Neuf Preux de Gourmandise*. This is one of the lesser-known works of Jean Molinet (1435–1507), a prolific poet and chronicler who spent most of his career in the service of the Valois Dukes of Burgundy and their Hapsburg successors. Most of Molinet's output concerns matters of serious import: he produced a substantial chronicle, a moralised prose version of the *Roman de la Rose*, a manual of versification, at least one theatrical piece, and a large body of moral, occasional, and devotional poetry.[2] However, there is also a ludic, carnivalesque, and bawdy strain in Molinet's verse, a strain that the *Neuf Preux* combines with a more familiar didacticism.[3] Composed in heptasyllabic *huitains* rhyming

---

[1] Paul Verlaine, 'Art poétique', in Paul Verlaine, *Œuvres poétiques*, ed. Jacques Robichez (Paris: Garnier, 1986), pp. 261–62 (vv. 1–4).

[2] Jean Devaux, *Jean Molinet, Indiciaire bourguignon* (Paris: Champion, 1996), provides a thorough general account of Molinet's career and, in particular, his ideological stance.

[3] On Molinet's bawdy verse, see Leonard W. Johnson, *Poets as Players: Theme and Variation in Late Medieval French Poetry* (Stanford: Stanford University Press, 1990), pp.

abaabbcc, the *Neuf Preux* constructs a pantheon of Old Testament figures who were brought low by drunkenness.[4] A stanza is devoted to each figure, while an introductory quatrain outlines the overall theme:

> La Bible fait mention
> De l'extreme vaillantise
> Que noef preux de gourmandise
> Firent par potation. (vv. 1–4)

The *Neuf Preux* is transmitted in various manuscript and printed witnesses from the early sixteenth century, most of which are substantial anthologies dominated by Molinet's work.[5] Five printed witnesses, however, are much more modest and, from a literary-sociological viewpoint, much more interesting. Each is an anonymous pamphlet, in which the *Neuf Preux* follows a brief satirical poem entitled *La Loyaulté des femmes*, and is in turn followed by one or more short pieces on light or amatory subjects.[6] Most significantly in these editions, the hepta-

---

231–87.

[4] Jean Molinet, *Les Faictz et dictz de Jean Molinet*, ed. Noël Dupire, 3 vol. (Paris: Société des Anciens Textes Français, 1936–39), II (1937), pp. 536–39. Further references are to this edition unless otherwise stated, and are provided. On the commonplace of the Nine Worthies, see Horst Schroeder, *Der Topos der 'Nine Worthies' in Literatur und bildender Kunst* (Göttingen: Vandenhoeck & Ruprecht, 1971).

[5] These anthologies are:

Tournai, Bibliothèque communale, MS 105 (destroyed in 1940), fols 155^r–56^v.

Arras, Bibliothèque municipale, MS 619, fol. 4^v.

Paris, Bibliothèque nationale de France, MS Rothschild 471, fol. 28^v.

Cambridge, Gonville and Caius College, MS 187:220, p. 274–fol. 121^r.

Jean Molinet, *Les Faictz et dictz de feu de bonne memoire Maistre Jehan Molinet* (Paris: Jean Longis and the widow of Jean Saint-Denis, 1531), fols P2^v–P3^r.

Jean Molinet, *Les Faictz et dictz* (Paris: Jean Longis and others, 1537), fols T7^v–V1^r.

Jean Molinet, *Les Faictz et dictz* (Paris: Alain Lotrian and others, 1540), fols x7^r–x8^v.

[6] These editions have very similar titles, and reliable information on their dates and places of publication is lacking. Accordingly, they are best distinguished through reference to the surviving copies:

La Loyaulté des femmes, avec les neuf preux de gourmandise et une recepte pour guarir les yvrongnes (n.d.o.p.), Paris, BnF, Rothschild 573.

La Loyaulté des femmes, avec les neuf preux de gourmandise et une recepte pour guerir les yvrongnes (n.d.o.p.), Paris, BnF, Rothschild 574.

La Leaulté des femmes, avec les neuf preux de gourmandise et une recepte pour guerir les yvrongnes (n.d.o.p.), Paris, BnF, Rés. Ye 2981.

La Leaulté des femmes, avec les neuf preux de gourmandise et aussi une bonne recepte pour guerir les yvrongnes (n.d.o.p.), Paris, BnF, Rés. Ye 4288.

La Loyaulté des femmes, avec les neuf preux de gourmandie et balades d'amours (n.d.o.p.); Paris, BnF, Rés. Ye 1203.

syllabic lines of the *Neuf Preux* are converted into octosyllables.[7] This chapter examines, firstly, the implications of this change in versification for the poem's reception, and secondly, the techniques by which the heptasyllables are extended and their effects upon sense, syntax, and rhythm. It thereby contributes to the understanding not only of the fortunes of Molinet's poetry, but also of non-scholarly editorial practices in the early decades of French printing.

The octosyllable is clearly much more common than the heptasyllable in late medieval verse: Henri Chatelain established a century ago that octosyllables were the most widely used line in all verse texts of the late fourteenth and fifteenth centuries.[8] So ubiquitous was this line in courtly poetry that, as Daniel Poirion observes, it 'a dû former l'oreille des poètes'.[9] While the most commonly used line of under eight syllables, the heptasyllable is only sparingly mentioned in the *arts de seconde rhétorique*, the manuals of versification which testify to prevailing conceptions of form in late medieval France. Isometric stanzas of heptasyllables are rarely adduced as examples in the important *arts* by Molinet and Pierre Fabri, and never in the found-ational text of the genre, Eustache Deschamps's *L'Art de Dictier* (1392), nor in the *art* transmitted in the important printed verse anthology *Le Jardin de plaisance et fleur de rethorique*.[10] Even in Molinet's poetic

---

For the Rothschild copies, see Emile Picot, *Catalogue des livres composant la bibliothèque de feu M. le baron James de Rothschild*, 5 vol. (Paris: Morgand, 1884–1920), I (1884), pp. 384–85; Picot dates both editions to *c.* 1530. BnF Rés. Ye 4288 is the base text for *Recueil de poésies françoises des XVe et XVIe siècles*, ed. Anatole de Montaiglon, 13 vol. (Paris: Jannet, 1855–78), II (1855), pp. 35–41; the *Neuf Preux* appears on pp. 38–41, without line numbering.

[7] The various octosyllabic texts are very similar, and may be regarded as a distinct branch of the textual tradition, though the filiation between them is unclear; they are thus considered as a single version. References to the octosyllabic *Neuf Preux* are to Montaiglon's edition, and appear within the text.

[8] Henri Chatelain, *Recherches sur le vers français au XVe siècle: rimes, mètres et strophes* (Paris: Champion, 1907), p. 234.

[9] Daniel Poirion, *Le Poète et le prince: l'évolution du lyrisme courtois de Guillaume de Machaut à Charles d'Orléans* (Grenoble: Université de Grenoble, Faculté des Lettres et Sciences humaines, 1965), p. 449.

[10] Jean Molinet, *L'Art de Rhétorique*, in *Recueil d'arts de seconde rhétorique*, ed. Ernest Langlois (Paris: Imprimerie Nationale, 1902), pp. 214–52 (for examples, see pp. 218–19, 225, 234–35); Pierre Fabri, *Le Grand et vrai art de pleine rhétorique*, ed. A. Héron, 3 vol. (Rouen: Société des Bibliophiles Normands, 1889–90), II (1889), pp. 59–61, 95–96; *Le Jardin de plaisance et fleur de rethorique: reproduction en fac-similé de l'édition publiée par Antoine Vérard vers 1501*, eds Eugénie Droz and Arthur Piaget, 2 vol. (Paris: Firmin-

output, which displays an outstanding formal variety, the heptasyllable is relatively unusual in isometric stanzas: indeed, the *Neuf Preux* is his only vernacular composition to consist entirely of heptasyllables.[11]

Less common and less prestigious than the octosyllable and decasyllable, the metre of the *Neuf Preux* also produces distinctive effects, and is apt to be used in specific types of poetry. Poirion notes that the heptasyllable resists smooth recitation, describing it in distinctly Verlainean terms as 'un vers qui ne permet pas de s'abandonner au "ronron" de la lecture courante.'[12] Perhaps because of this recalcitrant quality, the metre is used for satirical purposes by Deschamps and, with particular humorous effect, by Charles d'Orléans.[13] In Molinet's work, heptasyllables are of especial importance in his *fatras*, short fixed-form pieces which almost exclusively form part of longer texts, and which entail the ingenious, light, and sometimes bawdy treatment of an introductory distich.[14] But the most striking use of heptasyllables occurs much earlier in the fifteenth century, in the work of Christine de Pizan. The first narrative section of her *Chemin de longue étude* (1403) recounts in heptasyllabic couplets the grief of the first-person narrator Christine at her husband's death, and the consolation she draws from Boethius's *Consolation of Philosophy* (vv. 61–252).[15] Then, as Christine summarises the *Consolation*, the couplets shift almost imperceptibly to octosyllables, the metre used almost exclusively for the rest of the *Chemin*. The heptasyllables seem to connote a situation of intolerable loss, and to disappear once that loss is made bearable by the lessons of Boethius. Christine again connects heptasyllables with wrongness in her later *Livre du Duc des vrais amans* (1403–5), the story of a love relationship told in the voice of the

---

Didot, 1910–25), I (1910), fols a2ᵛ–c3ʳ; Eustache Deschamps, *L'Art de Dictier*, ed. and trans. Deboarh M. Sinnreich-Levi (East Lansing: Colleagues Press, 1994). On the relative frequency of different line lengths in this period, see Chatelain, *Recherches*, pp. 236–37.

[11] Noël Dupire, *Jean Molinet: la vie – les œuvres* (Paris: Droz, 1932), pp. 338–50, notes the other occurrences of isometric heptasyllabic stanzas in Molinet's work. By contrast, the heptasyllable is quite common in heterometric stanzas: Dupire, *Jean Molinet*, pp. 336–37.

[12] Poirion, *Le Poète et le prince*, p. 450.

[13] *Ibid.*, p. 451.

[14] See Gérard Gros, 'Les Fatras de Jean Molinet', in Jean-Charles Herbin (ed.), *Image et mémoire du Hainaut médiéval* (Valenciennes: Presses Universitaires de Valenciennes, 2004), pp. 99–111.

[15] References are to Christine de Pizan, *Le Chemin de longue étude*, ed. Andrea Tarnowski (Paris: Librairie Générale Française, 2000).

eponymous Duke. Heptasyllabic couplets are the *Duc*'s standard narrative metre, but the *Duc* is far from a standard love story. It sharply critiques courtly love and its destructive social effects: the Duke is a distinctly unreliable narrator, whose empty values are laid bare by a weighty prose letter that his lady receives from her former governess.[16] A generation after Christine and a generation before Molinet, two major poets use heptasyllables in ways that are less obviously value-laden but subtly significant. Chartier's *Livre de l'Esperance* (1428–30) is an unfinished *prosimetrum* allegory, in which a first-person narrator is saved from despair and enlightened by the theological virtues. Heptasyllables appear in many of the *Esperance*'s verse sections, which have often been described as evoking spiritual rebirth and divinely sanctioned order, not only in thematic terms but also in respect of their stanzaic forms.[17] But the metres and rhyme schemes of these sections are formally quite different from those commonly found in lyric and narrative verse of the period; what is important for spiritually uplifting poetry, it seems, is precisely that it should *not* partake of familiar verse structures. Chartier's heptasyllables, then, signify through the very distance that separates them from the *ballade*, the *rondeau*, the octosyllabic *huitain*. Michault Taillevent's *Régime de Fortune* (c. 1445), by contrast, depends on such forms. In seven *ballades*, followed by a *rondeau* and three closing quatrains, it outlines the dangers that Fortune presents to humanity, and recommends constancy and

[16] Christine de Pizan, *Le Livre du Duc des vrais amans*, ed. Thelma S. Fenster (Binghamton, NY: Medieval and Renaissance Texts and Studies, 1995). On the *Duc*'s status as critique, see Roberta L. Krueger, *Women Readers and the Ideology of Gender in Old French Verse Romance* (Cambridge: Cambridge University Press, 1993), pp. 217–46; Douglas Kelly, *Christine de Pizan's Changing Opinion: A Quest for Certainty in the Midst of Chaos* (Cambridge: D. S. Brewer, 2007), pp. 129–38; Allison Kelly, 'Christine de Pizan and Antoine de la Sale: the dangers of love in theory and fiction', in Earl Jeffrey Richards, with Joan Williamson, Nadia Margolis, and Christine Reno (eds), *Reinterpreting Christine de Pizan* (Athens/London: The University of Georgia Press, 1992), pp. 173–86 (p. 176); Judith Laird and Earl Jeffrey Richards, '*Tous parlent par une mesmes bouche*: lyrical outbursts, prosaic remedies, and voice in Christine de Pizan's *Livre du Duc des vrais amans*', in Earl Jeffrey Richards (ed.), *Christine de Pizan and Medieval French Lyric* (Gainesville: University Press of Florida, 1998), pp. 103–31.

[17] See Virginie Minet-Mahy, *Esthétique et pouvoir de l'œuvre allégorique à l'époque de Charles VI: imaginaires et discours* (Paris: Champion, 2005), pp. 507–08; Sylvia Huot, 'Refashioning Boethius: prose and poetry in Chartier's *Livre de l'Esperance*', *Medium Ævum*, 76 (2007), 268–84; François Rouy, *L'Esthétique du traité moral d'après les œuvres d'Alain Chartier* (Geneva: Droz, 1980), pp. 337–49.

detachment as antidotes.[18] The central six *ballades* are decasyllabic, but heptasyllables are employed for the introductory *ballade*, which explains the *Regime*'s content and justifies its relative brevity, and for the final *rondeau* and quatrains, which exhort readers to reflect upon the preceding lessons and identify Taillevent as the author. In other words, Taillevent's metrical variation establishes a formal distinction between his metadiscursive frame and his practical moral lessons. Teachings are underpinned by the gravity of the decasyllable, while the secondary status of the surrounding material – we might think of it as versified paratext – is reflected in its lighter and less prestigious metre.

Heptasyllables are thus associated in late medieval French poetics with a range of overlapping qualities: lack, subservience, disruption, instability, novelty, levity. It is doubtless symptomatic that they appear relatively frequently in heterometric stanzas, which Fabri among others regarded as the appropriate form for conveying emotional disorder:

> en lay l'en ne traicte que matieres de grande ioye ou de excessiue douleur,
> et, quasi, comme en furie, les lignes sont ou courtes ou longues, a la
> volunté du facteur.[19]

Taillevent's poetry is a case in point: not only do heptasyllables appear more frequently in heterometric than in isometric stanzas, but they appear in *all* his heterometric stanzas.[20] Hence, in various ways, the heptasyllable is a suitable line for the *Neuf Preux*. Its humorous, satirical connotations befit Molinet's construction of a semi-parodic set of Worthies, which places biblical figures in an unexpected context. Equally, its disruptive quality aptly conveys the poem's juxtaposition of high and low, sacred history and profane excess, comedy and didacticism. The metre's characteristic instability even serves a mimetic function, its challenge to recitation and its irregular rhythm (of which more below) making language reel and lurch drunkenly. Molinet's heptasyllable, then, appeals to an audience familiar with contemporary

---

[18] Robert Deschaux, *Un poète bourguignon du XVe siècle: Michault Taillevent (Édition et Étude)* (Geneva: Droz, 1975), pp. 230–40 (text), 323–26 (analysis).

[19] Fabri, *Grand et vrai art*, II, p. 51.

[20] See Deschaux, *Un poète bourguignon*, pp. 305–07. Besides the *Regime*, Taillevent's only use of heptasyllables in isometric stanzas is in a stanza of his 1446 poem *Lai sur la mort de Catherine de France* (*ibid.*, pp. 242–50). All eleven of the *Lai*'s other stanzas are heterometric and include heptasyllables. Given the affective intensity of this lament – of which half the stanzas begin with an exclamation, 'Ha' or 'Helas' – the heptasyllable's prominence testifies to its thematic valency.

poetic conventions, who can recognise the line's cultural associations and bring them into meaningful relationships with the poem's content. These relationships reveal, most importantly, that the *Neuf Preux* is not solely a didactic poem warning about the dangers of intoxication; its formal lightness, its avoidance of the monumentality of more common metres, suggest that it is also an exercise in ingenuity, whose meaning lies partly in the witty recontextualisation of biblical characters.[21]

Similar effects are produced by the technique of *epiphonema*, the use of proverbs to close stanzas, evident in all but the first of the poem's *huitains*:[22]

> Je suis le fier Oloferne,
> Qui assiegay Bethulie;
> Judich, de beaulté lucerne,
> Que mon oeul regarde et cerne,
> Me vaincquit par ma follie;
> Moy dormant, le panche emplye,
> Me trencha du corps la teste:
> Fort vin esmoeult grand tempeste. (vv. 53–60)

The combination of biblical episodes and collective proverbial wisdom is incongruous: the latter does not quite gloss the former as we might expect. But *epiphonema* also has a significant association with the heptasyllable elsewhere in Molinet's work. In his *Art de Rhétorique*, Molinet notes that many poems use heptasyllabic *septains* 'dont la derraine ligne chiét en commun proverbe', and supplies a stanza from what appears to be a serious didactic piece as an example. His own early political allegory, *Le Trosne d'Honneur*, closes with three stanzas of the same form, two of which use *epiphonema*.[23] These stanzas, however, are *septains* rhyming abaabbcc; those of the *Neuf Preux* are *huitains*, using a rhyme scheme pioneered by George Chastelain and widely used by

---

[21] Jean-Claude Mühlethaler, 'Le Vin entre morale et carnaval: Jean Molinet et François Villon', in Karin Becker and Olivier Leplatre (eds), *Écritures du repas: fragments d'un discours gastronomique* (Frankfurt: Peter Lang, 2007), pp. 51–74, shows that the *Neuf Preux* does not lend itself to univocal reading in either serious or comic terms. On the portrayal of drink in this and other poems by Molinet, see also Adrian Armstrong, 'Boire chez (et avec) Molinet', in Jean Devaux, Estelle Doudet and Elodie Lecuppre-Desjardin (eds), *Jean Molinet et son temps* (Turnhout: Brepols; forthcoming).

[22] On this technique in the work of Molinet and his contemporaries, see Paul Zumthor, 'L'Épiphonème proverbial', *Revue des Sciences Humaines*, 41 (1976), 313–28.

[23] Molinet, *L'Art de Rhétorique*, pp 218–19 (p. 218); *Le Trosne d'Honneur*, in Molinet, *Les Faictz et dictz*, ed. Dupire, I, pp. 36–58 (pp. 57–58).

Molinet himself, in both octosyllabic and decasyllabic versions, largely in serious political and didactic pieces.[24] Consequently, the *Neuf Preux* seems to truncate a stanzaic form typical of Molinet's work: once again, the heptasyllable reveals to a well-informed audience that familiar structures are being disrupted.[25]

The *Loyaulté des femmes* editions, however, are clearly not destined for a public well versed in courtly poetic practice. Octavo volumes comprising four leaves, occasionally adorned by re-used woodcuts, devoid of publication details and transmitting inaccurate texts, they bear all the hallmarks of cheap, ephemeral publications.[26] All the material evidence suggests that these editions' target audiences, and quite possibly their publishers, were untrained in the finer points of versification. And herein seems to lie an explanation for the change in the *Neuf Preux*'s versification: as cheap editions made Molinet's poem accessible to non-expert readers, the unfamiliar heptasyllables have been converted to a much more common metre so as to be more comprehensible. The literary expectations of a presumably wide, urban audience are not sufficiently developed to encompass the general thematic associations of the heptasyllable, let alone its subtle implications in the context of Molinet's own work: none of the *Loyaulté* editions names the author of the *Neuf Preux*, and it is unlikely that readers could easily have guessed his identity. Octosyllables, by contrast, have such a dominant presence in late medieval poetry that even relatively unskilled readers of verse would be able to negotiate them without difficulty. Readers of this kind might be presumed to have an awareness of a few basic poetic forms, but of little if anything beyond these: they may well have regarded a heptasyllable as a hypometric octosyllable.[27]

This is a prime example of the process which literary theoreticians have sometimes termed 'naturalisation', by which the thematic or formal strangeness of literary discourse is made familiar to its readers. Jonathan Culler, in an important study of naturalisation and its

---

[24] See Chatelain, *Recherches*, pp. 101–02; Dupire, *Jean Molinet*, pp. 340–42.

[25] Chatelain, *Recherches*, p. 101 identifies no precedents for heptasyllabic *huitains* rhyming abaabbcc, confirming the incongruity of the form.

[26] The woodcuts on the title-pages of the Rothschild copies are cracked, indicating that they have probably been re-used from existing stock: see Picot, *Catalogue*, I, pp. 384–85.

[27] I am indebted for this insight to a remark by Denis Hüe at the conference 'Poetry, Knowledge and Community in Late Medieval France', Princeton University, 1–4 November 2006.

workings, neatly encapsulates both its epistemological and its ideological stakes. On the one hand, texts must be made assimilable to readers' knowledge for any kind of meaningful interpretation to take place: 'The strange, the formal, the fictional, must be recuperated or naturalized, brought within our ken, if we do not want to remain gaping before monumental inscriptions.'[28] On the other, this assimilation relies upon existing cultural models, such as genres, which are so well-known as to appear natural, and which consequently minimise the threat which the assimilated text poses to established ways of perceiving: 'to naturalize a text is to bring it into relation with a type of discourse or model which is already, in some sense [e.g. by generic convention], natural and legible.'[29] In the case of the *Neuf Preux*, octosyllabic *huitains* are more legible, because more widespread, than heptasyllabic ones: the version in the *Loyaulté* editions has been recuperated for non-expert readers by having a more 'natural' form imposed upon it.

But the octosyllable does much more than ensure the poem's legibility. The loss of the heptasyllable's disruptive, unstable associations promotes a distinctly different reading, in which the elements of wit and levity in Molinet's pantheon are less immediately apparent. Not that the metrical change converts the *Neuf Preux* into a straightforwardly didactic piece; far from it. The *epiphonema* still contrasts comically with the biblical episodes, while the *Loyaulté des femmes*, which begins each eponymous edition and hence sets its tone, anaphorically accumulates absurd images to endow a misogynist commonplace with humorous verve:

> Quant les regnars seront sans espier,
> Quant les chiens aux loups trève feront,
> Quant les prescheurs n'aymeront dan denier,
> Quant les Normans de vin cure n'auront,
> Quant les buvrages demourront entonnez
> Sans que de riens soient advironnez … ;
> Lors verrez-vous en femme loyaulté. (ed. Montaiglon, pp. 36–37)

Nevertheless, the octosyllable lacks the clear tonal value of the line it replaces, and in this sense makes a straight-faced moral reading of Molinet's poem more likely. At the same time, it transforms the stanzas into a *carré* form (8 syllables x 8 lines), a structure widely regarded as

---

[28] Jonathan Culler, *Structuralist Poetics: Structuralism, Linguistics and the Study of Literature* (London: Routledge & Kegan Paul, 1975), pp. 131–60 (p. 134).

[29] *Ibid.*, p. 138.

more accomplished and aesthetically pleasing than those in which the number of syllables per line differed from the number of lines per stanza.[30] While less distinctive than its heptasyllabic source, the octosyllabic *huitain* is thus more prestigious according to broad contemporary canons of literary taste; moreover, in the form abaabbcc, it enjoys a high standing in the work of Chastelain and Molinet, as previously noted. Readers aware of these formal valencies – however dimly – may be more likely to subject the *Neuf Preux* to a serious reading.[31]

While the change in line length has permitted various connotative shifts to be identified, what cannot be evaluated on this basis alone is the difference in rhythm between the heptasyllabic and the octosyllabic versions, the extent to which the mimetic irregularity of the former has been conserved or attenuated in the latter. Consideration of this issue must be based upon detailed study of the linguistic means by which octosyllables have been produced, study which will also permit a suitably precise assessment of the changes' semantic and syntactic effects. The following table indicates, with reference to the seventy-one lines common to both versions and in descending order of frequency, the variants which produce additional syllables in the *Loyaulté* editions:[32]

[30] See, for example, the guidelines for composing stanzas of *ballades* in *Recueil d'arts de seconde rhétorique*, ed. Langlois, pp. 294–95.

[31] Unambiguously serious readings are also evident in two prose translations of Molinet's poem, printed in the early sixteenth century. Only one of these survives, an English text entitled *A lytyll newe treatyse or mater intytuled and called the ix. drunkardes* (London: Robert Bankes, 1523), which according to its colophon was translated from Dutch. Bibliographical and philological evidence suggests that Bankes's source was published by the Antwerp printer Jan van Doesborch. The English text, and presumably its Dutch source, amplify Molinet's accounts considerably, notably by quoting heavily from the Old Testament, and present the 'drunkardes' in heavily moralising terms. It is impossible to establish whether Van Doesborch's text was based on the heptasyllabic or the octosyllabic version of the *Neuf Preux*. See Peter J. A. Franssen, *Tussen tekst en publiek: Jan van Doesborch, drukker-uitgever en literator te Antwerpen en Utrecht in de eerste helft van de zestiende eeuw* (Amsterdam: Rodopi, 1990), pp. 40, 66, 113–16.

[32] Molinet's introductory quatrain, and v. 24, are absent from the octosyllabic version. The *Loyaulté* editions exhibit some textual variation: v. 70, for instance, is heptasyllabic in Montaiglon's edition ('Champion du roy divin', 36) but octosyllabic in BnF Rés. Ye 1203 ('Champion du hault roy divin', fol. A3ᵛ). To facilitate clear analysis, the text edited by Montaiglon is taken as the point of reference.

Table 1: Linguistic techniques producing octosyllables

Change	*Total lines*	*Numbers of affected lines*
No change (i.e. hypometric line)[33]	16	6, 10, 21, 22, 28, 32, 53–60, 63, 70
Addition of subject pronoun[34]	9	8, 12, 23, 29, 37, 41, 43, 45, 61
Addition of co-ordinating conjunction *si*	7	20, 26, 36, 47, 48, 67, 76
Addition of article[35]	6	7, 31, 35, 44, 49, 74
*Addition of *tout* (noun, adjective, or adverb)	5	15, 25, 30, 33, 75
Use of longer equivalent word or phrase	4	11, 40, 68, 72
*Introduction of new verb[36]	4	13, 14, 50, 69
Addition of temporal adverb[37]	2	18, 39
Addition of *en* (pronoun or preposition)	2	19, 64
*Change of adverbial expression[38]	2	27, 65

[33] A minority of the lines in question may be read as octosyllabic if diæresis is presumed (e.g. v. 54, 'Qui ass*ie*gay Bethulie'). These have not been considered separately, the important issue being that Molinet's language has not been changed. Among the unchanged lines is a complete stanza, that on Holofernes cited above.

[34] To the lines in this category may be added v. 69, which converts 'Moy, Simon Machabeüs' to 'Je suis Scymon Machabeus' (ed. Montaiglon, p. 41). The pronoun in this case is consequent upon the introduction of a finite verb.

[35] This category includes the introduction of partitive (vv. 7, 31), definite (vv. 44, 49, 74), and indefinite (v. 35) articles.

[36] The changes in vv. 13 and 14 are related, and appear to result from a misreading of a proper name in Molinet's text:

> Je Codorlahomor tins
> Cinq grands roix en mon command.

The version in the *Loyauté* editions reads:

> Je suis Godor Lohomortins,
> Qu'ay cinq grans roys à mon command. (ed. Montaiglon, p. 38)

[37] In v. 39 the adverbial expression is 'pour lors' (ed. Montaiglon, p. 39), producing a hypermetric line.

[38] The change to v. 65, transforming 'Mais de nuit guerre felonne' to 'Mais de moult grant guerre felonne' (ed. Montaiglon, p. 41), produces syntactic incoherence, as 'guerre' can no longer be subject of 'resveilla' in v. 67.

*Addition of adjective *bon* or adverb *bien*	2	34, 73
*Addition of relative pronoun	2	38, 71
Addition of co-ordinating conjunction *et*[39]	2	46, 51
*Change of verb tense	1	5
Addition of *de* before infinitive[40]	1	9
Addition of co-ordinating conjunction *mais*	1	16
Addition of possessive adjective	1	17
*Change to entire line of text	1	42
Pluralisation	1	52
Feminine agreement of epicene adjective	1	62
*Change of verb	1	66

Three aspects of the changes are particularly striking. Firstly, they are frankly inept as amendments to versification: fully a quarter of the lines in the revised version are either hypo- or hypermetric. While printing errors and other sources of textual variation must not be discounted, the metrical inconsistencies strongly suggest that the *remanieur* had little more expertise in matters of versification than did his target audience. Secondly, the changes produce few significant semantic differences between the two versions. The asterisks in Table 1 indicate the categories of change which do have an appreciable effect upon meaning; a rather approximate means of assessment, but suitable enough for the present purpose. Only eighteen lines, a quarter of the text, are affected in this way. In this sense, we are entitled to regard the *remanieur* as quite a faithful translator – for his work is indeed an example of what Roman Jakobson definitively termed 'intralingual translation' – of Molinet.[41] Thirdly, most changes involve introducing elements whose linguistic function is implicit in the syntax of the heptasyllabic text: co-ordinating conjunctions, subject pronouns,

[39] In v. 51 a verb is also changed to a noun phrase: 'Cause mauvais accidens' becomes 'Et cause de plusieurs accidens' (ed. Montaiglon, p. 40), producing a hypermetric line.

[40] On the optional use of *de* before infinitives, see Georges Gougenheim, *Grammaire de la langue française du seizième siècle* (Paris: Picard, 1984), p. 137.

[41] On intralingual translation, 'an interpretation of verbal signs by means of other signs of the same language', see Roman Jakobson, 'On linguistic aspects of translation', in Lawrence Venuti (ed.), *The Translation Studies Reader* (London: Routledge, 2000), pp. 113–18 (p. 114).

articles, temporal adverbs, and the feminine agreement of an epicene adjective. These alterations concern just over half of the fifty-five lines that have been extended. Just as Molinet exploited the syntactic flexibility of Middle French – its tolerance of the zero article, frequent omission of subject pronouns, and the like – to fit his text into an unusual stanzaic form, the *remanieur* has benefited from the same flexibility when attempting to naturalise that form.[42]

Hence, by inserting elements which the structures of Middle French do not necessarily require, the *remanieur* has made the language of the *Neuf Preux* more explicit. The addition of co-ordinating conjunctions has the additional effect of rendering the text less paratactic, and thereby attenuating Molinet's breezy concision. More obvious in this respect are the two additions of relative pronouns. One of these converts a main into a subordinate clause:

> Amon suis, filz de David,
> Ma sœur Thamar deflouray. (vv. 37–38)

> Je suis Amon, filz de David,
> Qui ma seur Thamar deffloray. (ed. Montaiglon, p. 39)

The other contributes to transforming a single main clause into a main and a subordinate clause:

> Moy, Simon Machabeüs,
> Champion du roi divin,
> Fus mallement descheüs. (vv. 69–71)

> Je suis Scymon Machabeus,
> Champion du roi divin,
> Qui fus trop mollement deceus. (ed. Montaiglon, p. 41)

Comparisons with Molinet's snappier exposition clearly reveal the more pedestrian quality of the octosyllabic version. This is not simply a matter of syntax; it is also evident in the relationship between syntax and versification. In the octosyllabic text, sense-units coincide with verse-units more frequently than in its heptasyllabic source. Explicit subjects, for instance, occupy entirely different lines from the verbs they govern at six points in the heptasyllabic text, while verbs and objects occupy entirely different lines twice; these occurrences fall to three and

---

[42] On the zero article, see Robert Martin and Marc Wilmet, *Syntaxe du moyen français* (Bordeaux: Sobodi, 1980), pp. 116–19.

one respectively in the octosyllabic version.[43] The *remanieur* consequently reduces Molinet's use of enjambement, a technique often regarded as generally enhancing the semantic and formal richness of verse, and which in the *Neuf Preux* contributes to the heptasyllables' mimetically drunken rhythm.[44]

More detailed attention can now finally be devoted to this rhythm, and to the changes it undergoes as the octosyllabic text is produced. I focus on the relationship between metre and prosody in the two versions, establishing the distribution of accents by applying Roger Pensom's analytical model. Having identified 'structured alternation of accent as a linguistic phenomenon' in Old and Modern French, Pensom sets out the principle that 'the matching of accent and ictus is normal in verse-texts.'[45] On this basis, he suggests the following guidelines for determining accent-distribution in verse:

MARK   1.   group accent (obligatory lengthening) at obvious
               syntactical junctures (traditionally cesura and line end);

          2.   intra-phrasal word accent (obligatory rise in pitch) on
               (in order of priority) (a) polysyllables, oxytonic or
               paroxytonic *and* diacritical accent on monosyllables of
               relatively low frequency of occurrence; (b) accent on
               the countertonic(s) of oxytones of more than two
               syllables and paroxytones of more than three.

---

[43] These figures concern only those lines common to both texts. Verbs occupying different lines from their explicit subjects appear in vv. 17, 41, 51, 57, 67, and 71 in the heptasyllabic poem, and those occupying different lines from their objects in lines 5 and 13. The occurrences in the octosyllabic text are in vv. 5, 17, 41, and 57: the latter is a hypometric line unchanged from the heptasyllabic source.

[44] For the implications of enjambement, and a stimulating analysis of some Middle French examples, see Peter V. Davies, '"Si bas suis qu'a peine/Releveray": Christine de Pizan's use of enjambement', in John Campbell and Nadia Margolis (eds), *Christine de Pizan 2000: Studies on Christine de Pizan in Honour of Angus J. Kennedy* (Amsterdam: Rodopi, 2000), pp. 77–90.

[45] Roger Pensom, 'Accent and metre in French', *French Language Studies*, 3 (1993), 19–37 (pp. 35, 36). The model is further developed, and applied to illuminating effect, in Roger Pensom, *Accent and Metre in French: A Theory of the Relation Between Linguistic Accent and Metrical Practice 1100–1900* (Bern: Peter Lang, 1997), and *Le Sens de la métrique chez François Villon: 'Le Testament'* (Bern: Peter Lang, 2004). For an application of the model to Molinet's verse, see Adrian Armstrong, 'Pattern and disruption in Formalist poetry: the example of Jean Molinet', *Neuphilologische Mitteilungen*, 98 (1997), 209–16.

DELETE any *intra-phrasal* accent juxtaposed to any other in accord with the above priorities.[46]

When applied to the first *huitain* of the heptasyllabic text, Pensom's model produces the following results:

˘ / ˘ / ˘ ˘ /
Je suis Noël qui plantay

˘ / ˘ / ˘ ˘ / (˘)
La vigne aprés le deluge:

˘ / ˘ / ˘ ˘ /
J'en tiray vin et goustay,

/ ˘ ˘ / ˘ ˘ /
Tant en mon ventre en bouttay

˘ ˘ / ˘ / ˘ / (˘)
Que dormir me fut refuge;

˘ / ˘ / / ˘ / (˘)
De Cham, mon fils, raillié fus je,

˘ ˘ / ˘ / ˘ / (˘)
Qui perchut mes genitoires:

/ ˘ / ˘ ˘ ˘ / (˘)
Mauldit fus par mes boittoires. (vv. 5–12)

Rhythmic variation is particularly effective in these lines. The regularity of the first three lines gives way to an erratic pattern of accentuation; appropriately enough, this is immediately after Noah 'goustay' his wine, the evaporation of rhythmic consistency reflecting that of the patriarch's sobriety. In the octosyllabic version, although two lines are hypometric and have the same accentuation as in the source, the patterning is significantly different:

˘ / ˘ / ˘ / ˘ /
Je suis Noé, qui *ay* plantay

˘ / ˘ / ˘ ˘ / (˘)
La vigne après le deluge;

˘ ˘ / ˘ / ˘ ˘ /
Je tiray *du* vin et goustay;

[46] Pensom, 'Accent and metre in French', p. 36.

/ ˘ ˘   / ˘ / ˘ /
Tant à mon ventre *j'en* boutay

˘ ˘ ˘ / / ˘ ˘ / (˘)
Que *de* dormir fut mon reffuge.

˘   /   ˘ / / ˘ / (˘)
De Cham, mon filz, mocqué fus-je,

˘ / ˘ /   ˘ / ˘ / (˘)
Qui *app*erceut mes genitoires.

˘ / ˘ / ˘   ˘   ˘   / (˘)
Maudit *il* fut par mes boittoires.
(ed. Montaiglon, p. 38; additional syllables italicised)

The opening lines lack the regularity of the heptasyllabic text: the first has been altered by the addition of an informationally important and therefore accented monosyllable (the auxiliary verb 'ay'), while the insertion of the partitive 'du' in the third entails a different accentuation of 'tiray', no longer juxtaposed to the low-frequency monosyllable 'vin'. In the absence of initial prosodic consistency, the irregular accentuation of the subsequent lines no longer mimes Noah's descent into intoxication. It might be claimed that the inconsistent rhythm throughout the octosyllabic stanza is generally expressive of drunkenness, and thus effective in its own right; however, the changes in accentuation tend to produce a different kind of regularity, one evident throughout the revised poem. In vv. 5, 7, 11, and 12, the additional syllables result in a more regular, 'iambic' alternation of accented and unaccented syllables.[47] This is entirely consonant with Pensom's general assessment of 'rule-governed alternation of accent' as characteristic of French;[48] the *remanieur*'s octosyllables are, in other words, more reminiscent of ordinary language than Molinet's heptasyllables.

As the *Neuf Preux* is naturalised for the non-expert public opened up by printing, much more is at stake than the partial effacement of an unusual metre. That metre's cultural associations are lost, and a more straightforwardly serious reading of the revised text is tacitly promoted. While the revision evinces relatively few major semantic differences from the source, the introduction of optional lexemes promotes

[47] Twenty-three similar instances of more regular alternation can be identified in the forty-nine other octosyllables of the revised version: vv. 13, 14, 15, 16, 25, 27, 29, 33, 37, 42, 44, 45, 46, 50, 51, 61, 62, 67, 68, 69, 71, 72, and 75.

[48] Pensom, 'Accent and metre in French', p. 34.

linguistic explicitness and reduces parataxis. The result of these processes is – at least to an informed reader – aesthetically less satisfying than the source, in respect not only of syntactic concision but also of metrical flexibility and expressiveness. Hence the reception of the *Neuf Preux* in the *Loyaulté* editions points to some intriguing editorial and translating practices in the early sixteenth century, which further research will doubtless illuminate much more fully. In the first place, as might be expected, there is the likelihood that printers will somehow recuperate unfamiliar texts for their public: the recuperation is primarily formal in the case of the *Neuf Preux*, though previous research indicates that for various other Molinet texts it involves ideological repositioning.[49] More specifically, the amendments to Molinet's heptasyllables are of a nature which suggests that a text's propositional content is regarded as more important, more central to its meaning, than its formal or syntactic properties; this attitude may not be universally shared, but may prove to inform the choices of various editors and translators in this period. Finally, the *remaniement* reveals much about the quality of its source. Though a brief and minor poem by comparison with many of Molinet's other works, the *Neuf Preux* bears witness to an admirable level of technical proficiency and expressive subtlety. Not for nothing was Molinet regarded as 'le chief et souverain de tous les orateurs et rhetoriciens de nostre langue gallicane'.[50]

[49] See Adrian Armstrong, 'Cosmetic surgery on Gaul: the printed reception of Burgundian writing in France before 1550', in David Adams and Adrian Armstrong (eds), *Print and Power in France and England, 1500–1800* (Aldershot: Ashgate, 2006), pp. 13–26 (pp. 18–22).

[50] Jean Lemaire de Belges, *Chronique de 1507*, eds Anne Schoysman and Jean-Marie Cauchies (Brussels: Palais des Académies, 2001), p. 139. This article contributes to a larger research project, 'Poetic Knowledge in Late Medieval France', based in the Universities of Cambridge and Manchester and supported by the Arts and Humanities Research Council (AHRC). I thank the members of the project team for their comments on previous versions of the text.

10

A question of paternity: Denis Sauvage, Philippe de Commynes and Olivier de La Marche

Catherine Emerson

François-René de Chateaubriand, who had given some thought to the matter, invited his compatriots to consider the question 'pourquoi n'avons-nous que des mémoires au lieu d'histoire, et pourquoi ces mémoires sont-ils pour la plupart excellents?'[1] The identification of the genre of *mémoires* as something in which the French nation particularly excels is not unique to Chateaubriand. The belief that French historical literature is particularly rich in memoirs was the origin of a number of projects in the mid-nineteenth century, beginning with Claude-Bernard Petitot's *Collection complète des mémoires relatifs à l'histoire de France*, and is a recurring theme in the work of later commentators.[2] For instance, Philippe Lejeune's work on autobiography quotes with approval the *Grand Dictionnaire universel du XIXe siècle*'s distinction between memoirs and autobiography and its observation that the latter genre is an English – rather than a French – development.[3]

---

[1] Chateaubriand, *Œuvres complètes*, 32 vol. (Paris: Pourrat 1836–39), XV (1836), p. 283.

[2] In his preface to the first volume of this extensive collection, the editor observes that '[i]l n'est point de nation qui possède, comme la nôtre, un nombre considérable de Mémoires particuliers [...] et tous remarquables, non seulement par des anecdotes piquantes, mais par des observations pleines de justesse sur les mœurs nationales, et par ces sortes de détails qui, donnant aux scènes historiques une face nouvelle, en font pénétrer les plus secrets motifs', *Collection complète des mémoires relatifs à l'histoire de France depuis le règne de Philippe-Auguste, jusqu'au commencement du dix-septième siècle*, 42 vol. (Paris: Foucault, 1824–25), I (1824), pp. v–vi. For a history of the impulse behind this and similar collections, see Pierre Nora, 'Les Mémoires d'État. De Commynes à de Gaulle' in *Les Lieux de mémoire, La Nation II* (Paris: Gallimard, 1986), pp. 357–59.

[3] Philippe Lejeune, *L'Autobiographie en France* (Paris: Colin, 2003 [1971]), pp. 10–11.

Having thus identified the genre of *mémoires* as a peculiarly French literary form, critics of French literature have naturally sought to identify the moment of the genre's birth and the identity of the literary father. This search has been hampered by terminological difficulties: can one really speak of the independent existence of a genre before the emergence of a terminology designating that genre? Paul Zumthor seems to suggest that this is possible when he designates Villehardouin, Robert de Clari and Philippe de Novarre as 'auteurs de Mémoires proprement dits', despite none of their works actually being called *Mémoires*.[4] However, as Zumthor also points out, there are differences between these approaches of those of their modern-day counterparts; not least in that the medieval writers refer to themselves in the third, rather than the first, person. Meanwhile, Zumthor says that writers of what he terms 'textes en prose d'argument historique que l'on pourrait qualifier de Mémoires', which are indeed written in the first person and of which Joinville is the sole medieval exponent in French, are more concerned with documenting universal experience as exemplified by their career than they are with supplying their readership with information about that career for its own sake. Neither of Zumthor's two categories – that which could be properly called *Mémoires* but is not and does not take the modern form, and that which could be called *Mémoires* but which does not share the same individual focus – seems to correspond exactly to what we would regard as *mémoires*, although they clearly prefigure the development. Even after the generic term *mémoires* appears, the actual level of personal authorial involvement in the narrative is much less than might be expected.[5] Nevertheless, the moment when a genre *called mémoires* emerges is a significant one, because it demonstrates that a separate literary category has been recognized along with the need for a separate terminology.

---

[4] Paul Zumthor, *Essai de poétique médiévale* (Paris: Seuil, 1972), p. 173.

[5] Michel Zink, *La Subjectivité littéraire* (Paris: Presses Universitaires de France, 1985), argues that 'même lorsqu'il se place au centre de son œuvre, un auteur médiéval écrit rarement une autobiographie au sens moderne, c'est-à-dire non seulement un récit systématique de sa propre vie, mais encore un récit conduit dans la perspective de sa propre vie, dans lequel le monde apparaît à travers le double regard qu'il a porté sur lui au cours de son existence et qu'il porte sur ce regard même au moment où il écrit' (p. 172). Zink is, of course, discussing the genre of autobiography, in which modern readers would expect an even greater degree of personal involvement than in mémoires, but it would be true to say that the focus of works entitled *Mémoires* is still the world around, rather than the author.

In French literature the author traditionally credited with creating the new terminology is Philippe de Commynes. Pierre Nora, for example, calls Commynes's *Mémoires* the 'bréviaire des hommes d'État et modèle du genre'.[6] However, as Nora acknowledges, Commynes's claim to having been the first to *call* his text *Mémoires* rests on an accident of publishing history which illustrates the extent to which the genre was in its infancy at the time. The author's *Mémoires* were first published posthumously in 1524 by Galliot du Pré, who eschewed the neologism and entitled the work *Cronique et hystoire faicte et composee par feu messire Phelippe de Commines.*[7] Subsequent editions followed the lead of the first editor, either using exactly the same title or employing a variant which featured one or both of the generic markers contained within this original title.[8] In fact, it was not until Denis Sauvage's edition of 1552, also published by Galliot du Pré, that the work appeared under the title *Les memoires de messire Ph. de Commines, sur les principaux faicts et gestes de Louis onzieme et de Charles huictieme son fils, Roys de France*[9] – and even this was not the last word on the matter. An edition of 1559 was entitled *Cronique et histoire, composee par Philippes de Commines*[10] and translations in Italian and Dutch continued to style the work as a history.[11] However, Sauvage's new title for the work came to be the most commonly used in French, eventually excluding all competing titles. The triumph of Sauvage's nomenclature was only partly due to acceptance of his

[6] Nora, 'Les Mémoires d'État', p. 357.

[7] *Commynes, Cronique et hystoire faicte et composee par feu messire Phelippe de Commines Chevalier seigneur Dargenton, contenant les choses aduenues durant le regne du Roy Loys XIe, tant en France, Bourgogne Flandres Arthois Angleterre que Espaigne et lieux circonuoisins* (Paris: Galliot du Pré, 1524).

[8] For example the *Cronicques du Roy Charles Huytiesme de ce nom par messire Phelippes de Commines* (Paris: Jacques Regnault, 1543) or the Italian *La Historia famosa di monsignor di Argenton, delle guerre et costumi di Ludovico undecimo, re di Francia, trans. Nicolas Raince* (Venice: Tramezino, 1544).

[9] *Les Memoires de messire Ph. de Commines, sur les principaux faicts et gestes de Louis onzieme et de Charles huictieme son fils, Roys de France*, ed. Denis Sauvage (Paris: Galliot du Pré, 1552).

[10] *Cronique et histoire, composee par Philipppes de Commines, Contenant les choses auenues, durant le regne du Roy Loys unziesme, et Charles huictiesme. Auec plusieurs notables mis en marge* (Paris: for Barbe Regnault, 1559).

[11] Another edition of *La Historia famosa* was published by Giglio in Venice in 1559, while the translation *Historie van coninc Lodowyc van Vrancryc de XI, ende hertoch Carel van Borgogne*, by Cornelis van Kiel, appeared in Delft in 1612, published by Adraen Gerritsen.

arguments that the work should be referred to using the title that the author had himself intended. Mainly Sauvage's title was preferred because Sauvage's work itself was regarded as an authoritative edition, and editions of Commynes's *Mémoires* which followed his were often reprints of the same text – the first to present the totality of Commynes's *Mémoires* in print.

It was, therefore, only the happy accident of a diligent editor in the sixteenth century that ensured that Philippe de Commynes has been identified as the author of *mémoires* and thus that Commynes can be considered the first author to make use of the generic term. And yet Commynes was not the first writer to do so. His older contemporary, Olivier de La Marche was also the author of *Mémoires* and also referred to his work as 'mes mémoires' in the earliest portions of his text, written around 1473.[12] Since Commynes did not begin his work until 1489,[13] La Marche's usage of the generic term precedes that of Commynes. However, La Marche's *Mémoires* were not published until 1561, by which time Commynes's work had been through a number of editions, so, while La Marche preceded Commynes chronologically, he arrived after Commynes in the literary consciousness.

It is not the aim of this chapter to argue that Olivier de La Marche should be considered the father of the genre of *mémoires* in place of Philippe de Commynes. It may be that they influenced each other in the formulation of the new generic terminology that they both used, or that they may each have borrowed the terminology from a third author. They may even have each arrived at the taxonomy independently of the other, although this seems unlikely. What I want to examine here is how readings of Olivier de La Marche were affected by the fact that Philippe de Commynes – and not La Marche – was regarded as the primary exponent of *mémoires* together with the factors which may have led to this reading. Not the least of these is the fact that La Marche's first editor was the same Denis Sauvage who had previously produced that influential edition of Commynes's work.

Rare are the commentators on La Marche's *Mémoires* who do not draw an explicit parallel between his work and that of Philippe de Commynes. Sometimes this comparison is to La Marche's advantage, as

[12] Olivier de La Marche, *Mémoires*, Henri Beaune and Jean d'Arbaumont (eds), 4 vol. (Paris: Société de l'Histoire de France, 1883–88), I (1883), p. 196.

[13] For details on the chronology of composition of Commynes's *Mémoires*, see Jean Dufournet, *Études sur Philippe de Commynes* (Paris: Champion, 1975), pp. 19–25.

in the comments in Georgina and Dorothy Stuart's preface to their unpublished translation of La Marche's *Mémoires*:

> In the Chronicles of Chastelain, Monstrelet, Commines, Le Maire, and other distinguished historians, we have ample and valuable information regarding the Burgundian Court and nation at that time, but, precious as their writings are, they can never have the worth and charm of the Memoires of Messire Olivier de la Marche.[14]

More usually, however, critics follow Michaud and Poujoulat in arguing that, whatever La Marche's merits, they do not equal those of his younger contemporary:

> Les compositions poétiques d'Olivier de la Marche n'auraient point suffi pour lui faire une durable renommée, et quoiqu'il soit très loin de Commines, son mérite, comme historien des ducs de Bourgogne et de la chevalerie, mérite incontestable, lui assure un rang parmi les plus curieux narrateurs du XVe siècle.[15]

Even among those commentators like Stuart and Stuart whose final preference is for La Marche, there is the suggestion that this is a novel point of view, and that – of the two – Commynes is the more respected author. The most critical of La Marche's editors, Jean Lautens de Gand, gives Commynes precedence to the extent that he is the first historian mentioned in the introduction to the 1566 edition of La Marche's *Mémoires*. Indeed, La Marche himself only appears halfway through the five-page text, which traces a history of calumny against the residents of the Low Countries back to its origins with Commynes, arguing that this is unsurprising, given that author's personal record of treachery.[16] Olivier de La Marche is, Lautens argues, somewhat less biased than other French historians in this regard, but most have taken their lead from Commynes, of whose history Lautens writes

---

[14] *The Memoirs of Messire Olivier de la Marche*, trans. with an introduction and notes by Georgina Grace and Dorothy Margaret Stuart, 16 vol. (London, British Library, Typescript, 09073.e.3 (1930?)), I, p. 2.

[15] Joseph François Michaud and Jean Joseph François Poujoulat, *Mémoires pour servir à l'histoire de France* (Paris: L'Éditeur du commentaire analytique du code civil, 1837) I.iii, p. 306.

[16] *Les Memoires de Messire Olivier de la Marche Auec les Annotations & corrections de I[ean].L[autens].D[e].G[and]. Ce qui est dauantage, en cest seconde edition l'Epistre aux Lecteurs le declairera* (Ghent: Gerard de Salenson, 1566), Introduction: 'si voullions commencer à la cronique de Philippe de Comines, qui ne la iugeroit du tout resentir le naturel de son autheur plain de desloyauté?'

> [P]ar faute de contradicteur, elle a esté receue de plusieurs auec meilleure foy, qu'elle ne meritoit, au gra[n]d preiudice de la verité hisoriale: d'aultant plus que la poison dudit auteur a esté co[n]tinuée par les croniqueurs de France, l'ayans en ce suiui comme à la trace.

This comment by La Marche's editor demonstrates the extent to which Commynes is considered the precursor of La Marche and not the other way around; and remarks by other observers confirm that, where a hierarchical relationship is perceived, it is almost always to the benefit of Commynes. It is true that Petitot considers La Marche's *Mémoires* 'un complément nécessaire aux Mémoires de Philippe de Comines',[17] but this is based solely upon the fact that La Marche's work covers years not described in Commynes's *Mémoires*, and the implication is that Commynes's work is the better of the two, needing supplementing only where it fails to deal with events of the year in question.

Philippe de Commynes is thus the author most often associated with Olivier de La Marche, but the relationship does not operate as frequently in the other direction. Discussions of Commynes and his work rarely cite La Marche as a comparison, still less do they accord any sort of precedence – whether hierarchical or merely chronological – to the older man. There are a few exceptions. Pierre-Daniel Huet, in his own *Mémoires* (published posthumously in 1722) justifies his choice of genre, saying

> Je n'ai pas cru qu'on pouvait justement me reprocher d'avoir fait ce qu'ont fait tant d'hommes remarquables parmi nos compatriotes: Olivier de La Marche, Philippe de Commines, les deux du Bellay (Guillaume et Martin), Blaise de Montluc, Gaspard de Coligny ...[18]

This suggests that La Marche is here being considered the first author of *mémoires*, but the matter does not arise in the course of a discussion of Commynes himself. One commentator who focuses primarily on Commynes, but who allows his argument to encompass speculation on the nature of the relationship between his author and Olivier de La Marche, is Jean Dufournet. However, like many readers of La Marche, Dufournet's comments ultimately serve to suggest that La Marche is the lesser memorialist since, while he admits La Marche's and Jean de

---

[17] *Collection complète des Mémoires relatifs à l'histoire de France*, IX (1825), p. 3.

[18] Pierre-Daniel Huet, *Mémoires de Daniel Huet*, trans. Charles Nisard (Paris: Hachette, 1853), p. 252.

Haynin's prior use of the generic designation, he describes this as their having, 'à un niveau inférieur, inauguré la même voie'.[19]

This situation, wherein Olivier de La Marche – the older man and certainly the first of the two to use the generic term *mémoires* – is viewed as inseparable from Philippe de Commynes is not only observable in the comments of subsequent critics, editors and literary scholars. Readers too appear to have perceived a connection. The British Library possesses an example which illustrates the point. It takes the form of a volume, 596.i.4(1–2), which was originally the property of the Royal Library and is a composite of two separate editions bound together. The first of these editions is a copy of Denis Sauvage's second revised edition of Commynes's *Mémoires* published in Lyon in 1559, while the second is Sauvage's edition of La Marche's *Mémoires*, published in the same city in 1561. While the current binding is relatively modern, it has never been the practice of either the British Museum Library or the British Library to bind large works together, and the decision to bind these editions in a single volume must therefore have been taken before 1753, either by a librarian of the Royal Library or by an earlier owner.[20] Clearly factors such as the format of the volumes played an important role in making this possible, since it would not have been feasible to bind volumes of very disparate sizes under the same cover. However, the underlying feeling must have been that the two works were in some way comparable and would gain from presentation in the same volume.

The role played by the editor Denis Sauvage in creating this identity between the two authors cannot be underestimated. The fact that he was the editor of both volumes is in itself reason to compare the two, particularly since Sauvage's editorial practices create a strong visual identity between the volumes, which were nevertheless issued by different publishers. Sauvage's frequent recourse to annotation, both on the page alongside the text and at the back of the volume, meant that the two books look very similar. Even at the level of title pages there are close parallels, despite the presence in each case of the publisher's mark

---

[19] Jean Dufournet, 'Commynes et l'invention d'un nouveau genre historique: les mémoires', in Danielle Buschinger (ed.), *Chroniques nationales et chroniques universelles* (Göppingen: Kümmerle, 1990), repr. in Jean Dufournet, *Philippe de Commynes. Un historien à l'aube des temps modernes* (Brussels: De Boeck, 1994), pp. 17-33 (p. 28).

[20] I am indebted to Des McTernan, curator of early printed books in French at the British Library, for his very detailed information as to how early volumes were catalogued and stored.

which should serve to distinguish the books. Both display the title set in a triangular format of type of decreasing size, followed by the editor's details in italics, the publisher's mark, the words 'A LYON' and the publisher's name in capitals followed by a blank line above the date in Roman numerals.[21] None of these elements in itself is particularly unusual but, taken as a whole, the overall impression is one of similarity rather than distinctiveness, and the near identical wording of the way in which Sauvage is described ('DENIS SAVVAGE de Fontenailles en Brie, Historiographe du treschrestien Roy Henry IIe de ce nom') reinforces the similarity around the identity of the editor. Furthermore, there are other cases in which Sauvage seems to have been used as an author figure: Guillaume Rouillé, the publisher of Sauvage's edition of La Marche's *Mémoires*, appears to have adopted the practice of presenting this work bound together with another of Sauvage's editions of French historiography, the *Chronique de Flandres*. The British Library possesses one such composite volume, while the Bibliothèque nationale de France has two, and Rouillé's initial royal privilege for the chronicle was issued in 1558 in a composite document embracing it and privileges for 'la continuation d'icelle et les mémoires d'Olivier de la Marche', suggesting that the project had always been to view these works as a whole.[22]

The editions of Denis Sauvage were therefore seen as a piece, at least within Guillaume Rouillé's enterprise. Hervé Baudrier suggests that Sauvage was himself an employee of Rouillé as well as an editor and translator published by him, and, if this was the case, it would explain why the publisher invested in creating a demand for the editor's work.[23] However, it is interesting to speculate that this may have spilled over into other areas, creating a demand for Sauvage's editions not published by Rouillé. This tendency to identify the editor with the works that he edited may be one reason why La Marche has traditionally been considered in terms of Commynes, since the first editor of La Marche's work had already produced an edition of Commynes's, and the

---

[21] The title page to the Lyon edition of Commynes's *Mémoires* is reproduced in Jean Dufournet, 'Les Premiers lecteurs de Commynes ou Les Mémoires au XVIe siècle' in *Philippe de Commynes*, pp. 145–91 (p. 149).

[22] Hervé Baudrier and J. Baudrier, *Bibliographie lyonnaise: recherches sur les imprimeurs, libraires, relieurs et fondeurs de lettres de Lyon au XVIe siècle publiées et continuées par J. Baudrier*, 13 vol. (Lyon: Librairie Ancienne d'Auguste Brun, 1895-1921; reprint, Paris: F. de Nobele, 1964), IX, p. 274.

[23] *Ibid.*, IX, p. 177.

comparison can only have been heightened by the fact that the title *Mémoires* was a novel one. Indeed, when La Marche's *Mémoires* first appeared, Commynes's work seems to have been the only similar work to bear this title. In the very rare cases where this term was used elsewhere, it appears to have been employed with the older meaning of a memo or note.[24] Readers approaching La Marche's work for the first time, therefore, had nothing upon which to base their horizon of expectations except Commynes's prior usage, and it is therefore not surprising that the two memorialists came to be closely linked in the minds of their readers.

It should not be forgotten that it was Denis Sauvage who had first taken the decision to use Commynes's generic designation of his work as its title, and we could therefore legitimately ask whether Sauvage – rather than either La Marche or Commynes – could rightly be considered the father of the genre. Sauvage himself justified entitling Commynes' work *Mémoires* by pointing out that 'le pere mesme en a esté le parrain (comme l'on dit communément) le nommant Memoires'. This affirmation has been misread as evidence that Sauvage considered Commynes to be the originator of the genre, rather than simply as the person best placed to name his own work, but it does serve to illustrate Sauvage's respectful attitude towards Commynes, which is in marked contrast to the way in which he writes about La Marche. This may go some way to explaining why readers who have considered La Marche in terms of Commynes have, almost as a matter of course, regarded Commynes as the senior partner. Sauvage never draws an explicit parallel between the two authors. In fact, he does not discuss La Marche in terms of any other named historian or memorialist in his editor's preface to the edition. However, he makes a number of remarks that leave his reader in no doubt as to what he thinks of Olivier de La Marche as a writer.

Denis Sauvage's attitude towards La Marche can best be seen in the following comment:

Touchant son stile (auqul ie luy ay laissé quelques maniéres de parler, & certains mots de son siécle, & du creu de son païs, pour difference du vray

---

[24] An example of the use of the term with this sense, which may predate Sauvage's work can be found in an undated work, apparently from 1527, catalogued in the British Library entitled *Mémoires des nouvelles que le Josne montrichart a apporté de Romme* (Antwerp: Jacques de Nesvelt; London, BL, 1057.h.9.(3.)). This appears, however, to be an isolated example of the word being used in the title of a work.

> François auec le Bourguignon) ie l'ay trouué assez passable, quand il a
> suyui son naturel: mais le voulant farder, & agencer d'artifice, il s'égaroit
> tellement, que l'on ne pouuoit tirer construction de ce qu'il vouloit dire:
> en sorte qu'il m'a souuent esté besoing de luy aider à s'expliquer.[25]

The memorialist is thus denigrated as not a proper Frenchman at all,
but a Burgundian, and consequently his French, even when submitted
to the care of an experienced editor, can never escape the 'creu de son
païs'. When he attempts to adopt an elevated style, all hell breaks loose
and the educated Sauvage has to intervene to make sense of La Marche's
ramblings. This tone is sustained in Sauvage's notes to his edition. At
one point he apologises to his reader for not having corrected one of La
Marche's grosser errors of fact, explaining that 'ne doy corriger mon
Auteur, que là ou il est manifestement dépraué', creating the impression
that La Marche's writing frequently suffers from this handicap.[26] In
matters of both fact and style, therefore, Sauvage tells us that La Marche
is lacking.

By contrast, his attitude to Commynes is much more deferential. In
the first preface to Sauvage's edition of Commynes's *Mémoires*, which is
addressed to Henri II, the editor explains that Commynes is 'le plus
excelent de voz Historiographes François, voire egal aux meilleurs de
toutes autres langues' and that he has been sadly mistreated by his
previous editors, to the point that Sauvage has had to abandon his
original project of writing a history of France (albeit an 'œuure tant
necessaire & honorable à la nation Fra[n]çoise') in order to take pity on
the traduced author. The marks of Sauvage's respect for his subject here
are manifold: he praises Commynes with superlatives, he stresses the
gravity of the wrong done to him and the utility of the task that has had
to be abandoned to answer this more pressing call. The same themes
can be seen is his preface to the general reader, which describes
Sauvage's attempts to restore the mutilated text to its former pristine
condition:

> vous entendrez aussi que tous les Cirurgiens du monde, s'ils auoyent
> entrepris la cure d'un corps autant cruellement nauré que ce liure estoit

---

[25] *Les Memoires de Messire Olivier de La Marche, Premier Maistre d'hostel de l'archeduc Philippe d'Austriche, Comte de Flandres: Nouuellement mis en lumiére par Denis Sauvage de Fontenailles en Brie, Historiographe du Treschrestien Roy Henry, second de ce nom* (Lyon: Guillaume Rouillé, 1561), ii.

[26] *Les Memoires de Messire Olivier de La Marche*, ed. Sauvage, p. 436, annot. 2.

miserablement corrompu, n'en pourroyent venir à chef, sans y laisser cicatrices à tousiours apparentes.

Whereas Sauvage holds Olivier de La Marche responsible for the majority of the errors contained in his *Mémoires*, therefore, he implies that Commynes has been let down by a succession of inattentive scribes and editors. As far as the younger author's ability to manage the French language is concerned, Sauvage does not subject Commynes to the same *ad hominem* criticism levelled at La Marche. He tells his readers that he has amended certain outmoded phraseologies, but he does not pronounce on whether these were originally introduced by the author or by the scribe, saying simply that they 'se rencontrent au vieil Exemplaire'. Furthermore, he does not seem to regard their appearance to be evidence of linguistic deficiency in Commynes, as he was to suggest a decade later in the case of La Marche.

Readers who contrasted Denis Sauvage's prefaces to the two authors' *Mémoires* – and there is bibliographical evidence to suggest that the works were read in this way – would have been left with the distinct impression that Commynes was the superior memorialist. It is a short step from this to the conclusion that he was the original proponent of the genre, especially since the date of composition is not in evidence in either text and has to be deduced from extradiegetic references. The fact that Sauvage's edition of Commynes precedes that of La Marche by nearly a decade could only strengthen the impression that Commynes was the father of the genre.

Olivier de La Marche is less well known than Philippe de Commynes, but even those critics who do know of the existence of both memorialists – and know that La Marche was the senior of the pair – tend to use Commynes as the standard against which each is judged. And, indeed, it is questionable whether Sauvage would have accepted the validity of the title *Mémoires* if La Marche had been the sole proponent, given his general disregard for that author's capacity for expressing himself in French. It was Sauvage's editorial decision which has ensured that both are regarded as writers of the same genre, it is arguably the fact of Sauvage's editorship which has led to their being compared to each other, and it is very probably the implicit value judgements in his editorial practice that has meant that Commynes is regarded as the primary memorialist – in terms of status if not of chronology. Denis Sauvage is, therefore, the editor who comes after and who has made sense of what had gone before, but it is only a certain sort of sense and it does not reflect the nature of the relationship between La Marche and Commynes as the two men themselves perceived it.

If Philippe de Commynes and Olivier de La Marche were not well acquainted, they certainly moved in the same circles: each was in the service of Charles the Bold prior to his accession to the dukedom of Burgundy. Indeed, Commynes appears twice in the *Mémoires* of La Marche. However, on each occasion he is a peripheral actor engaged in a collective action, and in each case it is in a section not originally written for inclusion in the *Mémoires*. In fact, one of the appearances by Commynes in La Marche's *Mémoires* is in a reproduction of the text of the Treaty of Soleuvre (1475), the terms of which specifically excluded Commynes and two other men from a general restitution of property following a period of conflict between the Burgundian duke and the French king and Commynes's desertion of the former and entry into the service of the latter.[27] On this event itself, La Marche is silent. Is this a case of the older memorialist concealing events which might reflect badly on his colleague? Were La Marche and Commynes even aware of each other's literary projects? Each man specifies in his preface that his work was to be used as source material for a chronicle, and La Marche states that this should take place after his death.[28] The very nature of the project, therefore, meant that the men's work was not publicly available until after La Marche's death, by which time Commynes was ensconced in the French court, so any correspondence which took place between them must have been on a personal level. Commynes's surviving letters have been published, but there is nothing in them to suggest that he was in touch with La Marche.[29] On the other hand, Commynes does mention La Marche in his *Mémoires*, and he does so in a way that could be read as his tribute to a fellow practitioner of *memoires*:

> Au saillir de mon enfance et en l'aage de pouvoir monter à cheval, fus amené à Lisle devers le duc Charles de Bourgoigne, lors appellé conte de Charroloys, lequel me print en son service, et fut l'an mil quatre cens soixante quatre.[30]

[27] La Marche, *Mémoires*, eds Beaune and d'Arbaumont, III (1885), p. 221.

[28] La Marche, *Mémoires*, eds Beaune and d'Arbaumont, I (1883), pp. 15, 185.

[29] Philippe de Commynes, *Lettres*, ed. Joël Blanchard (Geneva: Droz, 2001).

[30] Philippe de Commynes, *Mémoires*, eds J. Calmette and G. Durville, 3 vol. (Paris: Champion, 1924–25), I (1924), p. 4.

So runs the beginning of the opening incident in Commynes's *Mémoires* in a construction which is reminiscent of the opening of La Marche's text:

> au commencement de mon eaige, et du premier temps que je puis entrer en matiere, et bailler ramentevance digne d'escrire, la premiere chose dont je puis parler est devoste et de saincte mémoire.[31]

Three days after his entry into the Burgundian court, Commynes tells us, French ambassadors arrived demanding the liberation of a French nobleman who had been imprisoned in the Burgundian Netherlands and the arrest of the Burgundian advisor who had allegedly spread rumours about the murderous intentions of the French towards the future Charles the Bold. The Burgundian official whose arrest thus became central to Franco-Burgundian relations in 1464 was none other than Olivier de La Marche, whose *Mémoires* give a brief outline of the way in which events developed.[32] Commynes's account is, if anything, more detailed than that of La Marche. Does Commynes begin his *Mémoires* in this manner in order to signal his generic debt to La Marche: the court official who had preceded him?

It is tempting to conclude that this is the case, and that subsequent attempts by critics to link the two authors are based on a genuine contemporary relationship between the two men and their work which goes beyond their having shared a common editor half a century after their demise. However, if this is so, it must be recognised that La Marche does not explicitly acknowledge Commynes. As for Commynes's acknowledgement of La Marche, it too is implied in the way that he structures his narrative to foreground the senior memorialist from the start, but it is not an open recognition of La Marche's influence. Nevertheless, if any influence did exist, it was of the earlier memorialist on the later one, and the reverse move detectable in subsequent criticism is in large part due to the influence of the editor who followed them both.

---

[31] La Marche, *Mémoires*, eds Beaune and d'Arbaumont, I (1883), p. 187.

[32] La Marche, *Mémoires*, eds Beaune and d'Arbaumont, III (1885), pp. 3–5.

Bibliography

Manuscripts

Arras, Bibliothèque municipale, MS 619.

Berne, Bürgerbibliothek, MS 274.

Besançon, Bibliothèque municipale, MS 554.

Besançon, Bibliothèque municipale, MS 864.

Besançon, Bibliothèque municipale, MS 865.

Brussels, Bibliothèque royale Albert 1er, MS II 88.

Brussels, Bibliothèque royale Albert 1er, MS IV 251.

Cambridge, Gonville and Caius College, MS 187:220.

Cambridge, University Library, MS Hh.3.16.

London, British Library, MS Arundel 67.

New York, Pierpont Morgan Library, MS M.133.

Paris, Bibliothèque de l'Arsenal, MS 3523.

Paris, Bibliothèque nationale de France, MS fr. 837.

Paris, Bibliothèque nationale de France, MS fr. 1661.

Paris, Bibliothèque nationale de France, MS fr. 2650.

Paris, Bibliothèque nationale de France, MSS fr. 2663–64.

Paris, Bibliothèque nationale de France, MS fr. 6475.

Paris, Bibliothèque nationale de France, n. a. fr. 4513.

Paris, Bibliothèque nationale de France, n. a. fr. 15771.

Paris, Bibliothèque nationale de France, n. a. fr. 9605.

Paris, Bibliothèque nationale de France, MS Rothschild 471.

Stonyhurst College, MS 1.

The Hague, Koninklijke Bibliotheek, MS 71. E. 49.

Toulouse, Bibliothèque municipale (Bibliothèque d'étude et du patrimoine), MS 511.

Tournai, Bibliothèque communale, MS 105.

Vatican, Biblioteca Apostolica Vaticana, MS Reg. Lat. 1720.

Vatican, Biblioteca Apostolica Vaticana, MS Reg. Lat. 1363.

Primary Sources (Pre-1800)

A lytyll newe treatyse or mater intytuled and called the ix. drunkardes (London: Robert Bankes, 1523).

Cronicques du Roy Charles Huytiesme de ce nom par messire Phelippes de Commines (Paris: Jacques Regnault, 1543).

Commynes, Philippe de, *Cronique et hystoire faicte et composee par feu messire Phelippe de Commines Chevalier seigneur Dargenton, contenant les choses aduenues durant le regne du Roy Loys XIe, tant en France, Bourgogne Flandres Arthois Angleterre que Espaigne et lieux circonuoisins* (Paris: Galliot du Pré, 1524).

——, *Cronique et histoire, composee par Philipppes de Commines, Contenant les choses auenues, durant le regne du Roy Loys unziesme, et Charles huictiesme. Auec plusieurs notables mis en marge* (Paris: for Barbe Regnault, 1559).

——, *La Historia famosa di monsignor di Argenton, delle guerre et costumi di Ludovico undecimo, re di Francia*, trans. Nicolas Raince (Venice: Tramezino, 1544).

——, *La Historia famosa di monsignor di Argenton, delle guerre et costumi di Ludovico undecimo, re di Francia* (Venice: Giglio, 1559).

——, *Historie van coninc Lodowyc van Vrancryc de XI, ende hertoch Carel van Borgogne* trans. Cornelis van Kiel (Delft: Adraen Gerritsen, 1612).

——, *Les memoires de messire Ph. de Commines, sur les principaux faicts et gestes de Louis onzieme et de Charles huictieme son fils, Roys de France*, ed. Denis Sauvage (Paris: Galliot du Pré, 1552).

Le Debat de la damoiselle et de la bourgoise (Paris: for Guillaume Bignaux, 1510; Chantilly, Musée Condé, III. F. 23).

La Marche, Olivier de, *Les Memoires de Messire Olivier de La Marche, Premier Maistre d'hostel de l'archeduc Philippe d'Austriche, Comte de Flandres: Nouvellement mis en lumiére par Denis Sauvage de Fontenailles en Brie, Historiographe du Treschrestien Roy Henry, second de ce nom.* (Lyon: Guillaume Rouillé, 1561).

——, *Les Memoires de Messire Olivier de la Marche Auec les Annotations & corrections de I[ean].L[autens].D[e].G[and]. Ce qui est dauantage, en cest seconde edition l'Epistre aux Lecteurs le declairera* (Ghent: Gerard de Salenson, 1566).

Mémoires des nouvelles que le Josne montrichart a apporté de Romme (Antwerp: Jacques de Nesvelt [1527?]; London, BL, 1057.h.9.(3.))

Molinet, Jean, *Les Faictz et dictz de feu de bonne memoire Maistre Jehan Molinet* (Paris: Jean Longis and the widow of Jean Saint-Denis, 1531).

——, *Les Faictz et dictz* (Paris: Jean Longis and others, 1537).

——, *Les Faictz et dictz* (Paris: Alain Lotrian and others, 1540).

——, *La Loyaulté des femmes, avec les neuf preux de gourmandise et une recepte pour guarir les yvrongnes* (n.d.o.p.; Paris, BnF, Rothschild 573).

——, *La Loyaulté des femmes, avec les neuf preux de gourmandise et une recepte pour guerir les yvrongnes* (n.d.o.p.; Paris, BnF, Rothschild 574).

——, *La Leaulté des femmes, avec les neuf preux de gourmandise et une recepte pour guerir les yvrongnes* (n.d.o.p.; Paris, BnF, Rés. Ye 2981).

——, *La Leaulté des femmes, avec les neuf preux de gourmandise et aussi une bonne recepte pour guerir les yvrongnes* (n.d.o.p.; Paris, BnF, Rés. Ye 4288).

——, *La Loyaulté des femmes, avec les neuf preux de gourmandie* [sic] *et balades d'amours* (n.d.o.p.; Paris, BnF, Rés. Ye 1203).

Primary Sources (Post-1800)

Alain Chartier, The Poetical Works, ed. James C. Laidlaw (Cambridge: Cambridge University Press, 1974).

Alexandre de Paris, *Le Roman d'Alexandre*, pres. and trans. Laurence Harf-Lancner (Paris: Librairie Générale Française , 1994).

La Bataille Loquifer, ed. Monica Barnett (Oxford: Blackwell, 1975).

Le Batard de Bouillon, ed. Robert Francis Cook (Geneva: Droz, 1972).

Boccaccio, Giovanni, *Genealogie deorum gentilium*, in *Tutte le opere di Giovanni Boccaccio*, ed. and trans. Vittore Branca, 10 vol. (Milan: Mondadori, 1964–98).

Cayley, Emma (ed.), *Sleepless Knights and Wanton Women: constructing relationships in late medieval French debate poetry*, vol. 1: *The Debate Poems* (Tempe: Arizona Center for Medieval and Renaissance Studies, forthcoming).

La Chanson de Roland, ed. Cesare Segre, 2 vol. (Geneva: Droz, 1989).

Charles d'Orléans, *Ballades et rondeaux*, ed. Jean-Claude Mühlethaler (Paris: Librairie Générale Française, 1992).

Chartier, Alain, Baudet Herenc, Achille Caulier, *Le Cycle de 'La Belle Dame sans mercy'*, eds David Hult and Joan E. McRae (Paris: Champion, 2003).

Chateaubriand, François-René de, *Œuvres complètes*, 32 vol. (Paris: Pourrat, 1836–39).

Le Chevalier des dames du dolent fortuné: allégorie en vers de la fin du XVe siècle, ed. Jean Miquet (Ottawa: Les Presses de l'Université d'Ottawa, 1990).

La Chevalerie d'Ogier de Danemarche, ed. Mario Eusebi (Milan: Instituto editoriale Cisalpino, 1963).

178 Bibliography

Chrétien de Troyes, *Le Chevalier au Lion ou le Roman d'Yvain*, ed. David F. Hult (Paris: Librairie Générale Française, 1994).

——, *Cligés*, eds Stewart Gregory and Claude Luttrell (Cambridge: D. S. Brewer, 1993).

——, *Le Roman de Perceval ou le Conte du Graal*, ed. Keith Busby (Tübingen: Niemeyer, 1993).

Christine de Pizan, *Le Chemin de longue étude*, ed. Andrea Tarnowski (Paris: Librairie Générale Française, 2000).

——, *L'Epistre Othea*, ed. Gabriella Parussa (Geneva: Droz, 1999).

——, *Le Livre de l'advision Cristine*, eds Christine Reno and Liliane Dulac (Paris: Champion, 2001).

——, *Le Livre de la Mutacion de Fortune*, ed. Suzanne Solente (Paris: Picard, 1959–66).

——, *Le Livre du Duc des vrais amans*, ed. Thelma S. Fenster (Binghamton, NY: Medieval and Renaissance Texts and Studies, 1995).

Commynes, Philippe de, *Lettres*, ed. Joël Blanchard (Geneva: Droz, 2001).

——, *Mémoires*, eds J. Calmette and G. Durville, 3 vol. (Paris: Champion, 1924–25).

Coquillart, Guillaume, *Œuvres*, ed. M. J. Freeman (Geneva: Droz, 1975).

Deschamps, Eustache, *L'Art de Dictier*, ed. and trans. Deborah M. Sinnreich-Levi (East Lansing: Colleagues Press, 1994).

Deschaux, Robert, *Un poète bourguignon du XVe siècle: Michault Taillevent (Édition et Étude)* (Geneva: Droz, 1975).

Deux Moralités de la fin du Moyen-Âge et du temps des guerres de Religion: Excellence, Science, Paris et Peuple; Mars et Justice, eds Jean-Claude Aubailly and Bruno Roy (Geneva: Droz, 1990).

Diverres, A. H., *Froissart, Voyage en Béarn* (Manchester: Manchester University Press, 1953).

Du Bellay, Joachim, *Divers Jeux Rustiques*, ed. V. L. Saulnier (Geneva: Droz, 1965).

Esclarmonde, Clarisse et Florent, Ide et Olive, ed. Max Schweigel (Marburg: N. G. Elwert, 1889).

Fabri, Pierre, *Le Grand et vrai art de pleine rhétorique*, ed. A. Héron, 3 vol. (Rouen: Société des Bibliophiles Normands, 1889–90).

Froissart, Jean, *Chroniques*, ed. baron Kervyn de Lettenhove, 26 vol. (Brussels: V. Devaux, 1867–77).

——, *Chroniques. Troisième Livre. MS 865 de la Bibliothèque Municipale de Besançon*, ed. Peter Ainsworth (Geneva: Droz, 2007).

——, *Le Joli buisson de jonece*, ed. Anthime Fourrier (Geneva: Droz, 1975).

——, *Le Paradis d'amour – L'Orloge amoureus*, ed. Peter F. Dembowski (Geneva: Droz, 1986).

Gérard de Nevers: Prose Version of the Roman de la Violette, ed. Lawrence F. H. Lowe (Princeton/Paris: Princeton University Press/Les Presses Universitaires, 1928).

Gerbert de Montreuil, *La Continuation de Perceval*, ed. Marguerite Oswald, 3 vol. (Paris: Honoré Champion, 1975).

Girard de Vienne, ed. Wolfgang van Emden (Paris: Picard, 1977).

Guillaume de Lorris and Jean de Meun, *Le Roman de la rose*, ed. Félix Lecoy, 3 vol. (Paris: Champion, 1965–70).

——, *Le Roman de la Rose*, ed. Armand Strubel (Paris: Librairie Générale Française, 1992).

Huet, Pierre-Daniel, *Mémoires de Daniel Huet*, trans. Charles Nisard (Paris: Hachette, 1853).

Huon de Bordeaux, eds William W. Kibler and François Suard (Paris: Champion, 2003).

Le Jardin de plaisance et fleur de rethorique: reproduction en fac-similé de l'édition publiée par Antoine Vérard vers 1501, eds Eugénie Droz and Arthur Piaget, 2 vol. (Paris: Firmin-Didot, 1910–25).

Le Livre de l'espérance, ed. François Rouy (Paris: Champion, 1989).

La Marche, Olivier de, *Mémoires,* eds Henri Beaune and Jean d'Arbaumont, 4 vol. (Paris: Société de l'Histoire de France, 1883–88).

——, *The Memoirs of Messire Olivier de la Marche*, trans. with an introduction and notes Georgina Grace and Dorothy Margaret Stuart, 16 vol. (London, British Library, Typescript, 09073.e.3 (1930?)).

Le Franc, Martin, *Le Champion des dames*, ed. Robert Deschaux, 5 vol. (Paris: Champion, 1999).

Lehmann, Paul, *Die Parodie im Mittelalter*, 2nd ed. (Stuttgart: A. Hiersemann, 1963).

Lemaire de Belges, Jean, *Chronique de 1507*, eds Anne Schoysman and Jean-Marie Cauchies (Brussels: Palais des Académies, 2001).

Luce, S., G. Raynaud, Léon Mirot, and Albert Mirot (eds), *Jean Froissart, Chroniques*, 15 vol. (Paris: Société de l'Histoire de France, 1869–1975).

Mabrien, ed. Philippe Verelst (Geneva: Droz, 1998).

Machaut, Guillaume de, *'Le Jugement du roy de Behaigne' and 'Remede de Fortune'*, eds James I. Wimsatt, William W. Kibler and Rebecca A. Baltzer (Athens: University of Georgia Press, 1988).

——, *Le Livre du Voir Dit*, eds Paul Imbs and Jacqueline Cerquiglini-Toulet (Paris: Librairie Générale Française, 1999).

——, *Œuvres*, ed. Ernest Hoepffner, 3 vol. (Paris: Champion, 1921).

Le Manuscrit B. N. nouv. acq. fr. 15771: une nouvelle collection de poésies lyriques et courtoises du XVe siècle, ed. Barbara L. S. Inglis (Paris: Champion, 1985).

Michaud, Joseph François, and Jean Joseph François Poujoulat, *Mémoires pour servir à l'histoire de France* (Paris: L'Éditeur du commentaire analytique du code civil, 1837).

Milet, Jacques, *La Forest de Tristesse*, in *Le Jardin de plaisance et fleur de rethorique*, eds Eugénie Droz and Arthur Piaget, 2 vol. (Paris: Firmin-Didot, 1910–25).

Molinet, Jean, *L'Art de Rhétorique*, in Ernest Langlois (ed.), *Recueil d'arts de seconde rhétorique* (Paris: Imprimerie Nationale, 1902), pp. 214–52.

——, *Les Faictz et dictz de Jean Molinet*, ed. Noël Dupire, 3 vol. (Paris: Société des Anciens Textes Français, 1936–39).

Nicole de Margival, *Le Dit de la Panthère*, ed. Bernard Ribémont (Paris: Champion, 2000).

Octovien de Saint-Gelais, *Le Séjour d'honneur*, ed. Frédéric Duval (Geneva: Droz, 2002).

Omont, Henri, *Fabliaux, dits et contes en vers français du XIIIe siècle* (Geneva: Slatkine Reprints, 1973).

Petitot, Claude-Bernard, *Collection complète des mémoires relatifs à l'histoire de France depuis le règne de Philippe-Auguste, jusqu'au commencement du dix-septième siècle*, 42 vol. (Paris: Foucault, 1824–25).

The Pseudo-Ovidian de Vetula, ed. Dorothy Robathan (Amsterdam: Hakkert, 1968).

Pseudo-Ovidius de vetula. Untersuchungen und Text, ed. Paul Klopsch (Leiden: Brill, 1967).

Recueil de chansons pieuses du XIIIe siècle, ed. Edward Järnström, 2 vol. [(I) Annales Academiae Scientiarum Fennicae, Ser. B, t. III, 1; (II, with A. Långfors) Annales Academiae Scientiarum Fennicae, Ser. B, t. XX, No. 4 (Helsinki, 1910, 1927)].

Recueil de poésies françoises des XVe et XVIe siècles, ed. Anatole de Montaiglon, 13 vol. (Paris: Jannet, 1855–78).

Renaut de Montauban, ed. Jacques Thomas (Geneva: Droz, 1989).

Renaut de Montauban. Deuxième fragment rimé du ms. de Paris, B. N., fr. 764 ('R'), ed. Philippe Verelst (Ghent: University of Ghent, 1988).

Le Roman de la Violette ou de Gerart de Nevers, ed. Douglas Labaree Buffum (Paris: Champion, 1927).

Ronsard, Pierre de, *Discours des misères de ce temps*, ed. Malcolm Smith (Geneva: Droz, 1979).

——, *Œuvres complètes*, ed. Paul Laumonier, 20 vol. (Paris: Didier, STFM, 1968).

Tibaut, *Le Roman de la Poire*, ed. Christiane Marchello-Nizia (Paris: Picard, 1984).

Verlaine, Paul, *Œuvres poétiques*, ed. Jacques Robichez (Paris: Garnier, 1986).

La Vie Monseigneur Saint Fiacre, eds James F. Burks, Barbara M. Craig, and Marion E. Porter (Lawrence: The University of Kansas Press, 1960).

La Vie de P. de Ronsard de Claude Binet, ed. Paul Laumonier (Paris: Hachette, 1910).

Villon, François, *The Poems of François Villon*, trans. Galway Kinnell (Boston, MA: Houghton Mifflin, 1977).

——, *Le Testament Villon*, eds Jean Rychner and Albert Henry, 2 vol. (Geneva: Droz, 1974).

Dictionaries

Bidler, Rose, *Dictionnaire érotique: ancien français, moyen français, Renaissance* (Montreal: CERES, 2002).

Dictionnaire historique de la langue française, eds Alain Rey [*et al.*], 2 vol. (Paris: Dictionnaires Le Robert, 1992).

Godefroy, Frédéric, *Dictionnaire de l'ancienne langue française*, 10 vol. (Paris: Vieweg, 1881–1902).

Tobler, Adolf, and Erhard Lommatzsch, *Altfranzösisches Wörterbuch*, 11 vol. (Berlin: Wiedmann, 1925).

Secondary Sources

Abramowicz, Maciej, *Réécrire au moyen âge: mises en prose des romans de Bourgogne* (Lublin: Wydawnictwo Uniwersytetu Marii-Curie-Sklodowskiej, 1996).

Armstrong, Adrian, 'Boire chez (et avec) Molinet', in Jean Devaux, Estelle Doudet and Elodie Lecuppre-Desjardin (eds), *Jean Molinet et son temps* (Turnhout: Brepols, forthcoming).

——, 'Cosmetic surgery on Gaul: the printed reception of Burgundian writing in France before 1550', in David Adams and Adrian Armstrong (eds), *Print and Power in France and England, 1500–1800* (Aldershot: Ashgate, 2006), pp. 13–26.

——, 'The deferred verdict: a topos in late-medieval poetic debates?', *French Studies Bulletin*, 64 (Autumn 1997), 12–14.

——, 'Pattern and disruption in Formalist poetry: the example of Jean Molinet', *Neuphilologische Mitteilungen*, 98 (1997), 209–16.

——, *The Virtuoso Circle: Competition, Collaboration and Complexity in Late Medieval French Poetry* (Tempe: Arizona Center for Medieval and Renaissance Studies, forthcoming).

Armstrong, Adrian and Malcolm Quainton (eds), *Book and Text in France, 1400–1600. Poetry on the Page* (Aldershot: Ashgate, 2007).

Arn, Mary-Jo, *The Poet's Notebook. The Personal Manuscript of Charles d'Orléans (Paris BnF MS fr. 25458)* (Turnhout: Brepols, 2008).

Astell, Ann W., *The Song of Songs in the Middle Ages* (Ithaca/London: Cornell University Press, 1990).

Badel, Pierre-Yves, *Le Roman de la rose au XIVe siècle: étude de la réception de l'œuvre* (Geneva: Droz, 1980).

Balsamo, Jean, 'Galliot du Pré, éditeur de Guillaume Coquillart', in Jean-Frédéric Chevalier (ed.), *Les Mondes théâtraux autour de Guillaume Coquillart (XVe siècle)* (Langres: Dominique Guéniot, 2005), pp. 5–112.

Baroin, Jean, *De l'étranger à l'étrange ou la conjointure de la merveille* (Aix-en-Provence: CUER MA, 1988).

Baudrier, Hervé, and J. Baudrier, *Bibliographie lyonnaise: recherches sur les imprimeurs, libraires, relieurs et fondeurs de lettres de Lyon au XVIe siècle publiées et continuées par J. Baudrier*, 13 vol. (Lyon: Librairie Ancienne d'Auguste Brun, 1895–1921; reprint, Paris: F. de Nobele, 1964).

Bayless, Martha, *Parody in the Middle Ages: The Latin Tradition* (Ann Arbor: University of Michigan Press, 1996).

Bétemps, Isabelle, *L'Imaginaire dans l'œuvre de Guillaume de Machaut* (Paris: Champion, 1998).

Bloom, Harold, *Poetry and Repression: Revisionism from Blake to Stevens* (New Haven/London: Yale University Press, 1976).

Bourdieu, Pierre, *The Logic of Practice*, trans. Richard Nice (Cambridge: Polity Press, 1990).

Boutet, Dominique, 'Au-delà et Autre monde: interférences culturelles et modèles de l'imaginaire dans la littérature épique', in Denis Hüe and Christine Ferlampin-Acher (eds), *Le Monde et l'Autre Monde* (Orleans: Paradigme, 2002), pp. 65–78.

Brown-Grant, Rosalind, *French Romance of the Later Middle Ages: Gender, Morality, and Desire* (Oxford: Oxford University Press, 2008).

Brownlee, Kevin, *Poetic Identity in Guillaume de Machaut* (Madison: University of Wisconsin Press, 1984).

Burns, E. Jane, *Bodytalk: When Women Speak in Old French Literature* (Philadelphia: University of Pennsylvania Press, 1993).

——, *Courtly Love Undressed: Reading Through Clothes in Medieval French Literature* (Philadelphia: University of Pennsylvania Press, 2003).

Burr, Kristin L., 'Re-creating the body: Euriaut's tales in *Le Roman de la Violette*', *Symposium*, 56 (2002), 3–16.

Butterfield, Ardis, *Poetry and Music in Medieval France: From Jean Renart to Guillaume de Machaut* (Cambridge: Cambridge University Press, 2002).

Calin, William, *The Epic Quest: Studies in Four Old French Chansons de Geste* (Baltimore: Johns Hopkins Press, 1966).

Callahan, Christopher, 'A l'ombre du jongleur disparu. La grammaire de la performance dans deux romans lyrico-narratifs dérimés', *Revue des Langues Romanes*, 101 (1997), 211–33.

Castan, Auguste, 'Étude sur le Froissart de Saint-Vincent de Besançon', *Bibliothèque de l'École des Chartes*, 26 (1865), 114–48.

Cayley, Emma, *Debate and Dialogue: Alain Chartier in his Cultural Context* (Oxford: Oxford University Press, 2006).

——, *Sleepless Knights and Wanton Women, vol. 2: Gender and Voice in Late Medieval French Debate Poetry* (Tempe: Arizona Center for Medieval and Renaissance Texts Studies, forthcoming).

Cazenave, Caroline, 'L'Imagination au pouvoir: le décor onirique du périple de Huon dans la *Chanson d'Esclarmonde*', in Jean-Michel Racault (ed.), *Ailleurs imaginés: littérature, histoire, civilisations* (Paris: Didier, 1990), pp. 21–55.

Cerquiglini, Jacqueline, *'Un engin si soutil': Guillaume de Machaut et l'écriture au XIVe siècle* (Paris: Champion, 1985).

Cerquiglini-Toulet, Jacqueline, *La Couleur de la mélancolie: la fréquentation des livres au XIVe siècle, 1300–1415* (Paris: Hatier, 1993).

Chatelain, Henri, *Recherches sur le vers français au XVe siècle: rimes, mètres et strophes* (Paris: Champion, 1907).

Collet, Olivier, 'Le manuscrit BnF. f. fr. 837 et le laboratoire poétique du XIIIe siècle', in Milena Mikhaïlov (ed.), *Mouvances et jointures: du manuscrit au texte médiéval* (Orléans: Paradigme, 2005), pp. 172–92.

Colombo Timelli, Maria, 'Refaire Doutrepont? Projet pour un nouveau répertoire des mises en prose des XVe et XVIe siècles', *Le Moyen Français*, 63 (2008), 109–17.

——, 'Sur l'édition des mises en prose de romans (XVᵉ siècle): bilan et perspectives', *Le Moyen Français*, 44–45 (1999), 87–106.

Copeland, Rita, *Rhetoric, Hermeneutics, and Translation in the Middle Ages: Academic Traditions and Vernacular Texts* (Cambridge: Cambridge University Press, 1991).

Croenen, Godfried, 'La radition manuscrite du Troisième Livre des *Chroniques de Froissart*', in V. Fasseur (ed.), *Froissart à la cour de Béarn: l'écrivain, les arts et le pouvoir* (Turnhout: Brepols, forthcoming).

Croenen, Godfried, Mary A. Rouse, and Richard H. Rouse, 'Pierre de Liffol and the manuscripts of Froissart's *Chronicles*', *Viator*, 33 (2002), 261–93.

Culler, Jonathan, *Structuralist Poetics: Structuralism, Linguistics and the Study of Literature* (London: Routledge & Kegan Paul, 1975).

Curtius, Ernst Robert, *Europäische Literatur und lateinisches Mittelalter*, 2ⁿᵈ rev. ed. (Bern: Francke, 1954).

Davies, Peter V., '"Si bas suis qu'a peine/Releveray": Christine de Pizan's use of enjambement', in John Campbell and Nadia Margolis (eds), *Christine de Pizan 2000: Studies on Christine de Pizan in Honour of Angus J. Kennedy* (Amsterdam: Rodopi, 2000), pp. 77–90.

Defaux, Gérard, 'Facing the Marot Generation: Ronsard's *giovenili errori*', *Modern Language Notes*, 119, Supplement (2004), 299–326.

Delumeau, Jean, *Une histoire de Paradis. Le jardin des délices* (Paris: Fayard, 1992).

Demats, Paule, *Fabula: trois études de mythographie antique et médiévale* (Geneva: Droz, 1973).

Demaules, Mireille, '*Le Cycle de la gageure* au XVᵉ siècle: l'exemple français et l'exemple italien', in Danielle Böhler (ed.), *Le Goût du lecteur à la fin du moyen âge* [*Cahiers du Léopard d'Or*, 11 (2006)], pp. 85–99.

Derrida, Jacques, *Spectres de Marx: l'état de la dette, le travail du deuil, et la nouvelle Internationale* (Paris: Galilée, 1993).

Devaux, Jean, *Jean Molinet, Indiciaire bourguignon* (Paris: Champion, 1996).

Dixon, Rebecca, '"Homs sui je dame, vraiement": sex, chivalry and identity in *Jehan d'Avennes*', *French Studies*, 61 (2007), 141–54.

Dixon, Rebecca, and Finn E. Sinclair (eds), with Adrian Armstrong, Sylvia Huot, and Sarah Kay, *Poetry, Knowledge and Community in Late Medieval France* (Cambridge: D. S. Brewer, 2008).

Donaldson-Evans, Lance K., 'Ronsard's *Folies Bergères*: the *Livret des Folastries* [sic] and Petrarch', *Neophilologus*, 91 (2007), 1–17.

Dorais, David, '"Les Païens de la Pléiade": l'érotisme dans les *Folastries* de Ronsard et dans les *Gayetez* d'Olivier de Magny', *Renaissance and Reformation/Renaissance et Réforme*, 23 (1999), 65–79.

Doutrepont, Georges, *Les Mises en prose des épopées et des romans chevaleresques du XIVe au XVIe siècle* (Brussels: Palais des Académies, 1939; Geneva: Slatkine Reprints, 1969).

Doyle, Kara, '"Narratizing" Marie of Ponthieu', *Historical Reflections/Réflexions Historiques*, 30 (2004), 29–54.

Dubost, Francis, *Aspects fantastiques de la littérature narrative XIIe–XIIIe siècles. L'Autre, l'Ailleurs, l'Autrefois* (Paris: Champion, 1991).

Dufournet, Jean, 'Commynes et l'invention d'un nouveau genre historique: les mémoires' in Danielle Buschinger (ed.), *Chroniques nationales et chroniques universelles* (Göppingen: Kümmerle, 1990), pp. 59–79.

——, *Études sur Philippe de Commynes* (Paris: Champion, 1975).

——, *Philippe de Commynes. Un historien à l'aube des temps modernes* (Brussels: De Boeck, 1994).

Dupire, Noël, *Jean Molinet: la vie – les œuvres* (Paris: Droz, 1932).

Duys, Karen, 'Books Shaped by Song: Early Literary Literacy in the *Miracles de Nostre Dame* of Gautier de Coinci' (PhD dissertation, New York University, 1997).

Ferlampin-Acher, Christine, '*Larron* contre *luiton*: les métamorphoses de Maugis', in Danielle Quéruel (ed.), *Entre épopée et légende: Les Quatre Fils Aymon ou Renaut de Montauban*, 2 vol. (Langres: Dominique Guéniot, 2000), II, pp. 101–18.

François, Charles, 'L'Épisode interpolé du "Roman de la Violette"', *Revue Belge de Philologie et d'Histoire*, 11 (1932), 689–98.

Franssen, Peter J. A., *Tussen tekst en publiek: Jan van Doesborch, drukker-uitgever en literator te Antwerpen en Utrecht in de eerste helft van de zestiende eeuw* (Amsterdam: Rodopi, 1990).

Frappier, Jean, *Les chansons de geste du cycle de Guillaume d'Orange*, 2 vol. (Paris: SEDES, 1967).

Freeman, M. J., 'Les Éditions anciennes de Coquillart', *Bibliothèque d'Humanisme et Renaissance*, 36 (1974), 87–104.

——, 'Guillaume Coquillart ou l'envers de la sagesse', in Jean-Frédéric Chevalier (ed.), *Les Mondes théâtraux autour de Guillaume Coquillart (XVe siècle)* (Langres: Dominique Guéniot, 2005), pp. 11–26.

——, 'La Satire affectueuse dans les *Droitz nouveaulx* de Guillaume Coquillart', *Réforme Humanisme Renaissance*, 11 (1980), 92–99.

Freeman, Michael, and Jane H. M. Taylor (eds), *Villon at Oxford: The Drama of the Text* (Amsterdam: Rodopi, 1999).

Gaunt, Simon, *Gender and Genre in Medieval French Literature* (Cambridge: Cambridge University Press, 1995).

——, *Love and Death in Medieval French and Occitan Courtly Literature* (Oxford: Oxford University Press, 2006).

Girard, René, *Deceit, Desire, and the Novel: Self and Other in Literary Structure*, trans. Yvonne Freccero (Baltimore: Johns Hopkins Press, 1972).

Glasser, Richard, 'Abstractum agens und Allegorie im älteren Französisch', *Zeitschrift für romanische Philologie*, 69 (1953), 43–122.

Gougenheim, Georges, *Grammaire de la langue française du seizième siècle* (Paris: Picard, 1984).

Gros, Gérard, *Le Poète, la Vierge et le Prince du puy. Etude sur les Puys marials de la France du Nord du XIVe siècle à la Renaissance* (Paris: Klincksieck, 1996).

——, 'Les Fatras de Jean Molinet', in Jean-Charles Herbin (ed.), *Image et mémoire du Hainaut médiéval* (Valenciennes: Presses Universitaires de Valenciennes, 2004), pp. 99–111.

Gruber, Jörn, *Die Dialektik des Trobar: Untersuchungen zur Struktur und Entwicklung des occitanischen und französischen Minnesangs des 12. Jahrhunderts* (Tübingen: Niemeyer, 1983).

Halba, Eve-Marie, 'Hagiographie de saint Renaut de Montauban', in Jean-Luc Deuffic (ed.), *Reliques et sainteté dans l'espace médiéval* [*PECIA*, 8–11 (2005)], pp. 281–99.

Harf-Lancner, Laurence, *Les Fées au Moyen Âge* (Paris: Champion, 1984).

Heintze, Michael, 'Les Techniques de la formation de cycles dans les chansons de geste', in Bart Besamusca [*et al.*] (eds), *Cyclification: The Development of Narrative Cycles in the Chansons de Geste and the Arthurian Romances* (Amsterdam: Royal Netherlands Academy of Arts and Sciences, 1994), pp. 46–55.

Hindley, Alan (ed.), *Drama and Community: People and Plays in Medieval Europe* (Turnhout: Brepols, 1999).

Hofstadter, Douglas R., *Le Ton Beau de Marot: In Praise of the Music of Language* (New York: Basic Books, 1997).

Hult, David F., *Self-Fulfilling Prophecies: Readership and Authority in the First 'Roman de la rose'* (Cambridge: Cambridge University Press, 1986).

Hunt, Tony, 'Aristotle, Dialectic and Courtly Literature', *Viator*, 10 (1979), 95–129.

Huot, Sylvia, *From Song to Book: The Poetics of Writing in Old French Lyric and Lyrical Narrative Poetry* (Ithaca, NY: Cornell University Press, 1987).

——, *The Romance of the Rose and its Medieval Readers: Interpretation, Reception, Manuscript Transmission* (Cambridge: Cambridge University Press, 1993).

——, 'Refashioning Boethius: prose and poetry in Chartier's *Livre de l'Esperance*', *Medium Ævum*, 76 (2007), 268–84.

Ilvonen, Eero, *Parodies de thèmes pieux dans la poésie française du Moyen Âge: Pater – Credo – Ave Maria – Laetabundus* (Geneva: Slatkine, 1975).

Jakobson, Roman, 'On linguistic aspects of translation', in Lawrence Venuti (ed.), *The Translation Studies Reader* (London: Routledge, 2000), pp. 113–18.

Jeanroy, Alfred, and Eugénie Droz, *Deux manuscrits de François Villon: Bibl. Nat. f.fr. 1661 et 20041* (Paris: E. Droz, 1932).

Johnson, Leonard W., *Poets as Players: Theme and Variation in Late Medieval French Poetry* (Stanford: Stanford University Press, 1990).

Jung, Marc-René, '*Poetria*: zur Dichtungstheorie des ausgehenden Mittelalters in Frankreich', *Vox Romanica*, 30 (1971), 44–64.

Kay, Sarah, *Courtly Contradictions: The Emergence of a Literary Object in the Twelfth Century* (Stanford, CA: Stanford University Press, 2001).

Kay, Sarah, and Simon Gaunt (eds), *The Practice of Medieval Literature* [*Forum for Modern Language Studies*, 33 (1997)].

Kelly, Allison, 'Christine de Pizan and Antoine de la Sale: the dangers of love in theory and fiction', in Earl Jeffrey Richards, with Joan Williamson, Nadia Margolis, and Christine Reno (eds), *Reinterpreting Christine de Pizan* (Athens/London: The University of Georgia Press, 1992), pp. 173–86.

Kelly, Douglas, *Christine de Pizan's Changing Opinion: A Quest for Certainty in the Midst of Chaos* (Cambridge: D. S. Brewer, 2007).

——, 'Imitation, metamorphosis, and Froissart's use of the exemplary *Modus tractandi*', in Donald Maddox and Sara Sturm-Maddox (eds), *Froissart Across the Genres* (Gainesville: University Press of Florida, 1998), pp. 101–18.

——, *Internal Difference and Meanings in the 'Roman de la rose'* (Madison: University of Wisconsin Press, 1995).

——, 'Les Inventions ovidiennes de Froissart: réflexions intertextuelles comme imagination', *Littérature*, 41 (1981), 82–92.

——, 'Matière, sens et *compilacion* dans le *Dit de la panthère* de Nicole de Margival', in Anne Amend-Söchting, Kirsten Dickhaut and Walburga Hülk (eds), *Das Schöne im Wirklichen – Das Wirkliche im Schönen: Festschrift für Dietmar Rieger* (Heidelberg: Winter, 2002), pp. 125–34.

——, *Medieval Imagination: Rhetoric and the Poetry of Courtly Love* (Madison: University of Wisconsin Press, 1978).

——, 'La Spécialité dans l'invention des topiques', in Lucie Brind'Amour and Eugene Vance (eds), *Archéologie du signe* (Toronto: Pontifical Institute of Mediaeval Studies, 1983), pp. 101–25.

Kennedy, Elspeth, 'The scribe as editor', in *Mélanges de langue et de littérature du moyen âge et de la Renaissance offerts à Jean Frappier*, 2 vol. (Geneva: Droz, 1970), I, pp. 523–31.

Krause, Kathy M., 'L'Héroïne et l'autorité du discours: le *Roman de la Violette* et le *Roman de la Rose ou de Guillaume de Dole*', *Le Moyen Âge*, 102 (1996), 191–216.

——, 'The material erotic: the clothed and unclothed female body in the *Roman de la violette*', in Curtis Perry (ed.), *Material Culture and Cultural Materialisms in the Middle Ages and the Renaissance* (Turnhout: Brepols, 2001), pp. 17–39.

Krueger, Roberta L., *Women Readers and the Ideology of Gender in Old French Verse Romance* (Cambridge: Cambridge University Press, 1993).

Lacan, Jacques, *Les Quatre Concepts fondamentaux de la psychanalyse: le séminaire XI* (Paris: Seuil Points, 1990).

Lacy, Norris J., 'Adaptation as reception: the Burgundian *Cligès*', *Fifteenth-Century Studies*, 24 (1998), 198–207.

——, 'Motivation and method in the Burgundian *Erec*', in Keith Busby and Norris J. Lacy (eds), *Conjunctures: Medieval Studies in Honor of Douglas Kelly* (Amsterdam: Rodopi, 1994), pp. 271–80.

Laird, Judith, and Earl Jeffrey Richards, '*Tous parlent par une mesmes bouche*: lyrical outbursts, prosaic remedies, and voice in Christine de Pizan's *Livre du Duc des vrais amans*', in Earl Jeffrey Richards (ed.), *Christine de Pizan and Medieval French Lyric* (Gainesville: University Press of Florida, 1998), pp. 103–31.

Lausberg, Heinrich, *Handbuch der literarischen Rhetorik: eine Grundlegung der Literaturwissenschaft*, rev. ed. (Munich: Hueber, 1973).

Lechat, Didier, '*Dire par fiction*': metamorphoses du '*je*' chez Guillaume de Machaut, Jean Froissart et Christine de Pizan* (Paris: Champion, 2005).

Lecoy, Felix, 'Une mention du *Roman de la rose* au XVIᵉ siècle', *Romania*, 87 (1866), 119–20.

Lejeune, Philippe, *L'Autobiographie en France* ([1971]; Paris: Colin, 2003).

Lowe, Lawrence F. H., *Gérard de Nevers: A Study of the Prose Version of the Roman de la Violette* (Princeton/Paris: Princeton University Press/Libraire Édouard Champion, 1923).

Martin, Robert, and Marc Wilmet, *Syntaxe du moyen français* (Bordeaux: Sobodi, 1980).

Matter, E. Ann, *The Song of Songs in Medieval Western Christianity* (Philadelphia: University of Pennsylvania Press, 1990).

Minet-Mahy, Virginie, *Esthétique et pouvoir de l'œuvre allégorique à l'époque de Charles VI: Imaginaires et discours* (Paris: Champion, 2005).

Morris, Rosemary, 'Machaut, Froissart and the fictionalization of the self', *Modern Language Review*, 83 (1988), 545–55.

Mühlethaler, Jean-Claude, 'Le Vin entre morale et carnaval: Jean Molinet et François Villon', in Karin Becker and Olivier Leplatre (eds), *Écritures du repas: fragments d'un discours gastronomique* (Frankfurt: Peter Lang, 2007), pp. 51–74.

Müller, Otto, *Das lateinische Einschiebsel in der französischen Literatur des Mittelalters* (Zürich: Leemann, 1919).

Mus, David, 'François Villon: le drame du texte', in Michael Freeman and Jane H. M. Taylor (eds), *Villon at Oxford. The Drama of the Text* (Amsterdam: Rodopi, 1999), pp. 1–34.

Nora, Pierre, *Les Lieux de mémoire, La Nation II* (Paris: Gallimard, 1986).

Orr, Mary, *Intertextuality: Debates and Contexts* (Cambridge: Polity Press, 2003).

Palermo, Joseph, 'Vivien de Monbranc: personnage épique ambivalent', in *VIIIe Congreso de la Société Rencesvals* (Pamplona: Institución Principe de Viana, 1981), pp. 375–79.

Paris, Gaston, 'Le Cycle de la *gageure*', *Romania*, 32 (1903), 481–551.

Peckham, Robert, 'A la recherche d'un Villon perdu. Pour une histoire de sa réception au XVIIIe siècle', in Jean Dufournet, Michael Freeman, and Jean Dérens (eds), *Villon et ses lecteurs* (Paris: Champion, 2005), pp. 71–88.

Pensom, Roger, 'Accent and metre in French', *French Language Studies*, 3 (1993), 19–37.

——, *Accent and Metre in French: A Theory of the Relation Between Linguistic Accent and Metrical Practice 1100–1900* (Bern: Peter Lang, 1997).

——, *Le Sens de la métrique chez François Villon: 'Le Testament'* (Bern: Peter Lang, 2004).

Pettegree, Andrew, Malcolm Walsby, and Alexander Wilkinson (eds), *French Vernacular Books: Books Published in the French Language Before 1601*, 2 vol. (Leiden: Brill, 2007).

Phillips, Helen, 'Rewriting the Fall: Julian of Norwich and the *Chevalier des dames*', in Lesley Smith and Jane H. M. Taylor (eds), *Women, the Book and the Godly* (Cambridge: D. S. Brewer, 1995), pp. 149–56.

Picot, Émile, *Catalogue des livres composant la bibliothèque de feu M. le baron James de Rothschild*, 5 vol. (Paris: Morgand, 1884–1920).

Poirion, Daniel, *Le Poète et le prince: l'évolution du lyrisme courtois de Guillaume de Machaut à Charles d'Orléans* (Grenoble: Université de Grenoble, Faculté des Lettres et Sciences humaines, 1965).

Pope, Mildred K., *From Latin to Modern French with Especial Consideration of Anglo-Norman: Phonology and Morphology* (Manchester: Manchester University Press, 1952).

Quéruel, Danielle, 'L'Art des réécritures: de *Maugis* à *Mabrien*', in Jean Dufournet (ed.), '*Si a parlé par moult ruiste vertu': mélanges de littérature médiévales offerts à Jean Subrenat* (Paris: Champion, 2000), pp. 455–65.

Randall, Catharine, 'Poetic license, censorship and the unrestrained self: Ronsard's *Livret de folastries*', *Papers in French Seventeenth-Century Literature*, 23 (1996), 449–62.

Regalado, Nancy Freeman, '*En l'an de mon trentiesme aage*: date, deixis and moral vision in Villon's *Testament*', in Emmanuèle Baumgartner and Christiane Marchello-Nizia (eds), *Le Nombre du temps. En hommage à Paul Zumthor* (Paris: Champion, 1988), pp. 237–46.

——, 'Speaking in Script: the construction of voice, presence, and perspective in Villon's *Testament*', in W. F. H. Nicolaisen (ed.), *Oral Tradition in the Middle Ages* (Binghamton, NY: Center for Medieval and Early Renaissance Studies, 1995), pp. 209–23.

——, 'Villon's legacy from *Le Testament de Jean de Meun*: misquotation, memory, and the wisdom of fools', in Michael Freeman and Jane H. M. Taylor (eds), *Villon at Oxford: The Drama of the Text* (Amsterdam: Rodopi, 1999), pp. 282–311.

Ribémont, Bernard, 'Héros épique ou héros de cour? Une autre vision de l'héroïsme à la fin du Moyen Âge; Le cas de *Mabrien* (XVe s.)', *Cahiers de Recherches Médiévales*, 11 (2004), 63–73.

Riffaterre, Michael, 'Compulsory reader response: the intertextual drive', in Michael Worton and Judith Still (eds), *Intertextuality: Theories and Practices* (Manchester/New York: Manchester University Press, 1990), pp. 56–78.

——, 'L'Intertexte inconnu', *Littérature*, 41 (1981), 4–7.

——, 'La Trace de l'intertexte', *La Pensée*, 215 (1980), 4–18.

Rossi, Marguerite, *Huon de Bordeaux et l'évolution du genre épique au XIIIe siècle* (Paris: Champion, 1975).

Roussel, Claude, '*D'armes et d'amours*: l'aventure chevaleresque dans les dernières chansons de geste', in Dominique Boutet (ed.), *Le Romanesque et l'épique. [Littérales*, 31 (2003)], pp. 163–78.

——, 'Le Mélange des genres dans les chansons de geste tardives', in Carlos Alvar and Juan Parades (eds), *Actes du XVIᵉ Congrès International de la Société Rencesvals* (Granada: University of Granada, 2005), pp. 65–85.

Rouy, François, *L'Esthétique du traité moral d'après les œuvres d'Alain Chartier* (Geneva: Droz, 1980).

Schroeder, Horst, *Der Topos der 'Nine Worthies' in Literatur und bildender Kunst* (Göttingen: Vandenhoeck & Ruprecht, 1971).

Sedgwick, Eve Kosofsky, *Between Men: English Literature and Male Homosocial Desire* (New York: Columbia University Press, 1985).

Sinclair, K. V., '*Le Dit des patenostres de Gieffroy*: parodie d'un thème pieux', *Le Moyen Âge*, 103 (1997), 561–70.

Solterer, Helen, 'The freedoms of fiction for gender in premodern France', in Thelma S. Fenster and Clare A. Lees (eds), *Gender in Debate from the Early Middle Ages to the Renaissance* (New York: Palgrave, 2002), pp. 135–63.

——, *The Master and Minerva: Disputing Women in French Medieval Culture* (Berkeley/London: University of California Press, 1995).

Strubel, Armand, '*Grant senefiance a*': allégorie et littérature au moyen âge* (Paris: Champion, 2002).

Sturm-Maddox, Sara, and Donald Maddox, 'Renoart in Avalon: generic shift in the *Bataille Loquifer*', in Karen Pratt (ed.), *Shifts and Transpositions in Medieval Narrative* (Cambridge: D. S. Brewer, 1994), pp. 17–22.

Suard, François, 'Charlemagne dans les proses épiques imprimés', in Madeleine Tyssens and Claude Thiry (eds), *Charlemagne et l'épopée romane*, 2 vol. (Liège: Université de Liège, 1978), I, pp. 271–80.

——, 'Le Développement de la 'Geste de Montauban' en France jusqu'à la fin du moyen âge', in Hans-Erich Keller (ed.), *Romance Epic. Essays on a Medieval Literary Genre* (Kalamazoo, MI.: Medieval Institute Publications, 1987), pp. 141–61.

——, '"Meurvin" et "Mabrian", deux épigones de la "Chevalerie Ogier de Danemarche" et de "Renaut de Montauban"', in Wolfgang van Emden and Philip E. Bennett (eds), *Guillaume d'Orange et la chanson de geste. Essays presented to Duncan McMillan* (Reading: Reading University Press, 1984), pp. 151–66.

Swift, Helen J., *Gender, Writing, and Performance: Men Defending Women in Late Medieval France (1440–1538)* (Oxford: Oxford University Press, 2008).

Taylor, Jane H. M., '*Le Chevalier des dames du dolent fortuné*: image and text, manuscript and print', in Adrian Armstrong and David Adams (eds), *Word and Image: Studies in the French Illustrated Book from the Middle Ages to the Present Day* [*Bulletin of the John Rylands University Library of Manchester*, 81 (1999)], pp. 153–76.

——, 'Courtly gatherings and poetic games: "coterie" anthologies in the late Middle Ages in France', in Adrian Armstrong and Malcolm Quainton (eds), *Book and Text in France, 1400–1600: poetry on the page* (Aldershot: Ashgate, 2007), pp. 13–29.

——, 'Embodying the *Rose*: an intertextual reading of Alain Chartier's *La Belle Dame sans mercy*', in Barbara K. Altmann and Carleton W. Carroll (eds), *The Court Reconvenes: Courtly Literature Across the Disciplines* (Cambridge: D. S. Brewer, 2003), pp. 325–33.

——, 'Inescapable rose: Jean Le Seneschal's *Cent Ballades* and the art of cheerful paradox', *Medium Ævum*, 67 (1998), 60–84.

——, *The Making of Poetry: Poetic Anthologies at the End of the Middle Ages* (Turnhout: Brepols, 2007).

——, 'Order from accident: cyclic consciousness at the end of the Middle Ages', in Bart Besamusca [*et al.*] (eds), *Cyclification: The Development of Narrative Cycles in the Chansons de Geste and the Arthurian Romances* (Amsterdam: Royal Netherlands Academy of Arts and Sciences, 1994), pp. 59–73.

——, *The Poetry of François Villon: Text and Context* (Cambridge: Cambridge University Press, 2001).

——, 'The sense of a beginning: genealogy and plenitude in late medieval narrative cycles', in Sara Sturm-Maddox and Donald Maddox (eds), *Transtextualities: Of Cycles and Cyclicity in Medieval French Literature* (Binghamton, NY: Medieval & Renaissance Texts & Studies, 1996), pp. 93–123.

——, 'The significance of the insignificant: reading reception in the Burgundian *Erec* and *Cligès*', *Fifteenth-Century Studies*, 24 (1998), 183–97.

Traub, Valerie, *Desire and Anxiety: Circulations of Sexuality in Shakespearean Drama* (London: Routledge, 1992).

Van Emden, Wolfgang G., 'Le Personnage du roi dans *Vivien de Monbranc* et ailleurs', in Madeleine Tyssens and Claude Thiry (eds), *Charlemagne et l'épopée romane*, 2 vol. (Liège: Université de Liège, 1978), I, pp. 241–50.

Várvaro, Alberto, 'Problèmes philologiques du Livre IV des Chroniques de Jean Froissart', in Godfried Croenen and Peter Ainsworth (eds), *Patrons, Authors and Workshops: Books and Book Production in Paris Around 1400* (Leuven: Peeters, 2006), pp. 255–77.

Verelst, Philippe, 'L'Enchanteur d'épopée: prolégomènes à une étude sur Maugis', *Romanica Gandensia*, 16 (1976), 19–162.

——, 'Le Personnage de Maugis dans *Renaut de Montauban* (versions rimées traditionelles)', *Romanica Gandensia*, 18 (1981), 73–152.

Vitz, Evelyn Birge, '"Bourde jus mise"? Villon, the liturgy, and prayer' in Michael Freeman and Jane H. M. Taylor (eds), *Villon at Oxford: The Drama of the Text* (Amsterdam: Rodopi, 1999), pp. 170–94.

——, 'The impact of Christian doctrine on medieval literature', in Denis Hollier (ed.), *A New History of French Literature* (Cambridge, MA: Harvard University Press, 1989), pp. 82–88.

Wathelet-Willem, Jeanne, 'La Fée Morgain dans la chanson de geste', *Cahiers de civilisation médiévale*, 13 (1970), 209–19.

Zaganelli, Gioia, 'L'Orient du prêtre Jean et la tradition encyclopédique du Moyen Âge', in *La Géographie au Moyen Âge: espaces pensés, espaces vécus, espaces rêvés* [*Perspectives Médiévales*, suppl. 24 (1998)], pp. 97–107.

Zeikowitz, Richard E., *Homoeroticism and Chivalry: Discourses of Male Same-Sex Desire in the 14th Century* (New York: Palgrave Macmillan, 2003).

Zink, Michel, *La Subjectivité littéraire* (Paris: Presses Universitaires de France, 1985).

Zumthor, Paul, *Essai de poétique médiévale* (Paris: Seuil, 1972).

——, 'L'Épiphonème proverbial', *Revue des Sciences Humaines*, 41 (1976), 313–28.

——, 'Un problème d'esthétique médiévale: l'utilisation poétique du bilinguisme', *Le Moyen Âge*, 66 (1960), 301–36, 561–94.

Tabula gratulatoria

Peter Ainsworth

Rosamund Allen

Elizabeth A. Andersen

Adrian Armstrong

Mary-Jo Arn

Margaret Atack

Jeanette Beer

Jean Blacker

Michel-André Bossy

Geoffrey Bromiley

Rosalind Brown-Grant

Kevin Brownlee

Bill Burgwinkle

Keith Busby

Ardis Butterfield

Carleton W. Carroll

Emma Cayley

Carol J. Chase

Collingwood College, Durham University

Collingwood College JCR

Collingwood College SCR

Helen Cooper

Raymond J. Cormier

David Cowling

The Department of French Studies, University of Manchester

Rebecca Dixon

Carol R. Dover

Catherine Emerson

Hillary Engelhart

Melanie Florence

John M. Fyler

Russell Goulbourne

Linda Gowans

Joan Tasker Grimbert

Carol J. Harvey

Leofranc Holford-Strevens

Sylvia Huot

Martin Kauffmann

Sarah Kay

Douglas Kelly

Angus Kennedy

Roberta L. Krueger

Norris J. Lacy

James Laidlaw

Elizabeth Eva Leach

Richard Maber

Donald Maddox

Sara Maddox

Sally Mapstone

Nadia Margolis

Sophie Marnette

Peggy McCracken

Jean-Claude Mühlethaler

Andrea Noble

Linda M. Paterson

Rupert T. Pickens

Rhiannon Purdie

Nancy Freeman Regalado

Judith Rice Rothschild

Shigemi Sasaki

The School of Modern Languages and Cultures, Durham University

Harvey L. Sharrer

Lesley Smith

St Hilda's College Library, Oxford

Helen J. Swift

Mike Thompson

Adrian P. Tudor

Stephanie Cain Van D'Elden

Jocelyn Wogan-Brown

Michel Zink